10592

338
.76762
Mat

Mathias, Philip.
  Takeover; the 22 days of risk and
decision that created the world's largest
newsprint empire, Abitibi-Price. Toronto,
Maclean-Hunter, 1976.
  xiv, 287 p. illus.
  A Financial Post book.
  Includes bibliography.
  1. Abitibi Paper Company.
2. Price Company. 3. Paper making and
trade – Canada. T. Title II. Financial Post.
0888960379   0101540

TAKEOVER

The 22 days of risk and decision that created the
world's largest newsprint empire, Abitibi-Price

by Philip Mathias

a Financial Post book

Maclean-Hunter Limited

ISBN 0-88896-037-9 (casebound edition)
ISBN 0-88896-038-7 (soft-cover edition)

Printed and bound in Canada

For Laura Mathias, who made this
book possible a long time ago.

Contents

PHASE I: THE INVESTIGATION

Acknowledgments

The people who most deserve acknowledgment, certain sources of information and advice, can't be named here. Fortunately, *they* know who they are — and I thank them for their indispensable assistance. Thanks are also due to my wife Caroline for her steady support over many difficult months. And a special thank you to Robert L. Perry, Editor, Financial Post Books, whose patience and good humor came just when it counted most.

P.M.   Toronto, March 1976

x

Preface

This book is a reconstruction of the events that led to the takeover of Price Co. by Abitibi Paper Co. in November 1974. It's divided into two parts. The first is a narrative that focuses on the human aspects of the takeover, the drama, the comedy, the tensions, the challenges, the decision-making style of men at the upper levels of corporate life. The second part is an extensive analysis of the legal and financial issues, which appears as reference notes at the back of the book, keyed to the narrative by text numbers. The reader should refer to these notes to appreciate fully the complexity of the decisions thrust upon the executives caught up in the takeover.

The author has labored hard to attain accuracy of detail in this account, but it should be remembered that all conversations in the book have been reconstructed from memory or are fictional creations based on fact. They've been presented in quotation marks to establish immediacy and drama. The author wasn't present at any of the discussions described, and, if any tapes exist, they haven't been made available.

The sources for this book were all unofficial and, unfortunately, in some cases incomplete. Any opinions expressed or implied are the author's and shouldn't be construed as The Financial Post's or the official attitudes of any of the companies or persons named in the text. In particular, the lengthy analysis of Hon. Vere

Harmsworth's difficulties comes from the author alone. Harms-worth didn't bless this book with either his assistance or his im-primatur.

An introductory passage

The takeover condition, like the profit motive that fuels it, is fundamental to all corporations, and it most closely resembles the human sex drive — an irresistible urge to couple that is capable of creating new life. As with sex, the takeover drive is an integral part of the corporate psyche, intensified by a gland-like corporate-development department where MBAs feed into the corporate bloodstream esoteric financial analyses of suitable mating partners, tempting the executive head to want one.

Like the millions of sex acts performed on the dark side of the world each night, takeovers are neither all good nor all bad, but range from asset-stripping and rape, through the cheap-thrill promiscuity of conglomerates, to decent double-bed mergers after a gentlemanly abduction or nuptials. Neither are their results uniform: perhaps oppressive monopoly, or comfortable corporate stagnation, or maybe sanity in a competition-crippled industry. But takeovers are potentially more good than bad: the nation's precious productive capacity is concentrated in the hands of the best managers, though they may not choose to use their new power well.

"Seldom, or perhaps never, does a marriage develop into an individual relationship smoothly and without crises . . ."

Carl Gustav Jung

PHASE I

The investigation

Day One

Thursday, October 31
"Let's make a raid . . ."

Abitibi Paper Co. had been searching harder than usual for a takeover prospect. A huge, 61-year-old matriarch of a corporation, Abitibi was stodgy and conservative, even in the realm of pulp and paper which is probably the stuffiest of Canada's industries.[1] Abitibi's arteries had hardened in the 1950s under a strong-willed, autocratic chairman, Douglas W. Ambridge, who'd stifled initiative perhaps as an understandable reaction to a traumatic receivership in the 1930s and 1940s. Ambridge had built a strong team and he'd been badly needed when Abitibi was in disrepute after receivership, but he'd stayed too long. In the 1960s new management had livened the old girl a little, but a big company tends to have a personality all its own that takes decades to alter.[2] A takeover would give Abitibi a pleasant, rejuvenating jolt and propel profits upward in a year when there was no other way of doing that. At least, that was the way Abitibi's senior executives were thinking this Thursday morning in Toronto in the autumn of 1974.

"Let's make a raid on Federal Paper, Jack." It was nine o'clock, and Claude Harry Rosier, Abitibi's president and chief operating officer, was talking to John E. Haire, chief financial officer, in Haire's office. "The stock was down to $17 in New York yesterday," Rosier said. "With a bit of luck we could pick up control for $30 million."

Federal Paper, a paper board, cartons and glass manufacturer,

3

was the third American company Abitibi had looked at in the past few weeks, the other two having the improbable names of Bangor Punta and Superior Fiber Products. Abitibi wanted to expand in the United States because that was where the action seemed to be, despite the lacklustre performance of Abitibi's American newsprint and board subsidiaries. But it always came down to the same obstacles: a takeover might violate American anti-trust laws; and Abitibi shares might have to be given for stock of the target company, destroying Abitibi's "Canadian" status and leaving it no longer free to expand by takeover in its own country.

Haire and Rosier discussed the attractions and otherwise of Federal for half an hour, then Haire said suddenly: "You know, Harry, the takeover of a Canadian company would be much more flexible.[3] I think we should go after our old favorite, Price."

With these words, Haire, a mild and thoughtful man, touched off at 9:30 a.m. a train of events that would crown Abitibi as the world's largest newsprint manufacturer in the brief period of 22 days.

Even as Haire and Rosier spoke, Abitibi was sizable. Annual sales were $500 million; the company owned 18 pulp, paper and board mills in North America, and produced about two million tons of pulp, paper and building materials a year.

A hint of Abitibi's economic might could be seen in the furnishings of its executive suite, on the 22nd floor of the Toronto-Dominion Centre — a prestigious cluster of dark, square head-office towers that had permanently altered Toronto's skyline in the late 1960s. When Abitibi had moved into the new "T-D" in 1967 at a rent of about $500,000 a year, Paul Roberts, then the chairman, wanted to conjure up an opulence in the executive suite that would be an object lesson in status to the other head-office employees on the funereal 21st and 22nd floors.

Along one wall of the executive-suite hallway were pictures of Abitibi's mills, lovingly framed but ugly like all paper mills. The other wall wore flawless walnut paneling, set off by a row of elegant Queen Anne chairs, one outside each office door. Walnut had been used lavishly in the suite as if to make the point that wood was Abitibi's fortune. But the crowning touch of the decor lay on the floor — thick broadloom in color-of-gold to remind the servants of the company that Abitibi's purpose was wealth, not paper.

4

When Thomas J. Bell had succeeded the high-domed, aristocratic Roberts as chairman in 1968, the broadloom had spread out into the rest of the head office, but in orange, the color of democracy and motivation. Now, the employees affectionately referred to the executive suite as "The Gold Coast."

Through the large windows of their offices Abitibi's executives could see far out over Lake Ontario, on some days as far as the United States, where Abitibi sold most of the million and a quarter tons of newsprint its mills produce every year. As if in contempt of almost half a million annual tons of fine paper and paper board, few of the executive windows faced north into Canada where most of that is sold.

Harry Rosier and Jack Haire were talking takeover this morning because Abitibi was wrestling with a modern dilemma. The company needed more newsprint capacity, but, thanks to inflation, there was little profit potential in expanding by building new mills. The return simply wouldn't be big enough to justify the investment. Then, and in the years to come, Abitibi wanted at least a 15% return (after tax) from any new investment. The return from existing mills was 15%, but new mills would return only 8% to 10% because the cost of building mills had risen faster than newsprint prices.[4]

For example, in 1973, a year earlier, Abitibi's corporate development department had estimated it would cost $65 million to build an extension to a Thunder Bay newsprint mill, part of an Abitibi mill complex there. At the most economical size required by conditions in the mid-1970s, a new mill built from the ground up would cost $200 million.[5]

Current interest rates alone were a formidable deterrent to a project at the Lakehead. Rosier and Haire knew the 10% pre-tax interest payment on borrowed money wouldn't leave much of a new mill's return for the shareholders.

Besides, the timing would be all wrong. Construction costs, high as they were then, were going up by at least 12% a year. "It's murder finding labor in the woods these days, and Great Lakes[6] is already building at the Lakehead, so construction labor will probably be scarce as well.[7] It doesn't add up, Jack," Rosier said, shaking his head emphatically.

The irresistible force that drives corporations to greater profits had met an immovable object. New mills weren't profitable enough, and Abitibi's existing mills were running flat out in a temporary newsprint shortage, so no more profits could be squeezed out of them.[4] How could profits be kept growing? Rosier's idea was to buy additional, profitable, already-operating mills cheaply, not from the *company* owning the mills, but from the *shareholders* owning the company.

(On a smaller scale, the man in the street was making a similar decision about his automobile purchases. New-car prices had risen so fast due to recent manufacturing cost inflation that he was buying used cars, because the price per mile of transportation remaining in the vehicle was lower.)

One company that owned profitable, already-operating newsprint mills was the Quebec-based Price Co., and to Haire, the financial officer, it looked good in other ways.

"Price's shares have been selling at less than $15 lately," Haire told Rosier persuasively, picking up the Globe & Mail and glancing through the stock-market columns. "The high yesterday was $13. I figure Price will earn about $3.20 a share this year, so that should bring the book value[8] per share up to about $20," Haire observed. At $13, the market price was much less than book value, and the earnings of $3.20 per share would represent a handsome return on the price of the stock.

Price Co.'s and most other stocks were neglected and undervalued at the time. There was pessimism over a coming recession and apprehension about the way inflation would erode company profits, and investment cash was rushing into rocketing real estate. Hundreds of stocks were trading at historically absurd values, perhaps a half or a third of their values three years before, maybe 20% or 30% less than book value, probably only three to four times earnings per share. A buyer with a few million dollars in his pocket could pick off many a going concern for a fraction of the cost of building its manufacturing plants himself.[9] (Inflation had not only pushed the cost of "new cars" into the stratosphere, it had driven the price of "used cars" to ridiculously low levels).

But Price was attractive not only because of the low cost at which control could be purchased, but also because it had little debt and lots of cash — and this would bolster the debt-raising capacity of a company that went heavily into debt to buy it.

Haire quickly calculated it would cost about $100 million to buy 50% of Price's shares. For that money the buyer would get half ownership of Price's five mills at less than half the cost of building 2½ mills new. The saving: about $150 million.[10] But as Haire chatted about spending $100 million to do this and do that, he felt a sharp pang of apprehension. In 1958 Abitibi had spent $25 million on its board mill at Alpena, Michigan. In 1968 it had spent $50 million to buy Cox Newsprint in Augusta, Georgia, and often there'd been talk about building new mills for more than $60 million, but Haire had never sat around chatting about a *$100-million* stock-market takeover. "If we do this, it had better work — not like 1969 . . ." he thought.

In 1969, Abitibi and Price had tried to connect before. They'd eyed one another like two black-widow spiders trying to mate. After months of talks, Jack Haire and an Abitibi team had met a Price delegation in Montreal to work out the final mechanics of a merger. To smooth the way, Abitibi's chairman Tom Bell had agreed to step aside as chairman of the new company in favor of Price's chairman, who'd said he'd stay in office only three or four years. But the companies hadn't been able to agree on the relative values of their two stocks, which would have had to be exchanged for stock of the new umbrella company.[11]

At the last moment the bride had turned up her nose and stayed away from the church. There'd been desultory talks within Abitibi about a takeover since then, but they'd never been brought to the boil. Now a determined Abitibi was contemplating not rape, but abduction and forced nuptials, and this virile idea had been generated by 61-year-old Jack Haire, cautious by temperament, by corporate upbringing, and by the demands of his responsibilities.

Financial men are usually more resistant to change. They tend to realize more acutely than operating men how much a blunder can cost. But Haire's career indicated a man conservative by his very nature. An accurate, restrained, slightly old-fashioned executive, Haire had known only one home town — Toronto — and only one employer — Abitibi. He'd joined Abitibi in 1936 after a graduate's customary one-year kickaround to celebrate a bachelor of commerce degree at the University of Toronto, and had remained with a company that stayed on the defensive for 30 years following its near-ruin in the 1930s. This seemed to reveal a man who preferred safety to risk, a quiet haven to the open sea. Yet it was Haire who generated a vision of what could be the second greatest event in Abitibi's history.

This Thursday morning, Rosier and Haire chatted about a Price takeover for another 20 minutes as dully and mechanically as if they were going through a laundry list, then both went back to the day-to-day task of running a $500-million business.

At noon, Rosier went up in the elevator alone to the Fifty-Fourth, a dining lounge and executive rendezvous on the Toronto-Dominion Centre's top floor, where he was usually treated like an honored guest. He wanted to think quietly over lunch before talking to Tom Bell, Abitibi's chairman.

Rosier's basic responsibility, as president and chief operating officer, was the company's mills and sales rather than "corporate development" which, along with other non-operating staff departments, reported directly to the chairman and chief executive officer, Bell. But as Number Two in Abitibi, Rosier took a keen interest in every aspect of the company's future.

An outwardly placid Maritimer, and an engineer, Rosier had brought predictable but indispensable qualities to the presidential office: an elephantine capacity to absorb technical data, and a cutting, almost cynical perception. The latter could carve quickly down to the core of an issue, slicing away the seductive imagery that corporations often weave around and within themselves. Rosier also had good rapport with the employees, perhaps because they perceived him as being completely free of pretense. His attitude to management: "Everything goes on better than if I interfere. And I don't. They come to me when they need help or guidance."

Rosier had been an Abitibi executive for 15 years, but, typically, he was little known in the paper industry, a fitting reward for his contempt of stardom. But now he was trying to correct that presidential defect. His photograph would appear on the cover of the November issue of Canadian Pulp & Paper Industry magazine, and on the inside pages he'd tell its readers prophetically: "Spend to increase profitability, not capacity" — a theme that had obviously enthralled him for weeks. The interview with the magazine's editor had been completed in mid-October. Now, during lunch, the solitary Rosier thought hard about applying to his own

8

company the wisdom of his own widely proclaimed advice.

He returned to the office, worked on the phone for a couple of hours, then picked up a few papers and walked down the golden broadloom to the office of the chairman.

Thomas J. Bell looked a little like David Niven, the film actor, but large leprechaun ears added a touch of fun to Bell's long, grave, patrician face — a countenance well suited to the dignity of his office and the breaking of bad news at shareholders' meetings. Bell's style was quite different from Rosier's. Bell was a conscious socializer and charmer, the man with the money connections, and an executive who motivated people instead of worrying about how they felt. Bell's drive and leadership would become the main force in the coming takeover, while Rosier's concern for the people of Price promised to make the marriage congenial.

"Jack and I have been talking about what Abitibi should be doing," Rosier said, allowing the restlessness of months to come out in his voice. Since 1968 and the Cox Newsprint acquisition, Abitibi had been expanding by the construction of new capacity and the purchase of a few tiny companies of little significance. Everybody realized this approach was stale, and Bell had designated 1974 as the year for fresh ideas.

"We want to go after Price," Rosier said, and Bell listened intently to the information on share price, earnings and book value. Hadn't he been thinking along similar lines himself, though he hadn't got as far as identifying the company he wanted as Price?

"It's a well-run company, Tom," Rosier said. "There aren't many managers better than Charlie Tittemore, and I'd say all their mills are as good as or better than ours, except for Kenogami which they've never modernized."[12]

Bell asked his secretary to call Haire, who stepped in immediately from the next office.

Their conversation focused on a visit in the spring of 1974 by a Montreal investment adviser named Stephen Jarislowsky, who'd spoken to Abitibi's pension-fund investment committee. Bell, Rosier and Haire had surreptitiously picked Jarislowsky's brains: the analyst had argued that a corporation shouldn't build new manufacturing capacity while shares were available at low prices in the stock market. Later, Alf Powis, president of Noranda Mines Ltd., had completed the argument by telling Rosier that a company should spend its money buying the stock of its own publicly traded subsidiaries. The idea was to maximize, at the low prices available, the earnings contributed by the subsidiary to the parent.[13]

Abitibi had no public subsidiaries. Bell, Rosier and Haire agreed it would have to start from scratch and buy one — Price.

"Alf Powis had the right idea, with Fraser," Bell said with a note of admiration for his old friend and a fellow director on the board of Simpsons Ltd., the big national retail chain.

In early April that year, Noranda, a world-wide mining and metals company, had bought 23% of the stock of Fraser Cos., a fine paper and pulp producer based in Maine and New Brunswick. Then Noranda had made a surprise offer of $28.75 a share for more shares (the stock had been trading at $24.50), increasing its holdings to 51% and control. The book value of the stock had been $34 a share, well above the price paid by Noranda.

Noranda owned a junior forest-products empire in Western Canada, which was based on a partnership with an American paper company in British Columbia Forest Products Ltd., and Northwood Pulp Ltd. Into the little empire Fraser had fitted nicely.

When he'd heard the Noranda news in April, Bell had telephoned Powis and said: "You bastard, we've been studying a take-over of Fraser for a year and a half."

"Then why didn't you bid for it?" Powis had shot back.

"Because we didn't have $35 million," Bell had replied. Now, only six months later, Bell was warming to the idea of a takeover that would need three or four times that much money, perhaps within a few days.

"Let's get the file on Price, Jack," Bell said to Haire. The three men pored over the file's contents for 45 minutes until papers were spread all over Bell's desk and a nearby coffee table.

At 4 p.m. Bell said finally: "Jack, get the lawyers and the Wood Gundy people over here tomorrow and let's see if we can't pull this thing off."

Haire hurried out to use the phone. Rosier went back to work.

Ironically, only a few months before, another corporation had studied a takeover of Abitibi itself, which was just as vulnerable to attack as Price. Abitibi's shares had been trading at about $9 to $10, which was 30% less than book value, and Abitibi had no large shareholders who could have held out and prevented the company from being taken by storm. Any offer appealing to Abitibi's small shareholders, who usually hold stock for monetary rather than family or other emotional reasons, would probably have won control.

The company that had been stalking Abitibi was *none other than Price*, but by late October the scheme had been abandoned.

The idea had died because Price was effectively controlled by a British publisher whose 18% share of Price might be diluted to less than 10% of an Abitibi-Price — and that would result in painful British tax effects. Then there was the federal Foreign Investment Review Act in Canada. "We couldn't take over a sawmill without prior approval of the cabinet," as one Price director put it.

Now it was Price's turn to become an object of desire.[14]

Day Two

Friday, November 1
"We'd like to go the quickie route . . ."

Abitibi's youthful vice-president of corporate development, Ian McGibbon, walked into Jack Haire's office at 10 a.m. and sat down expectantly. "Ian, we're thinking of taking over another newsprint company," Haire told him casually, his eyes still fixed on the papers on his desk.

"Which?" McGibbon asked, surprised.

Haire looked up, and with a gleam behind his spectacles teased out the details: "Well, Ian, it has five newsprint mills with the same capacity as our seven. Let's see . . . it's almost as big as Abitibi, and would make us a fine complement. I'd say it's the only newsprint company in Canada we could consider buying. In fact, we looked at it a few years ago . . ."

McGibbon, as big as a pro quarterback, reached across Haire's desk, plucked a piece of paper from a dispenser, wrote "P R I C E" on it and slipped it across to Haire. After all, there were only three or four newsprint companies in Canada that Abitibi could have considered.

"Come to a meeting in half an hour," Haire said with a smile.

McGibbon left the room delighted to have sparked such a tremendous idea, or so he thought. Two days earlier he'd circulated to Haire, Rosier and others a memo with the intelligence that Price would spend $74 million over the next two years modernizing two of its newsprint mills in Quebec and Newfoundland.

12

The return on investment of the Price expansions would be good — 30% to 40% (before tax), more than Abitibi could have expected from any new building.[1] Oddly enough, Price had embarked on this program as an alternative to its abandoned Abitibi takeover scheme, though McGibbon didn't know that. Now, again ironically, Price's expansion program was becoming an appealing element in Haire's, Rosier's and Bell's decision to study a takeover of Price. But it wasn't the real detonator, as McGibbon thought. He knew nothing of Thursday's conversations, because he'd been out of town. When he did learn about them, he'd regret his premature self-congratulations and chastise himself for not coming up with Price as a takeover candidate. His corporate development department was continually looking for digestible prey, but McGibbon himself had laid down a limit on size, and that limit precluded Price.

As vice-president in charge of corporate development, McGibbon was responsible for the future rather than the present, an appropriate constituency for a 48-year-old mechanical engineer with boundless energy — a man who liked working in the outdoors on his farm, who smoked a pipe, who always dressed comfortably, who tackled hard work as eagerly as a game, who radiated a youthful exuberance among serious seniors in their 60s.

McGibbon, respected as a high-calibre support executive, would soon be providing sophisticated decision analysis at several crossroads on the way to Price. Normally, a takeover would be a McGibbon project, but Price was too big. Tom Bell, the chairman, would take this one over himself.

McGibbon's corporate-development territory included the newsprint market. On October 31, Day One, he'd been visiting Arthur D. Little Inc., the international consulting firm based at Cambridge, Massachusetts, to check Little's conclusions in a $230,000 study of the future of newsprint, done for 13 clients including Price and Abitibi.[2] Little had forecast that newsprint would be in tight supply until the 1980s, and newsprint prices would strengthen, giving greater opportunity for higher profits. However, the Little study also had projected that only 10 or 15

North American companies would have both the wood and the financial resources to capitalize on this future opportunity.

The study had accelerated a profound change already under way in Abitibi's thinking. Nine months earlier, the company had been somewhat pessimistic about newsprint, at least in the short term.[3] Now Abitibi was so confident that it wanted either to build new mills or double capacity by buying Price. Abitibi wanted to become one of the future's 10 or 15 giants, and McGibbon had gone to Cambridge to make sure the conclusions were sound.

Now, at 10:30 a.m., McGibbon and four other men were sitting in Haire's office: Haire, the financial man; Rosier, the president; Donald Bean, the Abitibi account executive from Wood Gundy Ltd., Abitibi's fiscal agent, where he was a vice-president; and James Baillie, a studious lawyer from Tory, Tory, Deslaurier & Binnington, a distinguished firm, entrenched in the Canadian establishment, that had been advising Abitibi since the days of receivership.

Haire laid out the question at hand in his usual, precise manner: "Gentlemen, we want to know if there's a legal, practical way of purchasing control of the Price company that will benefit Abitibi's shareholders."

Bean and Baillie murmured with astonishment. Neither had suspected that Abitibi was looking at a prize like Price.

Haire turned to Bean: "Don, we want to know how much Abitibi would have to pay for control of Price and whether we can finance the purchase." Bean started to take rapid notes, and Haire suggested that Tuesday might be a good day for some answers.

The Wood Gundy house held a special position in Canada's financial system — dominant, established, the country's largest, a house with a mystique all its own, heavy in underwriting muscle.[4] (The only major criticism of the firm occasionally heard is that it's less attentive than it should be to big clients of its less profitable securities trading department.) As Abitibi's fiscal agent, Wood Gundy would help to answer some very important questions. What would be the best way to accomplish the takeover? How to raise the money? Was Abitibi capable of paying the interest or fixed dividends on the securities issued for the long-term financing?

Wood Gundy would also be required to give its opinion on Abitibi's long-term financing ability to the bank that provided the "bridge" financing — a one-year loan to tide Abitibi over until it could go through the cumbersome long-term financing. Few investment houses could do the job as well. Bean, a highly articulate, poised corporate-finance expert, largely bald although only in his mid-30s, would lead the Wood Gundy shock troops into this Abitibi assault. He'd later be joined in the work by the president and other senior men from Wood Gundy to advise on strategy and make the final decisions.

Acting as chairman, since he'd called the meeting, Haire instigated a lively 30- or 40-minute discussion on the method of takeover. Should Abitibi send out an information circular to all of Price's shareholders and then buy the shares they wished to sell after 21 days? Or should Abitibi make a quick bid on the stock exchange? The quick stock-exchange route was a new and controversial technique.

Suddenly, Tom Bell walked into the room and joined the discussion. The chief executive had only five minutes to spare for it. "We'd like to go the quickie route," he said, picking up the conversation. "That circular route is like playing poker with all your cards on the table. I can think of at least four other groups that might like a go at Price — Argus, MacMillan Bloedel, Canadian Pacific and Cemp."[5] If Abitibi took 21 days to buy shares, any of these companies could also leap into the fray.

"Is the quickie route available?" Bell asked.

Baillie thought it unlikely, but he'd explore it. Bean promised to speak to Bob Morgan, another vice-president of Wood Gundy and at that time the chairman of the Toronto Stock Exchange, but he felt most of the people at Wood Gundy would say the rules were not well enough formulated even for small takeovers, and Abitibi was looking at a $300-million company.

"Well, let's take a good look at it, because that's what we want," Bell said, and he left as abruptly as he'd arrived.

The structure of Price's ownership made choice of a takeover strategy difficult, even considering the obvious advantages of a stock-exchange takeover accomplished so quickly that competitive

15

buyers wouldn't have time to enter a bid. The Price company had two major shareholders and 9,462 small ones. Effective control was exercised by the British press peer, Lord Rothermere, and his family, who owned 1% of Price's stock directly and voted 17% through their control of Associated Newspapers Group Ltd. and its sister companies, which owned that stock.

Associated was a British public company that published the Daily Mail, The Evening News and some provincial papers, and owned taxis, wharfage, restaurants, a furniture factory, even a North Sea oil company.

The second largest shareholder in Price — though unable to challenge Rothermere's control — was Domtar Ltd., a Canadian pulp-and-paper, building materials and chemicals conglomerate, which held 7% of the Price stock. Perhaps because Price was a competitor, Domtar had no representatives on Price's board.

"What would be the best way of taking out the Rothermeres?" Haire wanted to know. Their block of stock wasn't big enough to make a special deal absolutely necessary, but neither could they be treated exactly like the other 9,000 shareholders. In any case, it wouldn't do to take control of Price by simply buying out the Rothermeres, assuming they would sell.

The Price operation controlled by a British publisher concerned only with getting enough newsprint for his presses was one thing, Haire deliberated. "But if we bought the Rothermeres out and tried to exercise control with what they had, we'd have a battle royal on our hands." Other Canadian newsprint companies would resent the competitive threat posed by the Abitibi-Price combination and would probably fight for control of Price themselves.

"We'd have to get into a much safer position than 18%," Haire said. "Besides, we want a better participation in the earnings and we want the option of working towards an eventual merger, wouldn't you say, Harry?"

Rosier agreed. "There isn't much point trying to make a special deal with the Brits, because I'm sure it was Rothermere who buggered up the merger in 1969 with fancy ideas about how much his stock was worth. I'd like to say to hell with them," Rosier added.

Then Rosier rapped out two sharp rhetorical questions. "Could we just buy up the stock around them? Wouldn't they start increasing their own position or try and foul up our takeover some way?"

Baillie, the lawyer, replied quickly, almost abrasive in the smooth force of his delivery: "In my opinion you'd be ill-advised to make a private offer to the Rothermeres, because there's an implicit assumption that you'd offer them more than the other Price shareholders. Otherwise why speak to them privately at all? I'm sure you don't want to offer the English $20 a share, then offer $15 on the exchange."

"No, we don't." Haire interjected.

"Besides," Baillie continued, "if you make a deal with them and cross the stock through the exchange at a price above the market, the exchange would be annoyed — if they allow it." Later, Baillie would advise Abitibi not to involve Wood Gundy and the stock exchange in any special deal with the Rothermeres.

Jim Baillie was a pugnacious-looking securities lawyer in his late 30s, and reputed to be one of the best in Canada. His entire career had been with the Tory firm, apart from three leaves of absence, which he'd spent getting a master's degree in law from Harvard, working on the inside of the Ontario Securities Commission and doing a stint in the mutual funds industry, just to see how it worked. A bachelor, Baillie was as devoted to his work and his clients as a mountain shepherd to his flock. He devoted a lot of his time to Wood Gundy, in underwriting and other securities matters, but, secretly, he hoped he was still regarded as a general corporate lawyer.

Baillie was well aware of the sensitivity of the authorities to quick takeovers through the stock exchange. He recalled a manoeuvre in 1972 by Acres Ltd., a Toronto-based firm of engineering consultants, which had held 10% of Great Lakes Power Corp. and wanted more. While Great Lakes had been trading at $20½, Acres had bid $22 a share to a few shareholders for more stock. Word of the bid leaked out, and the Ontario Securities Commission promptly clamped a 15-day cease-trade order on the stock, citing lack of information on what appeared to be a takeover bid. In law, and in fact, perhaps it had been a takeover-bid. Acres wanted to go from 10% to 25%, perhaps for effective control. The Ontario Securities Act views 20% as the takeover point.

Neither the Ontario Securities Commission nor the Toronto Stock Exchange knew whether the Acres bid was "private" or "public" within their different meanings of the two terms. To the commission, "private" meant a bid to "fewer than 15 share-holders" and therefore exempt from takeover regulations, and "public" meant a bid to 15 or more and subject to the regulations. To the stock exchange, "private" meant a "cross"*[6] and "public" meant a bid on the exchange available to any shareholder. None of these categories had seemed to fit. The bid may have been a hybrid.[7]

The street had speculated that Acres had offered to more than 15 shareholders, and was going to cross the stock to qualify for the "exchange exemption" and avoid having to send a circular to all the shareholders, Baillie said. In other words, the law exempted exchange transactions (as it did private transactions) from takeover restrictions. And the Acres manoeuvre had shown how this "exchange exemption" could be used.

"What happened?" McGibbon asked.

"When the stock started trading again, the price rose to $22.50 and Acres backed away rather than increase its offer," Baillie said. After that episode, the exchange had laid down a requirement that it be given prior notice of any bid for stock that would raise the buyer's holdings to more than 20% a legal takeover. That was so the exchange staff could decide whether the offer should be made to all shareholders in the spirit of the Securities Act.

Baillie's conclusion from the Acres case was brief: "The stock-exchange route is controversial, and Wood Gundy would have to talk to the exchange before you use it."

The trouble with the quick exchange route was a legal flaw. The Ontario Securities Act defined a "takeover bid" as an offer to purchase stock that would take the offeror's holdings above 20% — an arbitrary level at which "control" of a company was taken to become possible for the purposes of the act. This narrow definition was combined with an exemption for private purchases and all offers to purchase made on the stock exchange. The "exchange exemption" was intended only to permit the routine buying and selling of big blocks of stock that don't involve control. (If shareholder A has 51% of a company, and absolute control, and shareholder B has 18%, B can increase his holdings by well more than 20% without ever gaining control.)

---

* A transaction between two principals, but made through a stock exchange.

The drafters of the law, principally the Ontario Securities Commission which also administers the Securities Act, had never dreamed that canny brokers would use the stock-exchange exemption for a quick kind of takeover that bypassed both the requirements of the Securities Act and, because of its speed, month-by-month and day-by-day disclosure requirements. By now, the commission was beginning to grow uneasy. What's more, some of the early exchange takeovers had been "smelly" — like the Acres business. For several ensuing days, Wood Gundy and Baillie and his firm would believe that the commission, and perhaps the Toronto Stock Exchange too, wouldn't allow Abitibi to try a quick exchange takeover of Price. But it wasn't up to a lawyer or a fiscal agent to make corporate decisions or to second-guess commissioners. The quick route was available in law, but could be used only after approval of the exchanges, and the final decision on how to take over Price had to be made by Abitibi's senior executives.[8]

Harry Rosier had been looking down thoughtfully at the copper-green spires of the Royal York Hotel nearby, and worrying about the reaction of Charles Tittemore, the president of Price, which would be crucial to any successful takeover.

"How much stock should we go after?" he asked suddenly. "We could exercise control with less than 50%"[9]

Baillie asked: "Does Price have much undistributed income?" Haire looked briefly at some papers on his desk. "Retained earnings are about $100 million," Haire said, "and $35 million of that is in cash and marketable securities. The debt/equity ratio is much better than ours and . . ."

"Then 49% would be much better than 51%, tax-wise," Baillie interjected, "because of designated surplus." At 51%, dividends paid to Abitibi from designated surplus would be taxable. Below 50%, they wouldn't.[10]

"Forty-nine percent would be better for morale too," Rosier said, cheering up. "Charlie might feel we were breathing down his neck if we took 51%." A ripple of amusement went around the room, Baillie laughing the loudest to provide moral as well as legal support. Rosier also pointed out that 49% would look better than 51% in the United States, from an anti-trust point of view. Whether or not Abitibi had absolute control of Price might color the official view of whether or not it was an unacceptable concentration.

"What about the combines and anti-trust question?" McGibbon asked, as the hands of five wrist watches approached noon.

"I'll need to know what share of the market the Abitibi-Price group would have in Canada and in the States," Baillie replied. "You don't have much to worry about in Canada."

"There's a risk in the U.S., though isn't there, Jim?" Rosier asked. "When we acquired Cox in '68, we were investigated. And back in '69, your firm thought the Americans might want to look at an Abitibi-Price merger."

"The climate has changed since then," Baillie assured him. "With all the Canadian nationalism of the last few years, it's unlikely the Americans would try exporting their anti-trust laws to Canada. I'll ask American counsel what the risks are and what penalties might be available to the U.S. government if they did decide they didn't like it. But I'll need the market-share data."

"I'll get that for you," McGibbon offered, starting to take on the role he would play in this takeover — that of intelligence officer and methods man.

The visitors got up to leave Haire's office.

"There's just one more thing," Haire began hesitantly. "I'm very concerned about security. We don't want any of this to leak out." He rose to his feet like the others at the door. "We need a code name and, well, there's this system I've used for a long time. I don't know where I got it. You use the second letter of the company's name. In this case it would be 'Project R.' "

"Oh, that's *really* imaginative, Jack!" McGibbon said, laughing. But Project R became the name of their game for a few days.

20

Day Three

Saturday, November 2
"Their last normal weekend . . ."

Each of the participants being drawn into the developing take-over spent Saturday in his usual way. It was to be their last normal weekend for three weeks, though they didn't know it at the time.

James Baillie, the lawyer, went into his office as usual, allowing himself the Saturday luxury of arriving a little later in the morning. In the evening he dined out, because he rarely kept in his bachelor pad any nourishment greater than a bottle of milk. Mellow before bed, he daydreamed about the camera safari in Africa on which he'd leave the following week. Would he have to come back early to help in the takeover?

Baillie had always emphasized that he was on call for Abitibi wherever he might be vacationing around the world, and he'd once flown from Britain to a job in Chile at a moment's notice. If the takeover really gathered momentum, he might cancel his African safari altogether, he thought.

Harry Rosier painted a canvas all afternoon on his sun porch in Oakville. The light was good today. (Abitibi people often said, "He's quite good at it" — in a surprised tone, as if an engineer was unlikely to have artistic sensitivity.) For exercise, Rosier liked to indulge in his favorite sport, fishing. But this wasn't the season.

Ian McGibbon worked happily on his farm at Erin in the Caledon Hills north of Toronto with a power saw and a hammer and a mouthful of nails, building an extension to the farmhouse with the

21

help of a neighbor. At 5 p.m. he came in to watch Bugs Bunny with his young children.

Jack Haire took some financial papers to work on in his study. At mealtimes he told his wife Ethel more than once that Abitibi was considering a very important step and he might be quite busy next week.

Day Four

Sunday, November 3
"The day would end
in tension . . ."

Late this afternoon, Thomas J. Bell picked up Charles Rathgeb, president and owner of Comstock International Ltd.,* at his home and drove him to the airport. There they met, a few minutes after his arrival from the West, a friend of Bell's — Ronald Williams, publisher of the Winnipeg Tribune, which buys newsprint from Abitibi's mill at Pine Falls, Manitoba. The three men boarded a Sabreliner borrowed (as was Abitibi's custom) from Northern & Central Gas Corp.,† whose president, Edmund C. Bovey, was on the executive committee of Abitibi's board of directors. Abitibi had sold its own aircraft a few years before for reasons of economy.

The aircraft would take Bell and his guests to Augusta, Georgia, where Bell was a member of the Augusta National Golf Club, a connection he'd made after Abitibi bought Cox Newsprint. All three friends were sportsmen. Bell vigorously enjoyed skiing and golf. Rathgeb was a well-known sporting luminary: In 1971 he'd borrowed a CL41 jet from Canadair (he was a director) to lead the Dominion Day Air Race across Canada. He'd also ballooned across the Alps, set up an international tuna fishing competition, and built up a stable of race horses.

*Formerly Canadian International Comstock Co.
†Later to become, through merger, Norcen Energy Resources Ltd.

23

The three men had planned an easy Monday at Augusta — some golf, relaxation and perhaps a little turkey talk. But for Bell the day would end in tension.

Day Five

At 11 a.m. the telephone rang in Harry Rosier's office. It was Robert Foster, a principal of Kernaghan & Co. and an investment analyst with many years' experience in forest-products securities. Kernaghan & Co. is an investment dealer, but in securities-industry parlance it's a "boutique" — a small firm with a clientele among wealthy institutional investors and a plentiful assortment of knowledge on special situations. The firm's style was to develop informal contacts with corporate decision makers like Rosier, to gain an inside understanding of the market.

Foster and Rosier had lunched together occasionally — Rosier to pick Foster's brains, Foster to attract a little business to Kernaghan despite Abitibi's traditional association with Wood Gundy.

"Have you noticed Price these days, Mr. Rosier?" Foster asked on the phone. "It's down to $13.50 — that's about 30% less than book value. You people should consider a raid on Price."

Rosier was caught off guard. "Well . . . ah . . . we can't, Bob," he muttered. "We looked at in 1969 and were advised it might be against the U.S. anti-trust laws. But that's a good idea, Bob. Thanks for calling."

Rosier hung up as soon as he courteously could.

Under pressure of work, Tom Bell's golf handicap had slipped

25

over recent years from an excellent two to a good six. That afternoon in Augusta, he'd played with Williams, beat him and won a small bet.

"Why don't you take a look at Price?" Rathgeb asked Bell over a pre-dinner martini in the lounge after the game. "The word is that Domtar is going to make a run at it."

Comstock, Rathgeb's company, was a $50-million Toronto-based mechanical and electrical contractor that specialized in paper-mill work, and Rathgeb had to keep his ear cocked for industry scuttlebut. Bell knew that Rathgeb was usually a good source of information.

"Where did you hear that?" Bell asked sharply. Rathgeb, surprised at the reaction, told him. Bell forced himself to calm down and changed the subject.[1]

Day Six

Tuesday, November 5
"He was, of course, one of the 'bastards' himself . . ."

At 9:30 a.m., the Project R team filed into the Abitibi board room, which lies between the president's office and the chairman's, for the first sleeves-up working session. Rosier, the senior man present, avoided the high-backed chair at one end of the long table, which even Bell ignored at board meetings, and went instead to the far end beneath a dramatic Thomas F. Chatfield painting of an Ontario forest under early snow.

The six others scattered themselves among the long, polished table's 16 chairs, whose green and gold striped cushions repeated the executive suite's theme of wood and wealth. New to the team was James Tory, senior partner of the Tory law firm. Jim Baillie was going away on vacation that Thursday and a replacement would be needed. In personality, Jim Tory was the kind of man who's relaxed and quiet, even diffident, during preliminaries, coming into his own in a crisis. He wouldn't say much on this first occasion.

Don Bean from Wood Gundy, the youngest man in the room, sat under a magnificent portrait of Abitibi's founder, F. H. Anson, on the long wall facing the western window, as if to seek his blessing on the part Bean would play in this great undertaking. The room was coolly lit by refracted morning sunlight.

"Let's deal with the nasty stuff first, Jim." Rosier said to Baillie. "Anti-combines and anti-trust. The market shares, Ian?"

"Yes, sir." Ian McGibbon was already opening a file containing several scraps of scribbled notes. The corporate-development man had been well prepared for this moment. During 1973 and 1974, he'd sat on a government-sponsored committee set up by five newsprint companies and Canadian National Railways to find ways of distributing Canadian newsprint in the United States at lower cost. The committee work had left him with a good idea of where the member companies, notably Price, were sending their newsprint and in what quantities. Like a good intelligence officer, he also had other sources of information.

McGibbon apologized for the state of his notes. "I finished the calculations this morning and didn't have time to get them typed up," he explained. "In Canada, Abitibi has 20% of the newsprint market, we know that. Price has about 12% at the outside. [Price's share was actually less.] The combined share of market would be 32% at the most."

He paused and looked at Baillie, who reassured him: "I don't think you have much to worry about in Canada. It would have to be a near-monopoly before the courts would consider an adverse ruling." Canadian law at the time was toothless, as far as mergers and takeovers were concerned.

Baillie recalled the Canadian Breweries case in the 1950s, which wasn't too relevant but nevertheless was the lead precedent in Canadian anti-combines jurisprudence. "In 25 years, Canadian Breweries took over about two dozen other breweries and closed half of them," Baillie recalled. "When the anti-combines people made their investigation, Canadian Breweries controlled more than half the Ontario industry and half the Ontario-Quebec industry. But the court ruled that the company had no power to fix prices because beer sales are regulated by the provincial governments.

"That case cost the government more than $100,000 and they've attempted little else since. Your shares of market are a lot less than Canadian Breweries' were. I don't think you have much to worry about in Canada," Baillie repeated. "U.S. law is much more stringent. Under the Clayton Act, if a merger brings the combined market share of the two companies above a certain level and there's a lessening of competition, that might be sufficient to cause an inquiry, depending on other circumstances. But I'm not knowl-

28

edgeable in this area. We'll have to give the market figure to Dick Rohr. He's coming up on Thursday and he might be able to give you an opinion them." Rohr was Abitibi's counsel in the United States.

"What could they do if it does exceed their damn guidelines?" Rosier asked belligerently from the end of the table.

Baillie gave a calm reply. "In prudence we should consider whether the U.S. Justice Department might have any means of exerting pressure to reverse the takeover in Canada," Baillie said, "but that's a remote possibility. I'd think the most they could do is force divestiture of Cox or of Price's half interest in the De Ridder mill in Louisiana, or both. But Rohr will have to give you the definitive answer on that too."

Rosier turned to Bean who was doing esoteric earnings calculations, compulsively, on his blotter. "Don, did we get anywhere with the quick route?" Rosier asked hopefully.

"Well, our initial feeling is that there's a 50-50 chance the Securities Commission or the exchange would disallow it," Bean replied. "It's a hard one to call. The commission didn't express very strong views about the exemption when Royce* was chairman. There's a new chairman now, and who knows what he thinks?' As for the exchange, I've asked Bob Morgan about it, but he's in a tough position. He can't consult anybody at this stage without giving the game away. We really need to know what Jack Kimber thinks."

The meeting broke into noisy chatter as three pairs of men talked about whom they knew at the Toronto Stock Exchange and how Jack Kimber, president of the exchange, might be induced to give a frank statement of his views without being told what was happening.

Rosier reimposed his authority. "Well, we'll have to think that one out. The next item is how much we'll have to pay. Jack?"

Jack Haire began without looking at the papers and files stacked tidily in front of him: "Well, $20 would be a good round figure to start with." The chief financial officer spoke slowly, each phrase packed with financial significance. "At today's market price

*Edward Allen Royce was chairman of the Ontario Securities Commission from July 1969 until September 1974.

of $13 a share (you'll have noticed the price has fallen slightly on low volume since Friday), $20 would give the Price shareholders a very nice premium of more than 50%. Also, $20 would be close to book value per share, which is a sound justification for that price, to my mind."[2]

Haire looked around as if expecting disagreement. "At the same time, $20 would be a fair price for Abitibi's shareholders to pay," he continued, using "shareholders" as a euphemism for the company. "We'd be buying Price at about six times 1974 earnings, which would give a quite acceptable return on investment of about 17%. With the downturn in the newsprint market we think is on the way, Price's earnings may be down for the next couple of years, but they'll come back up again, and that's a good price, nevertheless."[3]

He pursed his lips with conviction. Haire and Bean, the Wood Gundy man, then engaged in an arcane discussion of Price's earnings and what should be paid for them. But it didn't alter Haire's original figure.[4]

"The lowest we could offer would be $18 because of Domtar," Haire pointed out. Domtar's 7% of Price had been purchased by St. Lawrence Corp., a paper manufacturer, in the late 1950s from the estate of industrialist Isaak Walton Killam. Argus Corp., then under the command of E. P. Taylor,* controlled both St. Lawrence and Domtar, and had seemed to be planning a takeover of Price. The St. Lawrence block originally had been 10% of Price's shares, but Taylor lost interest and no more shares were purchased. Later, St. Lawrence became a subsidiary of Domtar, and the 10% block fell to 7% as various manoeuvres increased the number of Price's outstanding shares.

Haire went on: "Domtar carried those shares on its books for a long time at $18 a share, which is what they must have been purchased for.[5] In 1969 we had reason to believe Domtar would dispose of the stock at close to that value on its books, $18. That might still be the case."

"Eighteen 1974 dollars are worth a lot less than eighteen 1959 dollars," McGibbon interjected.

"Yes, it's really an accounting approach rather than any reflec-

*Edward Plunket Taylor, one of Canada's best-known financiers and industrialists, retired in 1966 to the Bahamas, where he remained active in housing and real estate.

tion of the real inflated cost of the investment," Haire replied. "It must have been trading at about $15 a share at that time and the price hasn't changed much since then. If they applied an inflation factor to the original price, they'd never sell it."

Haire concluded that Domtar might let the shares go for $18, but probably not for less. "To tell you the truth I'm surprised they haven't made a run at Price themselves, with the head start they've got," Haire added. Bell hadn't returned yet from Augusta with Rathgeb's news. In the days to come, Haire would be the one most worried about a Domtar takeover.

"Wouldn't you think they see greater opportunities in packaging and kraft liner than in newsprint?" Rosier asked him. "Don't forget, they closed Three Rivers in March '72."[6]

Competing corporations may look at the same market figures for the same commodity and come to different conclusions about the future, colored by their own experiences and problems. Domtar's view of newsprint may have been darkened by trouble at a newsprint mill in Three Rivers, Quebec, which eventually had been sold to Kruger Pulp & Paper Co., of Montreal, one of the biggest privately owned paper companies in the world. Kruger also had trouble with Three Rivers. And Domtar's view of newsprint wouldn't necessarily be the same as Abitibi's just because both companies had subscribed to the same Arthur D. Little study.[7]

Rosier's comment tailed off inconclusively. Throughout their study of the Price takeover, the Abitibi executives would continue to find it surprisingly difficult to call Domtar's moves.

Rosier was anxious to move on to another appointment. "Let's leave the price at $18 to $20 for today," he said.

"Harry, are we still going Greenshielding?" McGibbon asked him. He was referring to a luncheon appointment with analysts from Greenshields Inc., another large investment dealer. McGibbon had been an Abitibi vice-president for only four months, and he hadn't settled down to a consistent form of address for the president. Rosier was still "sir" one moment and "Harry" the next, as he always had been to McGibbon.

Don Bean, the Wood Gundy account executive responsible for preserving good relations between his firm and Abitibi, jumped at the reference to a rival firm on Wood Gundy territory. McGibbon teased him with the cryptic reassurance they were only going to talk about "Arab money." The intrigue of Project R and the prospect of exciting work had put McGibbon in a playful mood.

"What are you going to say to Charlie Tittemore when you meet him at the industry dinner tonight, Harry?"McGibbon asked.

Rosier came back hard. "I don't know how I can break bread with him when I know what you bastards are going to do to him," he said, and he walked out of the board room with a grim smile. Rosier was, of course, one of the "bastards" himself.

This week, the financial analysis department of Domtar Ltd. was bringing up to date the company's information on Price Co., which had last been reviewed one year before. Price's cash flow was assessed, and Domtar's assumptions about the future of newsprint were superimposed on Price's performance. Later, an attempt would be made to analyze the synergism of a Domtar-Price merger. What factors would make the earnings of the combined companies greater than the sum of the parts? The updated conclusions would be sent up into the executive suite where decisions were made. Several times over the next week or two, rumors of what was going on would trickle through Domtar's leaky security and reach Abitibi, adding to Rosier's and Haire's apprehension.

That night, Rosier and Bell, relaxing in the opulent Reed Paper Co. dining room at the top of the York Centre office tower, half a block from Abitibi's head office, met and chatted socially with Charlie Tittemore at an industry dinner.

Price's president noticed nothing abnormal until he casually referred to Price's earnings for the first nine months of 1974. He was puzzled when Rosier took a small black notebook and a pencil out of his jacket pocket in the middle of the dining room and asked him to repeat the figures. Tittemore found this very odd and would wonder about it for days afterward.

At dinner, Bell, who'd returned from Augusta that day, gave Rosier the news about Domtar in a forceful whisper, anxious and impatient for Abitibi to be on the move.[8]

Day Seven

Wednesday, November 6
"Let's get it from the Arabs . . ."

At 10 a.m. the Project R team assembled in Bell's office, many striking a casual, bored pose in the vestibule beforehand for the benefit of the rest of the staff. Behind Bell's closed doors each team member was given assignments from a list of compelling questions Ian McGibbon had been tormenting his brains over since Monday. McGibbon, with the help of the lawyers and the securities people, had covered every conceivable angle, including a few crazy ideas that were abandoned as soon as they were spoken aloud. The work list's value at this stage was as a thorough review of all the issues in the takeover, and it pulled together all the stray thoughts generated since Day One.*[1]

In case a copy of the worklist should fall into unfriendly hands, McGibbon adopted Haire's "second-letter" code. It worked well with Abitibi (B) and Price (R), but he was annoyed to find he had to use "D" for Domtar and even "Cox" for Cox because both had the same second letter (O). If a copy of the list got lost, anybody with a grain of knowledge would know what it was all about, he realized. But to hell with it; that was unlikely.

The assignments were given, then Bell delivered a brief pep talk. "Secrecy and urgency," he said, "are the two things that will

---

* The work list, in effect a short guide to the complex art of takeover, appears in its entirety in the reference notes.

33

make this project go. We've got a date — there's a board meeting called for next Thursday and we could pull it forward from 10 to eight o'clock and go when the exchange opens."

He wound up the meeting with: "Well, before we go any further we better make sure of the money."

"Let's get it from the Arabs," Rosier said cheerfully.

Bell was *not* amused.

At 11:30 a.m., Bell hurried out of the Toronto-Dominion Centre, along King Street, across busy Bay Street, which gives its name to Toronto's financial district, and up the steps into the Toronto headquarters of the Royal Bank of Canada, Abitibi's banker and Canada's biggest bank.[2] It was half an hour before a weekly meeting of Toronto directors of the bank, which Bell as a director was due to attend. The meeting would be chaired by W. D. Gardiner, the Royal's deputy chairman and executive vice-president.

Gardiner was a tall man with a small, cherubic face, and he wore thick horn-rimmed spectacles. (Some wags, noticing his high shoulders, said he'd once shrugged off an impossible loan and the wind blew cold, leaving him permanently in that position.) He received Bell warmly in his office.

"Doug, there's this project I have in mind," Bell said in his usual breathless manner. "It's a takeover of a big company, and I'll need a hundred to a hundred and fifty million. Is it available?"

"Holy Christmas!" Gardiner exploded. Then he remembered he was a banker. "That's a very unusual request," he said in a businesslike tone. "We don't have many like that. I'll have to phone Earle. Who is it?"

Bell pleaded for secrecy: "I'll tell you who it is, but this has to be handled in such a confidential manner you wouldn't believe it. You can tell Earle, but this just has to be respected. We don't know how we're going at this deal yet. We haven't made our final plans yet, but it might be a stock-exchange transaction and, if so, there can't be one speck of information leaked out." Then he identified the target.

Gardiner phoned W. Earle McLaughlin at the bank's head office in Montreal. McLaughlin made no bones about who ran the

Royal, taking unto himself the ultimate title in a corporation, "chairman and president," which men like Bell would avoid. And McLaughlin's management style matched his chosen appelation. McLaughlin wasn't sure about Bell's $150 million. "Maybe . . . I don't know," he told Gardiner. "Money has been tight. Give me an hour."

Money was tight all right. In the inflation-hot economy, interest rates had reached levels never before attained. The bank's prime rate for best customers was topping 10% and house-mortgage rates were up to a cruel 12%. This was the peak. In the months to come, interest rates would ease downwards as the economy cooled off. When McLaughlin hung up, Bell and Gardiner went on into the directors' meeting.

After lunch, Bell walked back to his office and ran into McGibbon. "The money's almost in the bag," Bell told him. In the days to come he'd often clear obstacles by mentally minimizing them.

"Wow! I know you work fast, but that's goddam fast," McGibbon gasped, a little overawed.

At 3 p.m. Gardiner called Bell back to the bank. "It's not quite all that easy," Gardiner told him. "We've phoned Chase Manhattan and one or two other American banks, and it's illegal for them, under current conditions, to advance money for takeovers in the United States. It's legal for them to do it in Canada. We could bring some Canadian money up here, but their money is still tight. They don't feel they could let us have any when they have restrictions on doing the same thing in their own country. We can't get access to American money and we consider we'd need a lot of it if you want $150 million. Can't you offer shares and cash and do it with half as much money?"

Bell replied impatiently: "I'm not sure we want a hundred and fifty because we haven't really finalized our planning, but it's close to that. It may be a hundred. It may be a hundred and twenty-five; we just don't know. But in that area. Is the money available?"

Gardiner hesitated. "Well, we're just not sure, Tom," he said. "But we'll keep looking at it. We'll look at the European situation and see if we can get Eurodollars."

Bell returned to head office and told the Project R team precisely but optimistically: "It looks as if we can get the money.

We're not *sure*, but the money isn't going to be as big a problem as maybe something else. So let's keep moving."

At 4 p.m., Charles Gundy, the white-haired, sprightly, 70-year-old chairman of Wood Gundy walked across from Wood Gundy's offices in the Royal Trust Tower to the neighboring Toronto-Dominion Centre at Bell's request. Bell had a delicate task: to inform Gundy of Abitibi's intentions toward Price — and thereby place him in a potential conflict of interest.

At this time, Gundy was a director of 10 companies in retailing, steel, farm machinery, power and cement, chosen by them for the experience of a long, active business life, and for the insight into the clockworks of the economy available to the head of Canada's biggest investment dealer.[3] Gundy, however, was a man who seemed to be impatient with all the high respectability surrounding him at the apex of the investment community. In the midst of the rarified ambience of Wood Gundy's offices, with teas served in silver pots and exquisite Chinese porcelain pieces on display in corner shelves, he liked to adopt a touch of the devil-may-care of a mining promoter. An awed visitor might enter his drawing-room office at Wood Gundy and be presented with a cigar and one match. After discreetly wondering what to do with the match, he'd likely be told: "Strike it on the bottom of the table, or on the sole of your shoe or on the seat of your pants if you want to." Gundy was full of such out-of-character surprises.

Tom Bell was under a compelling obligation to put him in the picture because Charlie Gundy was not only on Abitibi's executive committee (a core group of powerful directors), he was also the chairman of Abitibi's fiscal agent; and he was a director of Domtar, which, if what Charles Rathgeb had told Bell in Georgia was right, was also planning a raid on Price.

At other times and in other places, eyebrows had been raised over Gundy's serving on the boards of two competitive paper companies, but he'd usually shrugged the question off. "You just have to be careful not to spill the beans about one company at the other's board meeting. In any case, Canada has a shortage of good director material," Gundy would say. "Many young men today do not want to expose themselves to the tight legal responsibilities of a directorship at a time when shareholders' suits against directors are becoming the mode."

But in *this* situation Gundy seemed to be on the spot. If Domtar was indeed considering a raid on Price, Gundy might find himself at a takeover discussion at one board meeting with full knowledge of the other company's plans, which could not fail to influence his contribution to the debate, if he made any.

When it came to a vote, if Gundy voted "no" to either takeover, cynics might charge him with favoring the other company. If he voted "no" at Domtar, it would be tempting to point to the big commission his firm would earn in the Abitibi takeover as Abitibi's fiscal agent. If he voted "yes" to both takeovers it could be argued he was helping create costly competition between two companies whose interests he served.

The only course open to Gundy, it seemed, would be to abstain from the discussion and voting at both board meetings, but, since Bell already had an idea that Domtar was eyeing Price, that would give the game away, at least at Abitibi, and perhaps also at Domtar where they well knew Gundy's close connection with the Toronto company. Gundy might "fall sick" and "regretfully be unable to attend" any Domtar meeting, but then he'd have to ask himself whether he was fulfilling his duty to Domtar. Still, Gundy was a sharp old campaigner. He'd find a way out.

Tom Bell was also in a delicate position. It would be unfair to Charlie Gundy to spring the Price project on him at the next board meeting. Besides, the secret probably wouldn't keep that long. Wood Gundy was already hard at work on Abitibi's takeover, and Gundy shouldn't hear the news from within his firm before he heard it from Bell. Soon, Wood Gundy might be asked to give Abitibi assurances that it would underwrite the long-term financing of the takeover, and the firm's chairman should be party to them.

Bell quickly told Gundy, and made him the first Abitibi director, other than himself and Rosier, to know. He added: "Charlie, the important thing about this deal from here on in is that you as our underwriter will assure the bank that through financing you'll take them out. I've asked for this money for a year, and they've said that's too long. So what Wood Gundy has to do in this program is assure the bank you can underwrite them out of this deal in time. Now you're in it, Charlie, and our only concern in not bringing you in before was that you're on the board of Domtar." From his position on Abitibi's executive committee, Gundy was one of the *eminences grises* behind Abitibi. He'd discovered Thomas J. Bell in the mid-1960s and brought him into the company, and normally, as a member of the executive committee, he'd learn about anything important happening at Abitibi before other outside directors.

Gundy didn't think much of the takeover at all, and he doubted that the route of a quick takeover on the floor of the stock exchange could be used. It would be two days more before he would warm to the idea and throw all his elderly vitality behind it. The Abitibi chief executive would take this as a sign that, if Domtar *were* planning a raid on Price, Charles Gundy knew nothing whatever about it — a rather inconclusive conclusion.

Day Eight

Thursday, November 7
"Are you going to get this money or aren't you . . .?"

"The transaction you have in mind lies outside the jurisdiction of the Clayton Act, I'm confident of that. I also believe an American court would adopt the same attitude but, of course, there are no guarantees." This was the message Richard D. Rohr from Detroit, Abitibi's counsel in the United States, gave to a morning assembly of the four Abitibi executives, the two lawyers, Jim Tory and Jim Baillie, and the Wood Gundy people. "There have been no authoritative decisions that would guide the courts on the question of extraterritorial mergers and takeovers, but our firm's review of hundreds of pages of legislative history on section seven of the Clayton Act — you know, Senate hearings, House debates, that sort of thing — indicates a total concentration on the U.S. economy with zero attention to shaping the economic environment of other nations," Rohr said.

That was fairly strong, though qualified, reassurance from Rohr, but it would do little to assuage Abitibi's nervousness about anti-trust measures. The word "anti-trust" had been a bogeyman in the Canadian pulp and paper industry for almost a century because the industry's newsprint customers, powerful American publishers, had always been able to whip publicity-conscious politicians into attitudes hostile to the industry whenever there'd been a price increase, justified or not. Most pulp and paper executives had a deep-rooted, habitual fear of American anti-trust attitudes.[1]

39

Any Abitibi-Price takeover would raise questions in the realm of two American statutes. The Sherman Act (1890), section two, prohibited monopolies, but since Abitibi-Price wouldn't be a newsprint monopoly in the United States — no problem. Section seven of the Clayton Act prohibited acquisitions where "the effect of such acquisition may be substantially to lessen competition, or to *tend* to create a monopoly." In this way, the Clayton Act tried, so to speak, to head monopolies off at the pass.

If Abitibi and Price had been American companies, and if the joint company had held a share of the American newsprint market in excess of tight guidelines laid down by the Department of Justice, a takeover might have been attacked under the Clayton Act. Even small market concentrations created by the joining of two companies had been ruled to be in violation of the Clayton Act. On one occasion the Supreme Court of the United States had ruled that a combined market share of 7% of grocery sales in the Los Angeles area was unacceptable, and, on another, 4½% of the national beer market. There were places in the United States where Abitibi-Price might have more than 7% of the newsprint market.

Rohr, a partner in the Detroit firm of Bodman, Langley, Bogle, Armstrong & Dahling, and an expert on anti-trust law, clarified his opinion even more precisely. He wasn't confident, he told the meeting, that the United States government wouldn't litigate, at great expense to Abitibi, the question of whether an Abitibi-Price takeover came under the Clayton Act. And he could give no assurance that Abitibi and Price wouldn't be brought into court, though he thought both eventualities unlikely. Rohr was confident, though, that at any stage of any litigation, a successful argument could be put forward that the takeover, being in Canada, wasn't within the scope of the Clayton Act and that the courts would accept this argument. "This is what I believe a court should do," he warned, "not what precedent compels it to do."

While Rohr was talking, some invisible Canadian observer, provided he was neither a lawyer nor an Abitibi man, might have noticed a disturbing assumption underlying Rohr's exposition of the ramifications of American anti-trust law: that the United States might have jurisdiction over a Canadian takeover *if it so chose.*

"Abitibi must on no account seem to be taking protection behind the border," Rohr warned, as if Bell and his team were barbarians hiding in the hills, as if Abitibi were a juvenile playing hookey from a Washington school, as if an extraterritorial takeover action involving two Canadian companies that traded in the United States were a sneaky way of getting around American justice, instead of being a dignified question unresolved in international law and the relationship of sovereign states.

Later, Rohr would send a long legal letter to the United States Department of Justice, in which he would present argument that the Congress of the United States never intended the Clayton Act to have extraterritorial effect because, for example, it graciously [not Rohr's word] chose to recognize the independence of the legal system of the Philippines, which was then under its jurisdiction, by exempting the Philippines from the operation of the act. Therefore, Rohr would tell the Justice Department, "it cannot be argued that any different result would obtain with respect to the Sovereign Dominion of Canada or any other nation independent of the United States."

The only proper gesture for a Canadian engaged in a lawful transaction on his own soil to make to the Congress of the United States of America was to raise one digit of his right hand high in the air in the direction of Washington. But the Abitibi executives calmly digested Rohr's monstrous notion that Congress itself decided where its laws were applicable, and calmly viewed the transaction in that light for purposes of anti-trust. Business lies in the realm of power, not of reason.

What could the United States government do if it decided to attack an Abitibi-Price takeover? There was no precedent, Rohr repeated. "We are literally on the frontiers of U.S. jurisprudence." American courts had dealt with a takeover of an American company by a foreign company, and with the takeover by an American company of a foreign company trading in the United States, but Rohr's research had disclosed no cases involving combinations of two foreign companies accomplished outside the United States.

What about an attack on Abitibi-Price assets within the United States? Although both Abitibi and Price had newsprint interests in that country (Cox and de Ridder), Rohr said that neither of these was significant, either together or individually, under any section seven test. "And a divestiture case would be a meaningless exercise," he added.

In the unlikely event the United States government did obtain a court order forcing Abitibi-Price to divest itself of Cox or de Ridder, Rohr said, the judicial process would be time-consuming. The Department of Justice had been reluctant to force any company to sell an acquired company at a loss, thereby giving reasonable time for divestiture. A pinch-the-toe attack — fining the Cox and de Ridder companies for an indefinite period if the parents didn't separate — wouldn't be available to the government either, Rohr believed, because the Clayton Act was remedial, not punitive.

One avenue of attack on an Abitibi-Price takeover Rohr didn't cover (because it lies outside the realm of law) was an appeal by the American government to the Organization for Economic Co-operation & Development (OECD), which has a committee that deals specifically with business practices in one member nation that might cause harmful economic effects in another.

But conciliation before the OECD is voluntary; Canada wouldn't even be obliged to join any panel formed to consider Abitibi-Price. If it did attend, Canada could argue that its anti-combines legislation in force in November 1974 didn't prohibit an Abitibi-Price takeover. Canada could argue that new competition legislation, which had been under study for some time, wasn't applicable, even if an Abitibi-Price takeover were a violation of its provisions, because the law wouldn't be retroactive. Finally, Canada mightn't want to unwind an Abitibi-Price combination if there were benefits within Canada. The two companies didn't exist for the American market alone.

An appeal to the OECD by the United States would certainly carry political dangers. American anti-trust laws are based on a political philosophy that isn't necessarily espoused in other countries. The broad and durable vein of American political thought running through the Clayton Act is that small business is *per se* good and that concentration that threatens or eliminates small business is *per se* bad, a kind of business populism that ignores economies of scale that can deliver better, cheaper goods to the consumer. This small-business philosophy isn't peculiar to the United States; it was found in the New Democratic provincial governments of Western Canada, and it found expression in the Poujade Party in France in the 1950s. But the government of the United States is apparently the only major national government that now espouses it.

In Europe, for instance, governments come down hard on price fixing and they regulate oppressive monopolies, but they don't subscribe to the American "might is wrong" philosophy. Rather, many European governments encourage corporate size so that, nationally, they may compete more effectively in world markets. (In January 1976, Canada's Prime Minister, Pierre Trudeau, despite his heatedly debated attitude toward big business and the market economy, said in a national address that he and his government recognized that large corporations can be valuable to the country for this very reason.)

Besides, American anti-trust policy has a serious defect, attributable to a paradox that lies at the heart of competition. A company that competes vigorously is, in fact, being anti-competitive because the essence of competition is to try to win. The only companies that preserve the competitive environment are those that complete half-heartedly or not at all — those that don't drive competitors out of business. American anti-trust laws discriminate against small companies by preventing them from becoming bigger by takeover or merger and challenging their biggest competitors, the General Motors and the Kraft Foods that have become big internally through vigorous market competition and which now dominate large shares of their markets. Takeovers may be discouraged, but to discourage internal growth by good management and efficiency would be to discourage competition itself — which would be an absurd conclusion of competition policy. Therefore the competition policy must remain incomplete.

Each country tries to resolve these dilemmas in its own way, and any attempt by the United States to export its incomplete and distinctively American competition policy to Canada through the OECD would undoubtedly meet with resistance and criticism.

Because the question of an extraterritorial takeover was a novelty in the United States and because of his firm's failure to find any reported precedent despite vast literature coverage, Rohr promised the Abitibi group he'd check his conclusions through more research and personal contacts. Later, after returning to Detroit, he'd telephone a friend who was publishing a book on the international aspects of anti-trust law, and another knowledgeable friend in New York City. One of Rohr's partners, who was also active in anti-trust work, would call a distinguished professor in the field. Despite the "no-names" nature of these dicussions because of the secrecy involved, Rohr would be satisfied from the conversations that his conclusions were generally sound. Abitibi nevertheless would remain jumpy.[2]

The two Canadian lawyers present on Day Eight believed the Canadian anti-combines branch was much less likely to be exercised about an Abitibi-Price takeover than the United States Justice Department. Canadian competition law was much less restrictive than in the United States and was virtually toothless.

Besides, as Tom Bell pointed out eagerly to the gathering, Canadian governments are schizophrenic about corporate combinations. Corporate power within Canada was viewed with suspicion, but its national value was recognized in export markets. During the Depression, the governments of Ontario and Quebec had promoted higher, fixed prices and extensive co-operation among newsprint producers, to overcome the disastrous erosion of prices in the American market which had led many companies into receivership or bankruptcy and hurt many paper-mill towns.

Normally, such measures would be a criminal violation of competition law, but no action against the companies had ever been proposed. The main consumers of Canada's newsprint had been in another country, the United States, so the arrangements couldn't be said to act to the detriment of the Canadian public. The United States had a similar attitude to export markets. The Webb-Pomerene Act (1918) exempted American exporting corporations from anti-trust legislation, providing that any combinations or associations formed didn't lessen competition in the United States. The Webb-Pomerene Act had permitted associations that fixed export prices to Canada and other nations. Any Canadian combination of companies that reduced competition in the United States — such as an Abitibi-Price takeover — would be merely giving the United States a taste of its own medicine, though nobody at Abitibi dared to look at it in that light.

The historically dual attitude of Canadian government towards corporate concentration persists today. Tom Bell read to the meeting excerpts in turgid civil-service prose from a restricted document, *A Working Paper Concerning the Canadian Pulp and Paper Industry With Implications for Other Forest-Based Industries.* It was written by a committee representing federal and provincial departments of trade, industry and commerce in 1973.

"In the eastern Canadian newsprint sector," Bell read, "it's the Canadian-owned and controlled portion of this industry [part of the industry is foreign-owned] that's most exposed to cyclical swings in demand . . . Accordingly, any measures which serve to restore Canadian dominance in newsprint markets should be of particular benefit to the Canadian owned and controlled companies in the industry . . . Specific means of strengthening the Canadian presence within the industry might include encouragement of various forms of collective action by Canadian-owned companies to the extent permitted within the framework of competition policy."

Here Bell paused and spoke with heavy emphasis: "In addition, mergers of some of these companies *may be desirable*, both to promote functional integration and to develop stronger corporate entities better able to compete with foreign-owned competitors."

He stopped reading and looked around the room. "That's why a merger between Abitibi and Price would be good for both companies and for Canada," he said with finality. "And half the government bestows its blessing."[3]

At noon, Jim Baillie prepared to dip his toes in the waters of élite opinion to feel whether the quickie route might not be a little too hot for Abitibi. The availability of this controversial route in such a big takeover had been discussed ad nauseam by the Project R committee and fresh opinions were badly needed, particularly from the one man who would decide whether Abitibi could use it or not — Jack Kimber, president of the Toronto Stock Exchange.

Baillie left the Abitibi offices and strolled across the parking lot of the Royal York Hotel to the renovated but passé glory of the hotel's Imperial Room restaurant. There he met Kimber and Warren

M. H. Grover, a professor at Toronto's Osgoode Hall Law School.

Baillie and Grover were organizing a series of fall-evening lectures for 25 practising lawyers studying for master's degrees in law. Both men were seasoned lawyers — Baillie by practice, Grover as a teacher and authority. Grover had advised Ottawa on mutual funds legislation, written texts on income tax law and competition policy, and represented Canada on a mutual funds committee of the Organization for Economic Co-operation & Development.

Kimber, a leading Canadian authority on securities law, was to be persuaded at this lunch to lecture to Baillie's and Grover's students. Kimber had seen the securities industry from all sides. He served as chairman of the Ontario Securities Commission (1963-1967), was chairman of the Ontario Attorney-General's Commission on Securities Legislation (the 1966 Kimber Commission) which recommended the present Ontario takeover legislation, and he headed the body that was the focus of all the regulation — the Toronto Stock Exchange. Perhaps some of his securities sagesse could be made to rub off onto the evening-class students.

During soup, Baillie dropped his question as nonchalantly as he could: "By the way, what do you think about what's been happening with the stock-exchange exemption?" But it wasn't Kimber who took the bait, it was Grover, and he expounded on the subject for half an hour, clear through the soup, the club sandwiches and into the coffee.

Each of the five controversial exchange takeovers had seemed to be fairer than its predecessor, that was clear. But nevertheless the two that Grover felt most strongly about were two of the most recent.

When Noranda had raided Fraser, shareholders had been given only half an hour — between 10 and 10:30 a.m. — to trade in their stock. By 10:30 Noranda had all the stock it wanted, and the bid was terminated. The bid had been announced the previous evening, but many small shareholders either hadn't heard of it or had no time to contact their brokers. Analysis of insider trading reports published later showed that a large proportion of the stock bought by Noranda had come from major Fraser shareholders who, it was believed, had been approached individually at the time of the bid. Grover felt the Noranda bid had been unfair because of its first-come, first-served basis. That kind of bid was bound to favor the big shareholders and institutions with their superior brokerage services.

On the other hand, Grover felt that the takeover of Pacific Western Airlines by an anonymous bidder (the government of Alberta, as it turned out) acting through a broker, though often criticized, was fair, because the bid had been open for two days. That had given most shareholders a chance to hear of it. What's more, the bid had been for all the stock, which enabled shareholders to sell their entire holdings if they didn't like the idea of a new control group coming into the company.

What did Kimber think? Baillie asked ingenuously. Kimber agreed with Grover. Baillie took him a step further: "What would you do if there was a bid already on the exchange and a competing bid came along?" (Bell, Baillie and Tory believed an exchange bid for a company the size of Price was much more likely to generate competition than any of the previous exchange raids.) Kimber winced and said: "Let's cross that bridge when we come to it."

The lunch broke up at 2 p.m. and Baillie walked quickly back to the Toronto-Dominion Centre where Ian McGibbon was waiting to drive him to the airport. Baillie was off to Kenya on his three-week camera safari. During the drive, Baillie told McGibbon that the quickie route was still in favor at the exchange so that he could take back the good news to the Project R conspirators.

By 3:45 McGibbon was back in the office reporting on Baillie's lunch to Bell and the others who sat around stewing about all the specific items they had to settle in minute detail now that the scatter-gun approach of the work list was past. After a while Bell said: "We really haven't got a very good feeling for our bank financing. It's left in limbo. I know Doug Gardiner has gone away shooting and I'd better get him and ask him just where we stand — because we're running out of time." Bell phoned the Royal Bank, and he was told that Gardiner was shooting quail in Georgia.

At four o'clock Bell raised Gardiner on the telephone and said: "Doug, you may be having a good time shooting, but we're sweating here about this money. I don't think we're going to need quite as much as I told you, but that hasn't been decided yet. We don't know what price we're going to offer. Are you going to get this money or aren't you? Because if you can't, we're going to take a whirl at this thing and I've got to have a chance to go to some other bank for the dough."

Bell was whistling Dixie; the Royal was Abitibi's only bank. But Gardiner couldn't be *sure* that the Royal mightn't lose that big customer if it let Abitibi down on its once-in-a-lifetime opportunity.

After a long silence, Gardiner said: "Look, I don't know how the hell we're going to do it, but all I'll tell you is we'll do it." His voice came over the speaker-phone in Bell's office, marred by long-distance noises and speaker distortion, but distinct enough to reach all parts of the room.

Bell replied: "Well, that's great, because I've got three guys in my office who've heard you make that statement. It's all we want to know."

Bell was right to be jubilant. A banker of Gardiner's calibre was bound by his word.

PHASE II
The decision

Day Nine

Friday, November 8
"We either move on Thursday
or forget it . . ."

Tom Bell's directive to the Project R team, assembled in the
board room at 9:30 a.m., was this: "We've talked around this project for a week [as if that were an age for a $100-million decision].
Let's make up our minds. We're over the anti-trust hurdle. We
think the money is there — at least it won't be the most serious
problem. And we have a day — next Thursday. If we do it by the
stock-exchange route, we can't let another week go by without losing secrecy. We either move on Thursday or forget the exchange
route and go the circular route, change our method, financial plan,
everything."

In the teeth of Bell's impatience, the meeting had to first go
back over all the ground covered so far for the benefit of a new-
comer — lawyer John Tory, Jim's twin brother, who'd come along
to add another expert view of the Abitibi plan. The Tory twins
were sons of J. S. D. Tory, founder of the Tory, Tory, Deslaurier &
Binnington firm and legal adviser to Harry Gundy, Charles' father,
during the Abitibi receivership and reorganization.

The twins were in their early 40s and far from identical. Their
father had allowed them the rare opportunity of competing in the
same profession; most twins are separated early into different
areas of endeavor. Jim Tory had the build, height and physical assurance of a pole-vaulter, but was often reserved, and he tended to
be cautious in the corporate "games" in which he gave counsel.

51

John Tory, of medium height, lean and adventurous, was a hot-seat executive as well as a lawyer. He'd been drawn deep into the network of associations historically built up between Abitibi, the Tory firm, Wood Gundy and the enterprises of Lord Thomson of Fleet. John formerly had been the partner of the Tory firm appointed to act as counsel to Abitibi, and, by coincidence, also had been counsel to the Thomson group in Toronto, although Lord Thomson had his own links with Abitibi that went back to the 1930s.[1] (Thomson's salesmanship in radios in Northern Ontario had embarrassingly outpaced the growth of the broadcast medium, and Abitibi came to the rescue.) But a few years back, John Tory had given up counselling Abitibi to become the full-time lawyer-president of two Thomson companies, the international holding companies for the Thomson chain of newspapers, which bought 50% of their North American newsprint consumption from Abitibi. John Tory did, however, remain an Abitibi director, in company with Ken Thomson (Lord Thomson's son who'd succeeded his father on the Abitibi board in 1970) and Charles Gundy. The Tory firm had acted as legal adviser to Wood Gundy since the days when Harry Gundy was defending the stockholders of Abitibi in receivership.

As soon as John Tory, the adventurous twin, learned what was brewing, he became enthusiastic about the stock-exchange route. But Jim Tory, who could see the problems more closely because he was doing the work, argued that no takeover this big had ever gone through the exchange before. "It's a new ball game," Jim Tory protested. "The procedure may not be appropriate."

Nevertheless, John Tory soon infected the Wood Gundy people with his enthusiasm for the quick route, as well as the Abitibi executives who wanted to be persuaded it was best anyway. By now, the dreary task of answering Day Seven's work-list questions was done, and the two action men, chairman Tom Bell and Ian McGibbon, became energized by the prospect of the excitement and challenge the stock-exchange route would offer. Jack Haire, the chief financial officer, became excited too, but more by the risks and dangers of the immense step Abitibi was contemplating. Harry Rosier's witty but placid personality started to rise, like a deep lake under a freshening wind. But Jim Tory remained cool and critical.

By mid-evening the decision was made to go ahead, on Thursday, by the quick route. Bell asked everybody to come in the following day (Saturday) to prepare a presentation with which they could sell the project to the bank, the Wood Gundy firm (which would have to give an underwriting assurance) and the stock exchanges.

For the first time, Tom Bell was visibly taking personal command of the project. "We're going to have to bust our ass from here on in," he said at the end of the day-long meeting.

Day Ten

Saturday, November 9
"To hell with the Brits . . ."

"Any jackass can think up a good idea. Now we've got to sell it." That was Bell's slogan for the weekend, and it revealed his sharp appreciation of the importance of proselytizing in business. The Abitibi executives and their legal and fiscal teams gave themselves a tight two-day schedule, just Saturday and Sunday, to accomplish two things: to sell *themselves* on the scheme (was it really the best thing for Abitibi?), and to draw up on paper a persuasive presentation for the other organizations involved.

At 9:30 a.m., Bell and his three executives moved into the board room and started calculating, assembling and relating masses of data about Abitibi and Price and the whole newsprint industry. Jim Tory, the more circumspect lawyer twin, walked over to Wood Gundy's offices, where he sat down with Don Bean, the account executive, and Bean's boss, Ross LeMesurier. They continued — despite yesterday's tentative decision — the interminable discussion about whether Abitibi should take the quick route or use the 21-day circular, and about how Domtar and the British should be handled. John Tory, the other twin, had faded from the scene on a vacation.

Jim Tory was pleased to find that LeMesurier shared his uneasiness over the quick route. Ross LeMesurier, a senior Wood Gundy vice-president, was regarded as one of the most proficient and demanding minds in the Canadian securities industry when it

54

came to corporate law and the mechanics of takeovers and mergers. He was both a lawyer and an MBA, and he could work endlessly with fine detail that would bore or irritate others.

Both Jim Tory and Ross LeMesurier were inclined toward protest this Saturday morning. Those highly controversial exchange takeovers hadn't taken place five years before; they happened only weeks and months before. Besides, 25% of the stock could go against the Abitibi takeover. If Domtar and Associated Newspapers combined and made a competitive bid, there were no rules to predict what might happen. And so the debate continued.

Jack Haire, Abitibi's chief financial officer, should have been everywhere at once, but the best he could do was begin the morning with Tom Bell's fact-collecting group, then walk over to Wood Gundy to switch to an assessment of Abitibi's debt-raising capacity and the tone of the bond market.

Wood Gundy and Jack Haire with his staff had studied Abitibi's most restrictive covenants to previous lenders, and they were confident the company could take its total long-term debt up to about $200 million.[1] This meant that Abitibi could borrow $100 million more, which should be more than enough to finance a bank loan of $80 million to $100 million. But borrowing is a two-way street. It wasn't enough to have the debt-raising capacity; there had to be people who'd buy the bonds. Wood Gundy, through its normal coverage of investing institutions, sensed that Abitibi could raise from $40 million to $60 million of debt in three months' time (in February 1975), but beyond that the view was foggy. The bond market was becoming congested with too many issues, and investors were holding back from buying because 10%-11% coupons didn't return a real profit when there was 10%-a-year inflation. Wood Gundy's experts talked mysteriously about the market having "windows" when securities can be placed, and "gaps" when they can't. The firm was confident a window would come along in 1975 through which Abitibi could borrow the remaining money needed. Jack Haire and Don Bean talked for a couple of hours and satisfied themselves that everybody was making the same, correct judgment.

Back in the Abitibi offices, a "loose-leaf encyclopedia" of relevant information was slowly taking shape under the stern direction of Bell. Ian McGibbon started to head the final work sheets "Project R" but Bell told him peremptorily: "We don't want any more of that nonsense." And he changed the code name to "Operation Price," which had a more military ring. In World War II, Bell had fought as a lieutenant, later captain, with the 11th Field Regiment (Third Division). After a nasty action in Holland in which Bell's company commander was fatally wounded and Bell took command, Bell had been awarded the Military Cross. Military matters still held a large part of his interest. In the early days of Operation Price, he'd read Cornelius Ryan's *A Bridge Too Far*, an account of the Arnhem landings, and on this day (Day Ten) he started using the military time system in which a day is divided into 24 hours rather than two lots of 12. But his secretary, Barbara Mills, wasn't used to it and kept putting a colon in the middle of the numbers (14:00) instead of running them together (1400).

By mid-morning it was apparent there weren't enough hands available, so Bell called Bob Gimlin, Abitibi's American-born vice-president of newsprint, and asked him to come to the office. Gimlin knew nothing about Operation Price. He arrived with his wife (they were about to go to the golf course), listened to a briefing from Harry Rosier, and then explained regretfully to her that he'd be tied up all day on "business."

At midday the two groups at Abitibi and Wood Gundy came together in the Abitibi board room for sandwiches and coffee and a general verbal thrash that would last all afternoon. Jim Tory and Ross LeMesurier, who were next-door neighbors and had come in together that morning in Tory's car, hadn't fully appreciated the closeness of their positions until the working discussions had begun. Now they played devil's advocate and argued strongly against the stock-exchange route, mainly on the basis of the heavy opposition (25% of Price stock) that could line up against Abitibi. At this point opposition to the majority consensus was a greater service to the cause than acquiescence; it deflated any vague euphoria and sharpened the others' wits in favor of their own decision. By the end of the afternoon, the stock-exchange route was still in general favor, but the question of what to do about Associated Newspapers was, if anything, even more undecided than it had been earlier.

Tom Bell was inclined to say, more by temperament than logic: "To hell with them. We'll treat the English like everybody else." But he realized a lot of thinking was still needed.

56

The contribution of Ian McGibbon, Abitibi's vice-president of corporate development, to this pre-decision analysis was minor. He wasn't an expert in securities, finance or law, and Tom Bell was the centre-stage executive. Nevertheless, McGibbon drove back to his farm in the Caledon Hills that evening, resolutely thinking through his management training for a way in which that stubborn Associated Newspapers question could be resolved.

Day Eleven

Sunday, November 10
"They couldn't be asked to walk around with dynamite in their pockets . . ."

Could Abitibi safely approach Associated Newspapers in Britain early in the game with an offer to buy out its entire block and still succeed with the takeover? And *should* Associated be bought out? What was the route of optimum success for Abitibi? Tom Bell had decided on a clean entry into the stock-exchange route ("To hell with the Brits!"), but his advisers had reservations that needed clearing up.

Ian McGibbon arrived at the office this Sunday morning, confident he'd devised a logical approach to the problem. At first he intended to draw a decision tree — with possible courses of action branching off the trunk and from one another — but the other Abitibi executives mightn't be familiar with this newly fashionable management tool. So he wrote a sequence of questions that had to be answered each day until the bid on the exchange on Thursday, and hung it up on the board-room blackboard. It was a masterful analysis of a complex problem.

Question	Yes	No
Does Associated have a quick decision maker?	Test him with an offer.	Do not approach Associated early.

Abitibi's best chance of success lay in springing into a takeover from a position of established strength. The existence of a quick decision maker at Associated would not only determine whether Abitibi could take Associated out of its stock early and begin the takeover with 17% of Price, but it would also weight other options.

Abitibi could approach a quick decision maker and say: "You have six hours to act. We'll buy all your stock now and accumulate the rest, either by 21-day circular or slow accumulation in the stock market. If you won't sell now, we're going to make an exchange raid tomorrow morning and you'll be treated like everybody else." (Without a 17% start the slow routes would be too risky.)

If Associated didn't have a quick decision maker, however, Abitibi would do best to ignore Associated and go the quick route from a zero-holdings start. Associated couldn't be given an early choice, to give its executives time to ponder a slow decision, because that would also give Associated the time to thwart Abitibi. The mere leaking out of Abitibi's intentions could drive the price of the stock up to a level Abitibi couldn't afford. So, if Abitibi were unable, because there was no quick decision maker, to buy 17% early, the quick exchange route was best. The slow routes threatened too much competition, particularly with Associated holding a 17% advantage.

The decision-making styles of corporations varied immensely. The $400-million, world-wide paper-mill builder, Parsons & Whittemore Inc., of New York, could act in an instant because decisions could be made by one man, the tycoon-proprietor Karl F. Landegger. At Domtar, decision making was presumed to be slow because the president, Alec Hamilton, had been in office only seven months since the death of a strong manager, T. Norbert Beaupre. In between the two extremes lay Abitibi, whose chairman, Tom Bell, was familiar with the company but still had to answer to the board. Bell wouldn't have authority to decide alone whether to sell a block of stock for $35 million. Did Associated Newspapers have a man who could do that? John Tory, who had international newspaper contacts through his Thomson affiliation, was telephoned in Florida and asked. Yes, he replied, Hon. Vere Harmsworth, Associated's chairman, was just such a man. The first question was answered. Associated could safely be approached before the bid.

Questions for Monday	**Yes**	**No**
Will the stock exchanges and the securities commissions accept a quickie in principle?	Keep going.	Abort raid plans.
Would they permit the offer to remain open for an acceptably short time span (hopefully no more than one or two days)?	Keep going.	Abort raid plans (if offer has to be kept open an absurd time like 15 days).
Will Abitibi be permitted to buy no shares if less than a control block is tendered? (At least 30% — a safe margin above Associated's 17% plus Domtar's 7%.)	Keep going.	Do we risk being "mousetrapped?" — spending millions for non-control? Possibly abort raid plans.

Ross LeMesurier of Wood Gundy and lawyer Jim Tory, the two devil's advocates, had warned that the quick exchange route wasn't favored by the Ontario Securities Commission. The views of the Quebec Securities Commission were little known, and the exchanges might have specific reservations about the quick route, though Baillie's conversation with Kimber over lunch on Day Eight seemed to indicate the exchanges would not object in principle. On Monday, Abitibi would have to call on all these bodies and ask if the exchange route would be open.

Question for Tuesday	**Yes**	**No**
Will the bank provide financing?	Keep going.	Abort all plans.

Question for Tuesday	**Yes**	**No**
Will the Abitibi executive committee (which has the power to act for the board) approve a takeover in principle and a $35 million expenditure for Associated's stock?	Keep going.	Abort or delay all plans, or only an early approach to Associated.

The executive-committee question was the key one on which a go-ahead on Thursday would turn (or so it appeared). The executive committee mightn't like to make this momentous decision without the full board around it. It could "act on behalf of," certainly, but it had to be able to foresee the board's wishes accurately. The full board meeting was scheduled for 8 a.m. on Thursday. If the Tuesday meeting of the executive committee couldn't, or wouldn't, approve an early purchase of the Associated block, there would be no authority for an approach to Harmsworth on Wednesday evening. If the committee thought the takeover a crazy stunt, it was unlikely the full board would approve at 8 a.m. Thursday a raid that had to begin just two hours later at 10 a.m. And the full board couldn't be called to meet a day or two before the raid because 17 people couldn't be asked to walk around with dynamite in their pockets. The whole thing hinged on approval by the executive committee.

Question for Wednesday	**Yes**	**No**
Will Associated agree to sell its block this day?	Keep going, or alternatively slowly add to the 17% block by buying on the market or by 21-day offer.	Move quickly with raid before Associated or Domtar can organize a defense, or abort depending on other circumstances.

61

By laying out these questions Ian McGibbon had located all the stepping-stones on which Abitibi would have to pick out its takeover route. Only one question was left unclarified: if Associated agreed to sell on Wednesday night, should Abitibi take the quick route or a slow route?

Jim Tory provided the answer. In his view Abitibi couldn't buy out Associated completely and then plunge into a quick bid on the stock exchange, because only a *proportion* of the other shareholders' stock would be bought (Abitibi didn't want 100% of Price, only 49%) and that was inequitable treatment.* The authorities wouldn't like that, Tory felt, and wouldn't give approval for such a quickie bid.

The questions had served their purpose. Abitibi's options were now seen to number only two: go the quick route and tell nobody in advance, or buy out Associated Newspapers and use a slow route. The first alternative was far superior. Why create an advantage by buying out Associated, only to lose it again by going the slow 21-day or creeping route? Besides, was there a courteous way of persuading Harmsworth to make a quick decision?

Ian McGibbon summed up the call on Harmsworth in the worst possible way, to see how it might look. "Bell and Rosier would fly into London on Wednesday afternoon," he said to the group in the board room, "and tell Harmsworth: 'You've got six hours to make up your mind!' "

Tom Bell was irritated by McGibbon's bluntness, but he took the point. He swept aside the questions, accepted Jim Tory's equitability premise and terminated the discussion with: "To hell with Associated! As a courtesy we'll arrange for somebody to be in London to see them coincident with release of the offer in Canada. We'll tell them: 'We'll do for you what we'll do for the others.' "

But later, as the takeover developed, Associated Newspapers would find it difficult to part with a proportion, with anything less than all its stock, for tax and other reasons. In hindsight, Abitibi might have been able to buy the entire Associated block by offer-

* Abitibi would purchase some shares from every Price shareholder who tendered, but only enough to obtain the 49% interest it wanted. If, say, eight million shares in total were tendered on the exchange and Abitibi wanted only five million, the company would buy only five eighths of each tendering shareholder's holdings.

62

ing the British a *lower price for the entire amount* — thus preserving equitability with other shareholders receiving more for a proportion of their stock. But on Sunday, Day Eleven, that didn't occur to the Abitibi team.

The planners worked most of the day on the presentation and the nuts and bolts of the takeover. A tentative $18.50 bid price for 49% of the stock was settled upon, with the conviction that the anti-trust atmosphere in the United States might be better if Abitibi took less than absolute control of Price. Bell asked McGibbon to have the presentation in final display form for noon the next day, when he'd try it out on senior executives of Wood Gundy.

On the 45-mile journey back to his farm in a rented car, Ian McGibbon stopped off at Georgetown, close to his home, to visit a small Abitibi mill that made high-quality coated paper. The mill manager left his supper and opened the mill. McGibbon strode across to the sheeting machine, grabbed a stack of paper six inches thick, and took it back to his farm so that he'd be able to work on the presentation that evening and first thing in the morning at the office.

Day Twelve

Monday, November 11
**"They even cleaned the ashtrays
to destroy evidence . . ."**

In his office, at 8:30 a.m., Tom Bell met with lawyer Jim Tory and Bob Morgan, a Wood Gundy vice-president, to work out what they'd say that morning to Jack Kimber, president of the Toronto Stock Exchange, who'd have to approve a quick takeover. Morgan had been exposed to the project briefly a couple of days before and he'd adopted it warmly. By good luck, Morgan also happened to be that year's elected chairman of the stock exchange. He'd make it clear to Kimber, however, that on this occasion he was acting only as an officer of Wood Gundy.*

At 9:30, Bell and the two advisers walked into Kimber's office at the exchange where Kimber introduced them to Lester Lowe, vice-president responsible for stock listings, and Harold Gibson, director of market surveillance, who'd both be involved in the organization of an exchange bid. Bell gave a persuasive account of what Abitibi wanted to do, why it was good for Abitibi, why the price was fair to Price shareholders, and why they wanted to use the exchange. Then he took a deep breath and suggested that the Abitibi bid should open on Thursday morning and close Friday afternoon.

On that basis the bid would have been open for two days — a

---

*Morgan later was appointed to the Ontario Securities Commission as a commissioner.

lot longer than Noranda's bid for Fraser, and about the same time as the Alberta government's bid for Pacific Western Airlines. But was it long enough for all of Price's 9,464 shareholders to hear of the bid and decide whether to tender? In retrospect, it was probably even a dangerously *short* time for Abitibi if 49% of Price was to be secured. But Bell was so fearful an opposing bid would be entered by Domtar, Canadian Pacific, Argus or one of the other big pools of Canadian capital, that in his heart he wanted to stampede the Price shareholders into accepting the Abitibi bid in a rush. He wanted to create a feeling that if they didn't act fast to grab the $18.50 per share, they'd lose their chance. After all, Bell had a legal responsibility to guard and further the interests of the Abitibi shareholders, but none towards the Price shareholders.

After Bell's presentation, Kimber discussed the proposal with his two advisers and eventually told Bell that, yes, Abitibi could use the exchange, it was within the rules, but Bell would have to be reasonable about the time.

"I don't think we can justify two days," he told Bell firmly. "A few weeks ago, the three exchanges [Toronto, Montreal and Vancouver] agreed that any more takeover bids would be kept open for at least three business days. That would take it to Monday night, and your bid could close Tuesday morning at 9:45.* There are financial newspapers in Canada on Saturday and in England on Sunday that can publicize the offer over the weekend, and that would make the entire five days useful for dissemination. By closing Tuesday, the bid would also remain open after the budget on Monday. The budget might include measures that would affect the Price shareholders' decisions."

Bell was disappointed, but said: "Well, if that's the best you can do, okay." The three left Kimber and walked a few yards to King Street and along to the Toronto-Dominion Centre.

Almost all the official approvals were to be obtained today, so Bell immediately tried to get in touch with Arthur Pattillo, the often irascible chairman of the Ontario Securities Commission, who'd been in office only two months. (Jack Kimber also had in-

---

*Trading began daily on the Toronto Stock Exchange at 10 a.m. But special transactions such as takeover share tendering, which would disrupt the operation of the exchange, were scheduled outside normal trading hours.

sisted that Abitibi obtain the commission's approval before the bid went through.) But it was Armistice Day and Bell discovered the commission was closed. He telephoned Pattillo's home — not in. Then the Toronto Club — not there — so Bell left a message in case he turned up at the club for lunch. But lunch time came and there was no call, and Bell began to believe that Pattillo was taking the long weekend in the Maritimes, his native region.

In fact, Pattillo was mentally in ancient China — at the Chinese exhibition on display in the Royal Ontario Museum in Toronto, gazing at the 2,000-year-old jade suit of a long-dead princess and marveling at exquisite porcelain miniatures of celestial horses rearing and plunging motionlessly forever.

Unable to raise Pattillo, Bell had his secretary telephone Harry Bray, vice-chairman of the Securities Commission, at home. Bray combined physical corpulence with a keen, agile mind. He'd been with the commission for almost a quarter of a century and had developed into such a capable legal technician that he'd virtually *become* the commission. Under an undistinguished previous chairman and in the midst of mediocre immediate advisers, he'd generally been the *tour de force*. (A high point of comedy had been reached a few years back, when one of Bray's senior advisers, believing the commission's investigators needed more training, invited a nurse from a veneral-disease clinic to lecture them on how to find missing persons. Everybody was red-faced when all she could advise the assembled investigators was, "Call the police.")

As the mainstay of the Securities Commission, Bray would have been deeply involved in drawing up the Ontario Securities Act which embodied the takeover legislation through which Noranda and the others had driven such a wide path. The phone call found him at home. Jim Tory took the phone from Bell's secretary and asked Bray for an appointment to see Pattillo. But the call developed into a half-hour outline of the plan. To Jim Tory's surprise, Bray didn't oppose it. "It would be better if you went the circular route and gave the shareholders a chance to make up their minds before they have to tender their shares," Bray said. "You know, we have a change in the legislation under consideration. But under the present law you have the right to go ahead. We won't prevent you from doing this. We'll be a bystander, perhaps not an

66

enthusiastic one, but we'll let you go." Tory hung up relieved that his apprehension over the commission's reaction was groundless.

At noon, Tom Bell and Jim Tory — who was acting as Bell's advocate in obtaining the approvals — met with Michel Bélanger, president of the Montreal Stock Exchange, who happened to be in Toronto for the day on other business. Bélanger previously had distinguished himself in the Quebec government as a rare phenomenon — an adventurous, innovative civil servant.* He raised no objections to Abitibi's plan and felt less uneasy than Kimber or Bray. As the planning progressed, Abitibi would discover that the authorities in Quebec generally were much more positive than in Ontario.

At 1 p.m., Bell called together the Abitibi-Tory team and invited over the Wood Gundy people for a trial run through the full presentation. Exposed to Bell's dominating vision for the first time would be C. E. (Ted) Medland, Wood Gundy's president, a man of cool, almost acid temperament and decisive mind. Having worked so hard on the early stages of the project, Don Bean of Wood Gundy identified with Abitibi during the presentation, hoping his firm's senior officials would see the project in the same optimistic way he did. Ross LeMesurier tried to listen as if he'd heard nothing about it before, at the same time packing away the detail. Charles Gundy was such an independent old-timer that he had no trouble judging the project again on its merits — even though he'd been partly won over days before.

Bell expounded on the takeover with gusto for an hour, putting McGibbon's charts on an easel one after the other and pointing proudly to the sweep of Abitibi-Price's mills from Manitoba to Newfoundland, and the deep penetration of North American newsprint markets the joint group would enjoy, then he asked with his best, enthusiastic, engaging smile: "What do you think?"

Everybody waited tensely for Ted Medland to give his verdict, which he did in a deliberately measured voice to belie the enthusiasm he obviously felt. So everybody was in favor; the collective persona of Canada's top investment firm agreed it was a good transaction all around.

In the middle of the afternoon, Abitibi's president, Harry Ro-

*Bélanger later became president of the Provincial Bank.

sier, almost lost his composure. At about three o'clock he received a telephone call from W. F. H. Gillespie, a young analyst with Fry Mills Spence Ltd. who specializes in forest-products securities. Bill Gillespie and his predecessor at the firm had the distinction of holding the least enthusiastic views in the securities industry about paper companies and their stocks.

Bill Gillespie told Rosier: "I've heard from several sources that Abitibi has a very important announcement to make in the immediate future." At his end of the phone, Rosier blanched. Abitibi's security had been airtight, he thought. There'd been no hint of a leak anywhere. The secret had been so well kept that the price of Price stock had quietly drifted downwards while Abitibi had been working out its plans — evidence, surely, that no one in the outside world was aware of what might happen.

"What the hell are you talking about?" Rosier asked angrily.

"I don't know," Gillespie replied, deflated. "And the people I talked to didn't know, but it's certainly supported by the fact so many of Abitibi's top brass worked over the weekend."

Fry Mills Spence's office was also in the Toronto-Dominion Centre, and Rosier began to assume that Gillespie himself had come in over the weekend and noticed the signatures of the Abitibi executives in the security book everybody signed — and now he was fishing.

Rosier felt a surge of relief, and counterattacked: "This time of year, all we're really trying to do is make up our budgets and find out what's going to happen in 1975 — so we can make a fool out of you for your pessimistic forecasts."

That pacified Gillespie, and he promised: "I'll do what I can to stop the rumors circulating." He didn't mean it literally, rather as an attempt to warn Rosier to do whatever he planned to do quickly.

Gillespie's call left Rosier disturbed at the ease with which an alert observer could twig. Abitibi's security precautions had been meticulous. Since Sunday, Day Eleven, all documents had been locked away after each meeting, even those destined for the shredder. And, after a prolonged meeting in the board room, Rosier and McGibbon even cleaned the ashtrays and threw out the sandwich wrappings to destroy evidence of a lengthy, secret conference. (This had given rise to an exclusive joke about Rosier and

McGibbon easily getting jobs as cleaning staff if anything went wrong with the takeover.) But security can never be total. There may be leaks — through a secretary's husband or a gossipy employee. Rosier was mistaken in thinking Gillespie was just a good detective. Gillespie had heard the rumor from two sources: a Fry Mills Spence salesman, and a client in Montreal. The word was trickling out.

It was now D-Day Minus Three and the financing still hadn't been secured. Late in the afternoon, Tom Bell telephoned the peripatetic Doug Gardiner, but the Royal Bank offices were closed for Armistice Day. Gardiner had returned from his quail shooting in Georgia over the weekend and was now shooting pheasant north of Toronto. Bell called Gardiner's home; his wife said he'd be home at six o'clock. Bell began to realize a sense of urgency.

Bell phoned again a little after six and Gardiner came to the phone. "Doug, I've absolutely got to spend three or four hours with you and *fast*," Bell said anxiously.

Gardiner replied: "I've got my father-in-law over here for dinner. Can it wait for an hour?" Bankers have private lives, too, and a family reunion may have to be conducted in the middle of a $100-million deal.

Bell was getting agitated: "Yes, but, Jesus, you've *got* to come over after that."

Gardiner was cool and soothing: "All right, I'll come over right after dinner." Bell went home and tried to quietly digest his own meal, without tasting it.

When Gardiner arrived, Bell told him happily: "We won't need as much money as we thought. It looks like only about $80 million." By now Abitibi had decided it wanted 49% of 9.8 million shares at about $18.50 a share and would pay for part with its own cash. "We want it for six months to a year," Bell said, leaning far forward from the chesterfield, smiling, "and we'll need it okayed this week."

"Oh, look, there's no way we can do it that fast," Gardiner said, appalled.

"Why not?" Bell replied, more keyed up by the moment. "Last Thursday you told me there was *some* way, you didn't know what."

Bell was having to come down out of the clouds to face reality. What Gardiner had been trying to tell him politely all along was this: "Yes, we'll try to get you the money, *some time soon*. But we can't give you a hard commitment to deliver it immediately."

"We can't get that much money that fast!" Gardiner told him. "Money's very tight. Besides, all the documentation and things we have to be sure of, *that* will take a week or 10 days." At a time of very high demand for money, the Royal Bank could hardly lend $80 million to one big company, when the same sum could be lent to many small businesses across the country. Bell had known money was tight when he embarked on Operation Price.

"We just can't do it that fast, Tom," Gardiner said finally.

Bell had phoned Ted Medland, president of Wood Gundy, three times that evening to tell him how he was getting along with the bank, and now he said to Gardiner: "Look, Wood Gundy are prepared to stand behind this underwriting. They believe in it, and you'll be taken out for this much money . . ."

But it was no use. Bell and Gardiner talked it over intensely till past midnight, but Bell still didn't have the commitment he wanted. And he went to bed with the adrenalin pouring through his veins and his mind obsessively churning over what he would say when he called on Earle McLaughlin, the Royal Bank's chairman, in the morning.

Day Thirteen

Tuesday, November 12
**"McLaughlin said quietly:
'Okay, we'll try . . .' "**

At 7 a.m., Tom Bell was at Toronto International Airport boarding the Sabreliner once again borrowed from Northern & Central Gas. With him were lawyer Jim Tory and Bob Morgan, the Wood Gundy vice-president who also was chairman of the Toronto Stock Exchange.

When the plane landed in Montreal at eight, Bell rushed to a booth in the terminal building and placed a call to the home of Earle McLaughlin. The chairman and president of the Royal Bank had already left for the office, his wife told Bell. "Would you phone his office and say I'm on my way into Montreal and I have to see him between nine and 10 o'clock?" Bell asked her. He had no appointment. "Certainly," she agreed.

While Bell was talking to Mrs. McLaughlin, an employee of Wood Gundy's Montreal office was phoning the home of Robert Demers, chairman of the Quebec Securities Commission. "Please stand by at this number for an important call. I can't give you the details," the Wood Gundy man said. Demers finished his breakfast, went upstairs to select a tie to wear that day, then sat patiently by the telephone, thumbing through the Saturday comic supplement which had been left beside the bed.

But the phone didn't ring. At 8:40 he decided he could wait no longer and left for the office.

Bell, Tory and Morgan, not knowing arrangements had been

made for them to telephone Demers on arrival, took a cab to the Quebec Securities Commission to meet him, arriving at about nine o'clock. Demers, they were told, was surprisingly late. Bell was pleased, and he told Tory and Morgan: "I'm so uptight about the money, I'd better leave you here and get over to the bank, because Earle has got a very tight schedule and he can't see me for long." And off he rushed. Demers arrived at 9:20 and spent an hour and a half with Tory and Morgan in a helpful discussion.

"Yes, there's no question about doing this on the stock exchange. The timing is right and everything is okay as far as I'm concerned," Demers told them.

Later he'd quip to friends about the half hour of his morning wasted waiting at the phone: "If that's the way they treat the chairman of the Quebec Securities Commission, what are they going to do to Price's minority shareholders?"

On arrival at the Royal Bank's executive offices in the Place Ville Marie office tower, Bell was shown immediately into McLaughlin's office.

On Monday morning, when he'd thought the bank's financing was fairly secure, Bell had arranged for the Abitibi team to run through its presentation to senior Royal Bank officials on Tuesday in Toronto, where all the paperwork and legal intricacies of the financing would have to be finalized. Now, on Tuesday, Bell was in the confused position of negotiating with two senior executives of the bank at almost the same time. He was in Montreal that morning to plead with the chairman for the money, because he seemed unable to get any further with Doug Gardiner, the deputy chairman and executive vice-president in Toronto. And Bell had to be back in Toronto by 1 p.m. to show Gardiner and the bank's Toronto brass, who'd handle the still-ungranted loan, how well the money would be used.

McLaughlin told Bell: "I haven't got long. I've got people coming in all morning, appointments I made a long time ago, plus a board meeting at 12 o'clock." The several million dollars of interest that Abitibi would pay on the loan was small potatoes to McLaughlin, considering the Royal Bank had assets in excess of $21 billion. Besides, McLaughlin probably preferred delegations of this kind to be received at a lower level, at a distance from which he could make the decisions more freely. Tom Bell was a friend and a Royal Bank director, but, all the same, it was unseemly to have borrowers in his office.

"If you've talked to Doug, you know our problem," Bell said.

"Yes, it's difficult raising that sort of money, right now," McLaughlin replied.

"Well Earle, we've come a long way down the road. This is a plan that's good for Abitibi," Bell said. "We were prepared to move this Thursday. I'm terribly disappointed. We can go the circular route and plan to offer stock and money, but I think we've gone too far to back away from this deal, because I think we're going to get it this way and we'd miss it the other way."

Bell added hopefully: "Are there any alternatives?"

"Just a minute," McLaughlin said, and he asked Rowlie Frazee, executive vice-president and chief general manager of the bank, and Alan Taylor, newly appointed deputy general manager of the international division, into the office to join in the discussion.

"Tom's presented us with this request for something like eighty million," McLaughlin said curtly, to bring them into the picture. "One of the other problems," he added, turning again to Bell, "is that the Bank of Canada has recently given us instructions that because of the tight money supply in Canada we should not be using it for frivolous purposes — and frivolous includes a takeover like this. You're not contributing anything."

"We *are* contributing!" Bell retorted indignantly. "We're contributing a hell of a lot to making this joint venture a much stronger and more competitive unit in international sales . . . Are there any alternatives?" he repeated, calming down.

"It's hard to raise this money," McLaughlin reiterated. "The Americans have said they can't give money for takeover bids, and we tried two or three banks there. But there is one thing," he said. "In the last three or four days money has loosened up very dramatically. It looks as if the trend is going to be like that. At least it's not as bad as it was going to be three or four weeks ago." Gardiner hadn't known this in Toronto on Monday; the report had only just come in.

Bell brightened at McLaughlin's optimism and pressed his point: "Let's look at the alternatives, because I'm not going to give up." McLaughlin turned to Frazee and Taylor and asked: "Is there any other way to do it?" They discussed international money markets in arcane bankers' language in front of Bell, and finally McLaughlin said: "Yes, we could get Eurodollars, but we'd have to form a group. We'd have to form a consortium with some European banks, and we think we could raise that much money. But it would involve disclosure of the principals, and, for us to get an English bank or a French bank or a German bank into this, they'd have to know who they were lending the money to and what the purpose was."

When Gardiner had first assured Bell he would "get the money somehow," Gardiner had thought that, money being tight in Canada, the Royal would be able to bring back some Canadian money from the United States. But there had been a lot of static from the American banks about not being able to lend for takeovers. The Royal could now try two other possible sources of the funds: the Eurodollar market (American dollars held outside the United States) and Orion Bank Ltd., in Britain. Orion was an international banking and leasing-finance group based in London but owned by the Royal Bank of Canada (Canada's biggest), Chase Manhattan (third biggest in the United States), National Westminster (Britain's second biggest), Westdeutsche Landesbank (West Germany's third biggest) and Japanese and Italian banks.

The Royal owned 20% of Orion, which had assets in excess of $1 billion. The trouble with going to Orion was that the international bank would probably reply: "Well, Royal, you take it if it's so good." Then, to prove that the loan to Abitibi was a good one, the Royal would have to present its Orion partners with documentation about the company — *and* its project.

"Well, there's no way we can do that," Bell exclaimed. "There can be no disclosure of this information or else the deal's dead, Earle. For heaven's sake! You've got a board meeting at 12 o'clock. Could you ask the board in principle if they'd approve a loan like this without saying who's making the application, and what other company is involved in the takeover?"

The Royal Bank had 46 directors from many areas of the economy including the oil industry, engineering, food, power, steel and chemicals. It was normal practice for the board to be asked to approve a big loan without the details being disclosed so that the customer's business plans weren't revealed to a competitor.

"Yes, I guess I can do that," McLaughlin admitted.

"We're going back to make this plea to your Toronto office," Bell said, not without appreciating the irony of his explaining how they'd use money they didn't have. "You know, this is your problem, not theirs. We think this is a wonderful deal for our company and I can't impress upon you how much this will do for us and for our future, and we think it's just one of those great deals. It may not happen again for a long time."

(It was all very well for Bell to deliver a sales pitch at this point, but, from a banker's position, the pitch and the details would have been more useful if the bank had been involved much earlier.)

"We'll work on it," McLaughlin replied. "At least money's a bit easier. But I've told you we can't get any money from the States and there isn't enough money in Canada to do that . . ."

"'Well, try," Bell asked fervently, "and once you've had your board meeting and you've looked at the situation, call Toronto, will you?"

McLaughlin said quietly: "Okay, we'll try."

By this time, Abitibi had arranged everything except this stubborn financing and the approval of its own board, which if they could get the money should prove a formality easily won by a little silver-tonguing from Bell, so attractive was the prospect of Abitibi governing Price. But would they get the money, or would they have to try it some other way?

As Abitibi's chief operating officer, Harry Rosier saw that his role in the affair was beginning to alter. The previous week he'd provided philosophical, human and practical observations while the takeover was still in the pre-decision stage. On Saturday he'd begun to seek a new function as Bell took charge. Haire, the chief financial officer, maintained a narrower role as financial adviser, and McGibbon, the corporate-development man, became tactical executive floating around behind Bell like a busy, gravity-free astronaut. Now Rosier realized what his contribution would be: to create a front of normality in the executive suite, which would soothe the suspicions of a widening group of executives and secretaries who sensed something very important was going on. From now on Rosier made a point of being as normal and placid as possible, making himself as accessible to as many people as he could, hoping this would cover the glaring preoccupation of Bell, McGibbon and Haire — by now almost totally incommunicado.

That morning Rosier, to avoid any suspicion, went ahead with a regular meeting of the Abitibi management committee.

After leaving McLaughlin, Bell met Tory and Morgan in the Royal Bank reception area. They rushed back to Montreal airport and boarded the Sabreliner, arriving at the Royal Bank offices on King Street in Toronto at exactly one o'clock. Sitting around the big table in the board room were eight bank officials, all the Wood Gundy people in the know, lawyer John Tory, Rosier, Haire and McGibbon — waiting to hear Bell's presentation.

Before he started, Bell said to Gardiner, seated at the front: "Doug, I've had a bad night with you, last night, and a bad morning in Montreal. I want to ask you, before I waste my breath, is there any point my making this presentation?"

Gardiner replied: "Go ahead, make it. Make it."

For half an hour Bell turned over on the easel chart after chart depicting the industry, Price, Abitibi, Abitibi's objective, Abitibi-Price internal financing, the bridge financing, long-term financing, expected benefits, plans for the bigger company, the risks and a summary of conclusions.

When the presentation was over, the bank officials asked questions for a quarter of an hour, mainly on the security Abitibi could offer. The bank wanted the Price shares, the Abitibi-owned shares of Mattabi Mines Ltd., a general assignment of accounts receivable and inventory — and, they wanted to know, what else? The Abitibi executives were taken aback by the bank's demands for security. The Price shares were understandable, and, because their value would probably fall back to $12 after a raid, the bank would naturally want more than that. But the Mattabi shares . . . and even more again . . . wasn't that going too far? But the bankers had Bell in a corner.

"We'll provide whatever you need," he finally told them.

When the questions petered out, there was a brief silence, then

Gardiner said, smiling: "Well, subject to a lot of documentation and a lot of effort, we'll get you the money." Because of the recent softening of loan demand, it would come out of the Royal after all. Bell gave a loud sigh and his entire body slackened with relief.

Bell thought to himself: "You son of a bitch, you knew all along you were going to give me the money." But he beamed at Gardiner, nevertheless. "That's great!" he said joyfully. "But the timing's still very important."

Gardiner told him sternly: "There's no way we can do it. This is Tuesday. You couldn't go through all the necessary things by Thursday."

"All right," Bell said, conceding the point for a moment, to attack it better later. "At least we've got the money, that's one hurdle past, so let's go and have a drink."

Cocktails and lunch had been arranged for two o'clock in the big Royal Bank board room, and all the participants in the presentation relaxed for an hour. They talked about the takeover, not as businessmen discussing a massive piece of cold financing, but as onlookers marveling at a daring corporate coup and the guts and balls of Bell.

At 3 p.m., Bell said in a loud voice so all could hear: "Just before we leave this lunch . . . We still have a tremendous desire, because of the timing we've developed, for this plan to go Thursday morning. I can arrange everything if you fellows will stay in this office and give us a list of the documents the bank has to have, and nobody from our side leaves this goddam building till you've got every detail you have to have from us."

Bell turned to Gardiner. "If you have those details, can we go Thursday morning?" he asked.

"Sure," Gardiner agreed easily. "But you'll never do it!" Bell would look foolish if the documentation weren't completed in time, and Gardiner wanted to keep things on a realistic basis.

"Okay," Bell said, with determination. "Our people, Wood Gundy and the lawyers stay with you and you tell us every document you have to have."

Tom Bell, Harry Rosier and Jim Tory then went back to Abitibi for the 4 p.m. executive committee meeting. Abitibi's legal and fiscal advisers (minus Tory) remained at the Royal Bank and, late that afternoon, held a preliminary meeting with the bank's lawyers. But the lawyers weren't ready to draw up a list of the required documents, and everybody went home that evening without telling Bell that the documentation process hadn't begun.

Perhaps approval by the executive committee was a foregone conclusion, despite the beauty of McGibbon's Sunday logic about what would happen if it did or didn't say yes. The only committee member unable to attend was Ed Bovey, chairman and chief executive officer of Northern & Central Gas. Bovey was vacationing in Hawaii and out of reach. Paul Roberts, who'd been Abitibi's chairman from 1965 to 1967, came up from his retirement home in Florida. He was the only member of the committee in attendance who wasn't already enthusiastic about the plan, and that was only because he'd heard nothing about it. The other members of the committee were Tom Bell, Harry Rosier, Charles Gundy and John Tory who were already committed. (John Tory broke his vacation to attend.)

Now the committee had to test its enthusiasm by approving the raid in principle on behalf of the board, a serious responsibility. Roberts' individual reaction was lost in the confession-like confidentiality of the meeting, but the collective decision was: "Let's go. If the directors' meeting at eight o'clock Thursday morning can approve the plan by 9:30, the offer can be at the exchange at a quarter to 10 and we're in business."

Day Fourteen

Wednesday, November 13
"His night's lodging was in
a dirty little motel . . ."

Only one day to go. Arrangements had to be made to tell Charles Tittemore, the president and chief executive officer of Price, and Hon. Vere Harmsworth, the chairman of Associated Newspapers Group in Britain, the moment the bid was made. It would seem hostile to let them find out from others.

At an early-morning meeting of the project team, Ross LeMesurier of Wood Gundy was elected to travel to London and notify Harmsworth. It was thought better to send a Wood Gundy man rather than an Abitibi official, or both, because LeMesurier, a financial securities expert, wouldn't be expected to answer the difficult operating questions that Harmsworth was sure to ask. One would certainly be: "What are you going to do about my newsprint contracts when they terminate?" Abitibi didn't know whether Associated Newspapers, as a major shareholder, was getting a special arrangement on the newsprint it bought from Price. Before Abitibi was forced to give an answer about the continuation of Associated's contracts, the newsprint company wanted to know the facts.

LeMesurier specifically was chosen to go to Harmsworth because he'd been involved in the takeover planning and was a senior vice-president of Wood Gundy, which would be a fitting tribute to the chairman of Associated. In preparation, LeMesurier was loaded down with photocopies of notes and documents, so that he could read them on the plane, an Air Canada flight that would leave at nine o'clock that night. A few minutes before three London time the following afternoon (nearly 10 a.m. Toronto time), LeMesurier would be telephoned that the offer was public. He'd then present himself to Vere Harmsworth.

Because of their old friendship and his demonstrations of personal concern, Harry Rosier had been chosen to break the news to Charlie Tittemore of Price — and to try to win him over quickly to a positive view of the potential for the bigger newsprint group. Rosier had been thinking about the problem for several days. He hadn't felt he'd be able to call Tittemore on the Monday or Tuesday and say: "I have to see you tomorrow morning." That would have necessitated either a lie or some such formula as, "I can't explain what it's about right now." Tittemore might have cottoned on, one or two days before the raid began. Although Rosier didn't know it at the time, it had been only two or three months since Tittemore and the Price board had had exactly the same thing in mind for Abitibi. No, it was too risky to approach Tittemore early.

On Monday morning when Rosier had been wondering aloud what he could do about Tittemore, McGibbon had suggested facetiously: "Oh, why bother, let's arrange a goose-hunting trip for Tittemore and get him out of the country so he can't come back and spoil the raid. That'll put him in a state of disarray." Ironically, Tittemore had conveniently arranged something similar himself.

At about 11 a.m. Rosier asked his secretary to call the Price head office in Quebec City and find out where Tittemore was. She was told he was out of town and wasn't going to be back for a week, and that was all the Price people would say. Rosier puzzled over the news for a while, then phoned a mutual friend, William E. Soles, former president of Anglo-Canadian Pulp & Paper Ltd., another newsprint manufacturer in Quebec, and now head of the industry's industrial relations group. Soles told him: "Charlie's gone to have a forward-planning session along with the rest of his management organization. They've hidden themselves way up north where nobody can get hold of them. I know, because I've been trying to get him to come to a meeting and his secretary won't put a phone call through to him. But she says he calls in once a day at four o'clock, and, if there are any special calls, he'll return them if he wants to."

Rosier still didn't want to risk leaving a message for Tittemore, particularly since he wasn't sure what he'd say to him if he called back. So Rosier let the problem simmer for a few hours, in the back of his mind.

On and off during the week, Rosier and Bell had talked about the price at which the bid should be made without coming to any conclusion narrower than the $18 to $20 recommended by Haire, except that there was a tendency to regard $18.50 as a likely price. Rosier still favored an offer of $20 per share because that was what Price's book value per share would be at the end of the year. Rosier was afraid that a smaller offer might give Abitibi perhaps only 30% of Price, rather than the 49% they now believed they had to have to exercise clear control, safe from another raid.

Complicating the decision about the bid was a drift downward in the market price of the Price stock. A week before it had been $13¼. Now it was hovering around $12. At about 11:30, Rosier prodded Bell about the bid price again and Bell replied: "We've got professional talent working for us and they know more about the stock market than we do. Why don't we see what Wood Gundy will come up with by way of a recommendation? We won't do anything to influence them."

Wood Gundy recommended an offer of $18 per share as the lowest price likely to attract 49% of the stock, and nobody was unhappy with it. The offer was a good 50% above the market and it was at Domtar's psychological "sell level." Also, it represented an investment in Price stock on which Abitibi would make an excellent return.

During the afternoon, Price Waterhouse & Co., Abitibi's auditors, were brought in to start certifying current information, subsequent to the last audited public report, which the bank would need within its documentation for the loan.

At about 4 p.m., lawyer Jim Tory, Jack Haire of Abitibi and some Wood Gundy executives held a progress meeting with Royal

Bank lawyers. It wound up quickly, to continue again later in the evening. The bank's advisers still weren't ready with a list of what they needed.

At 4:15, McGibbon of Abitibi, Don Bean of Wood Gundy and a lawyer from the Tory firm went over to the Toronto Stock Exchange to meet with its listings vice-president, Lester Lowe, and Harold Gibson, its director of surveillance. Since Monday, the two exchange officers had been closely watching the trading of Price stock for indications of a security leak or any sneaky buying by any of the people privy to Abitibi's plans. That afternoon, the stock had closed at 11⅞ bid and 12 asked. This price was not only below the October 31 level, but the volume of trading had also been low — as few as 600 shares on one day. If there were rumors on the street, nobody had attempted to profit by them.

Lowe and Gibson also went over the draft of an Abitibi press release that had been drawn up in the Tory firm's office to make sure it was up to exchange standards of disclosure. Then they switched to a technical discussion between themselves about the mechanism to inform other exchanges about the Abitibi offer and the halt-trading order on Price stock that would have to go out immediately.

When the meeting broke up, McGibbon took a dozen or so copies of the press release from the Tory lawyer handling them and made a mental note to give them to Abitibi's public relations department the following day when the bid was general knowledge.

At 5:45 p.m., when the Price office had closed for the day, Rosier again phoned Quebec City and got through to a late-working secretary. "I don't want to bother Mr. Tittemore during the planning session," he began, and he was about to say: "Can you tell me when he'll be back?" But he sensed that the secretary wanted to be helpful, so he took a chance instead, and asked: "Where can I reach him in the evenings?" The friendly French-Canadian secretary said she didn't know his telephone number, but Tittemore was staying in La Sapiniere Hotel in Val David. She was very sorry, but she couldn't help him any further.

"Thank you," Rosier replied, uttering the understatement of the day.

McGibbon, born in Montreal, remembered that Val David was

somewhere north of Ste. Agathe, and after he and Rosier pored over maps for a while they found the town. Val David was in the heart of French-speaking Canada and Rosier was strictly unilingual, so McGibbon arranged for Guy Brousseau, a fluently bilingual Abitibi sales manager in Montreal, who had a summer cottage near Ste. Agathe, to book a hotel room in Montreal for Rosier that night and drive him to Val David in the morning. Brousseau was told only that he would drive Rosier up the Laurentian Autoroute the next morning to the Ste. Agathe area, and would then receive further instructions. He was asked to arm himself with road maps of all the outlying areas around Ste. Agathe. After spending an hour at home that evening, Rosier left on an 8:30 flight for Montreal.

Rosier found his night's lodging had been arranged at a dirty little motel, whose only virtue was that it lay between the airport and the Laurentian Autoroute and was a good location for an early start northward in the morning. At 11:30 as he was preparing to go to bed, he set his traveling alarm clock for 4:30 a.m. — and then a worrying thought struck him. If the girl he'd spoken to had been foolish enough to tell him where Tittemore was, she might have given him the information after Tittemore had gone elsewhere. Close to midnight, Rosier phoned La Sapiniere in Val David and reached the night clerk on the front desk, whose English was little better than Rosier's French. Eventually Rosier made himself understood. The clerk looked up the register and said: "Yes, he's in Room 305. Just a moment, I'll call him." "Oh, no!" Rosier said. "Don't do that. I just wanted to know he was there." He hung up, relieved.

At six o'clock that evening in Toronto, the Royal Bank's lawyers, after considering the matter all day, had finally laid down a definitive list of the documents needed for the loan. Haire had returned to Abitibi to scare up the data needed for them, and the Tory law firm had started grinding the papers out.

At midnight, while Rosier was phoning La Sapiniere, Jack Haire, Jim Tory and another lawyer and two secretaries were still working hard, though the end seemed to be in sight. Soon one of the women was allowed to go home, and Haire left the office at about 1 a.m. Jim Tory left at about 2 a.m., but shortly afterwards the remaining lawyer realized the amount of work left had been underestimated. He and the lone secretary remained at the Tory office working on the papers till about four o'clock in the morning.

Alec Hamilton, the president of Domtar, and his wife were at a cocktail party in Montreal and about to leave. It was 7:30 in the evening, while Haire and the lawyers in Toronto were deep in work.

As Hamilton approached the door, a man from Wood Gundy stopped him and said: "Something big's going to happen tomorrow. I can't talk about it now, but can I call you sharp at 10 o'clock tomorrow?"

"Sure, I'll look forward to it," Hamilton replied, and he and his wife went out to a taxi. As the cab pulled away from the curb, Hamilton's wife asked him: "What was all that about?"

"Oh, probably MacMillan Bloedel going to take over Price," Hamilton said, jocularly.

PHASE III
Takeover

Day Fifteen

Thursday, November 14
"He's already gone. The
die is cast..."

Tom Bell arrived in the Abitibi office at 7 a.m. with an hour in which to sign 19 documents in triplicate before the eight o'clock board meeting. This morning every step of the borrowing procedure would have to click into its proper place. The bank would have to receive the proper documents, duly signed, before it could release a letter of commitment. Then the board would approve the borrowing when the letter of commitment said the bank was prepared to lend the money. The bank would finally authorize the line of credit when the Abitibi board had authorized the company to borrow the money. The bid would be made on the exchange when the bank had extended the line of credit.

Bell was the last to arrive at the office. Ian McGibbon, Jack Haire, and Abitibi's legal and fiscal advisers and three Royal Bank loan officers were already there, fussing over the papers typed during the night, occasionally arguing about a legal point, anxiously making inked corrections and initialling the changes, and shuttling between three offices where the papers were being handled, to check and re-check one another's checking. Only three secretaries had come in: Bell's, Haire's and McGibbon's. Rosier's wasn't yet in the know, and her boss was driving north in Quebec. In the office, tension was building everywhere, especially around Jack Haire, the chief financial officer, who was much more at home with thoughtful, measured decisions than with this kind of upheaval, which was a special kind of torture to him.

Abitibi wanted to buy 4,830,000 Price shares at $18 each for a total price of $86.9 million. The bank had agreed to extend to Abitibi an $81-million line of credit. Abitibi would raise $14 million from internal sources, draw the remainder needed from the Royal Bank, then lend the money to a subsidiary, which would spend it buying the Price stock. To do the job, Abitibi Finance Ltd., a dormant shell company incorporated for some fogotten financial purpose, was taken off the shelf, "dusted" and put to use. The 19 documents Bell was now signing legalized the step-by-step movement in opposite directions of cash and security between the bank, Abitibi Paper, Abitibi Finance, and Wood Gundy (which would actually disburse the money).

At 7:45 the pace of moving documents from one signing group to another was quickening, but in the centre of it all the pressured rhythm of the bank men patiently scrutinizing each document before acceptance gave them a firm authority in the midst of the growing tension.

By now, intrigued directors were beginning to arrive. Long before, the board meeting had been scheduled for 10 a.m., then, a week ago, brought back to 8 a.m., ostensibly because Bell had arranged a pheasant shoot at a club on Griffith Island in Georgian Bay, and the shooting party would have to leave by mid-morning. What puzzled the directors was being asked to keep the new time quiet — because of a *pheasant shoot!* And then to arrive and find the place swarming with strangers.

When Tom Bell had become Abitibi's president and chief executive officer and took the reins of power in the company in 1967, (he wouldn't be named chairman until 1973), the board had been stuffy and elderly. Directors' meetings had about them the air of a leisurely game of bowls on a Sunday afternoon. A stock-market raid on Price then would have been too shocking to contemplate.

But in six years Bell had rejuvenated the board. He'd brought in Hon. John P. Robarts, ex-Premier of Ontario (for a sensitive appreciation of Canadian federal and provincial politics), and Gen. Lauris Norstad, once supreme commander of NATO (to provide Washington connections and a knowledge of American business politics). Charles Gundy, still a fighting cock at 70, had remained;

88

his departure would be unthinkable. Regrettably, Lord Thomson of Fleet, still a powerhouse of financial imagination, had resigned at 70, in keeping with new rules, but he'd been replaced by his son, Ken.

By 8 a.m., almost the entire board of 17 directors had assembled — an unusual turnout, perhaps because nobody knew what it was all about. Norman J. MacMillan, ex-chairman of Canadian National Railways, was down from Montreal; Paul Roberts had remained in town after the executive committee meeting. And Gen. Norstad had flown up the night before in a plane specially provided to pick him up after a Washington meeting of ex-commanders of NATO the night before. The only two directors missing were Ed Bovey, still in Hawaii, and Rosier, in Quebec. Sitting in to answer questions were Jack Haire and Jim Tory. John Tory was already there by right of his own directorship.

From his chair in the middle of the long table, Bell called the meeting to order, and waited impatiently while the corporate secretary, James Flintoft, went through the routine procedure of asking for a proposer, a seconder and a vote on the acceptance of the minutes of the previous board meeting held in Montreal on October 24, which had been mailed to each director. While this went on, Bell eyed a sheet of paper in front of him. On it was typed in large letters, so he wouldn't have to peer at it, a little speech by which he would introduce the proposal to the board. Everyone in the room sensed Bell had something momentous to say and hardly heard the opening rituals. As soon as Flintoft had finished, Bell began:

"Gentlemen, I am bringing to you, at this unusual time, a matter of extreme importance to Abitibi. For the success of this venture, *speed and secrecy* were essential. We have achieved both . . ." His tone conveyed a mixture of relief, pride and apology to those directors to whom this announcement would come as a bombshell.

"The project, *a major one*, has been in our minds for the past six years. We negotiated in the late '60s for a merger with this same company and it was unsuccessful . . ." Bell spoke slowly to build up the suspense, and impart emphasis and dignity to what he'd say.

"We have been looking at various possibilities for acquisitions or mergers, and 10 days ago, Harry Rosier, Jack Haire and myself decided that the timing was right to mount 'Operation Price.' " He paused and looked around the room, beaming. A loud murmur went around the meeting and one board member said loudly, "Oh, great, Tom!"

"I apologize to you for asking you for a quick decision," Bell continued, "but the senior management and the executive committee are recommending to you, for approval, a stock exchange offer for up to 49% of the shares of the Price Co. This decision must be reached by 9:30 a.m., and I will endeavor to cover all the salient points, and would ask you to bear with me until finished before we get into discussion.

"First, you have all known me for some years. I came to Abitibi from a very happy and secure position because Paul Roberts excited me with the challenge and forget to tell me a few of the problems that might arise." Roberts chuckled and Bell smiled at him.

"I am not an empire builder, nor imbued with size is might or right. We, the senior officers of your company, believe this to be a unique opportunity and one that might not arise again, because of proposed changes in the Ontario securities legislation.

"I might say, personally, that I have not felt as I do this morning since 12 o'clock noon on the 5th of June when we set sail from Portsmouth harbor to be one of the invading forces to land at Courseille-sur-Mer in Normandy. Right this minute on the 6th we were on the beach and it was very heavy going." (Bell's brigade was off the beach in two hours and was the first that day, among the British and the Americans on either side, to reach its objective, the Carpiquet airport, 13 miles inland.)

"It was 30 years ago, and I have the same awful flutters going on in my tummy. Well — to Operation Price." Bell then gave a rundown of Price's mills, their sites and capacity, and the mine at Buchans, Newfoundland. For most board members, Bell's rundown was a formality more than an education. Bell then threw the meeting open for questions.

"Can we really finance it, and pay for it?" one director asked, even though the presentation had answered that question.

Bell was at a loss for a new way of giving reassurance. "I'm on tricky ground," he said, trying to be frank. "All I can say is, I think we can. That's in the lap of the gods, but the economics are so good we'll get over this. Wood Gundy have looked at all the facts and said, yes, they can underwrite it . . ." Bell was gaining strength. ". . .

90

We're talking about $100 million. The present Price dividends are enough to carry our charges because the interest on our debt is before tax, so we're on fairly secure ground. We might have one bad year — you know, a recession — but looking at all these facts, in the future we're fairly safe."

"Could you go over the anti-trust side of it again," another director asked. Bell did, which prompted Gen. Norstad to reciprocate and look at the Canadian deal with American eyes. After explaining that a stock-market raid wasn't possible in the United States or anywhere else that he knew of, for that matter, Norstad asked the Canadian directors at the meeting, "Is anybody here troubled by the ethics of the quick stock-exchange raid?" Norstad's question was answered by two directors with, "We are not troubled." The others made the same point with silence.

After further discussion and questions, Bell apologized once again. "I know this is a hell of a thing to throw at you at eight o'clock in the morning but we think this is very good for the company and it'll be the most important step ever taken by Abitibi."

He then submitted to the meeting, by handing them to secretary Flintoft, the documents that had been so hurriedly prepared and signed. Flintoft then read point by point a resolution divided into eight bite-sized legal chunks for easier digestion, and, as each point was read, the board was asked to vote: that Abitibi Finance make the bid; that Wood Gundy be the agent; that Abitibi borrow the money; that it lend the money to Abitibi Finance; that the Royal Bank commitment letter be accepted; that the finance agreement be accepted; that Abitibi give the bank undertakings; and, as a safety blanket, that Abitibi's officers be able to do all acts and execute all documents as are necessary to give full effect to the resolution. All motions were proposed, seconded and carried unanimously.

At 9:30 a.m. the board meeting was adjourned for 15 minutes to enable the bank letter saying that Abitibi had the money (it waited on a certified "approved" copy of the board resolution) to be given to Bell. Receipt of that letter would permit Ian McGibbon and Don Bean to rush over to the stock exchange to make the offer.

McGibbon had risen at 6 a.m. and come into the office early to set up the presentation in the board room, ready for Bell's exposition to the directors. During the hour and a half of the board meeting, McGibbon established telephone connections with Rosier in Quebec and LeMesurier through Wood Gundy's London office, so there'd be no delay in getting through to them once the announcement had been made. Then he sat back with Don Bean and waited for Bell's signal to hurry to the exchange — about four minutes away — and trigger the bid.

At 9:30 a.m., Jack Haire came out of the board room ahead of the others, flushed and breathless, and shouted: "Go, Ian, go!"

McGibbon and Bean rushed out the door, down the elevator, and over to the stock exchange, with two documents: a press release announcing the bid, and a letter from Bell stating that the press release was a valid document. In effect, the documents said: "Put the wheels in motion."

Both in the Toronto-Dominion Centre and in the stock exchange, McGibbon and Bean were in dread of some unforeseen event — like the elevator getting jammed or stopping between floors because of a power failure. But they arrived quickly at the executive floor of the exchange, and McGibbon handed the two documents to vice-president Lester Lowe, who was waiting for them. Then McGibbon left Bean there to phone him at Abitibi when the exchange had done what was necessary, and rushed back to Abitibi faster than he'd come.

Back at the office, McGibbon sat beside his phone waiting for it to ring. It soon did. It was Godfrey Palmer, an investment dealer with Burns Bros. & Denton Ltd.

"Now I see what your budgets are all about," Palmer exclaimed. He'd seen the announcement of the stop-trade and the bid on the ticker. Palmer, a neighbor in the Caledon Hills who'd been helping McGibbon build a cottage, had been told the previous weekend McGibbon had to go into the office to work on the "1975 budget."

"Get off the line," McGibbon shouted at him.

The phone rang again, and it was Bean reporting that the announcement had gone out. McGibbon then phoned Rosier and told him: "Okay, Harry, go!" McGibbon was about to speak to London on another line when his secretary came into the office and said: "Mr. Bell is looking for you. Quickly." McGibbon's and a couple of other executives' offices are out of sight of the main executive-suite vestibule. McGibbon jumped out of his office and caught Bell in the corridor coming to see him. Bell told him like a commander:

"We're almost ready to go, Ian. We're not quite finished signing these documents."

"What the hell do you mean?" McGibbon exclaimed loudly, stepping back as if he'd been hit. ". . . Sorry. What do you mean? *I've gone and been!"*

Both men were appalled, and they strode back towards Bell's office trying to sort out what had happened. As they approached Haire's office, next door to Bell's, McGibbon looked in and shouted: "Hey! . . ." But he needed go no further. Haire, red-faced, came out and said to Bell: "Jeepers, Tom, I didn't realize . . ." ("Jeepers" was the strongest expression Haire ever used.) But Bell had no time for explanations.

"He's already done it," Bell shouted to the bank officials who were in an office nearby dickering with Jim Tory over a legal technicality. Bell managed to remain calm. He called Tory over and said more quietly, though with trepidation: "He's already gone. The die is cast."

It was soon apparent, however, that no permanent harm had been done. Jumping the gate clarified everybody's minds. The legal technicality was quickly settled, the agreement closed, and the line of credit opened.

Rosier had risen at 4 a.m., shaved, washed and dressed and checked out of the Montreal motel to meet Brousseau at the front door at five. After a four-hour journey northwards through the worst blizzard of the winter, Rosier and Brousseau found themselves driving past La Sapiniere, a rambling old resort lodge in Val David, at about 8:45 a.m. The Price executives' meeting had already begun in a ground-floor room with a big bay window. As Rosier drove past, he thought he could see, through the swirling snowflakes, the back of Tittemore's head near a blackboard. Assured now that Tittemore was available, Rosier asked Brousseau, who still hadn't been told what was going on in case there was a hitch, to drive five miles back down the road where they'd seen a motel. On arrival there, they rented a room for the day as a base of operations, and Rosier, still in his topcoat, occupied it to test telephone communications.

First he placed a call to McGibbon to give him his number and say he was ready. That call went through without trouble. Then he placed a call to Domtar in Montreal to make an appointment with Alec Hamilton, the president, later in the morning to persuade him to sell Domtar's stock. But in the middle of the call the line went dead. Rosier started to panic. That goddam phone. McGibbon would be calling at any minute and he wouldn't be able to get through. Rosier jiggled the cradle pins up and down, but the phone was dead. Slamming the receiver down, he went rushing out across the snow to the motel office and demanded a room with a telephone that worked — and quick. The pretty French-Canadian receptionist explained sweetly she'd pressed the wrong button down, and the phone would work now. Rosier rushed back through the snow to his room and stared at the phone, not daring to lift the receiver to see if it was working for fear he'd cut off an incoming call.

The phone rang and it was McGibbon. "Okay, Harry, go!" he said. "I've delivered the documents to the stock exchange. The stop-trade and the announcement are out. Good luck!"

"Right!" Rosier said. He put the phone down and ran out to the car where Brousseau already had the engine running, as instructed. Off they went to La Sapiniere at a speed in excess of the 60 m.p.h. limit.

On arrival in the forecourt, Rosier, deliberately a little quieter by now, walked to the front desk to find it was manned by two girls who either couldn't or wouldn't speak English.

"I must get on the phone and speak to Mr. Tittemore," he kept saying slowly, and eventually they agreed to understand.

"But we've been told not to disturb him," one of the girls explained fluently.

Exasperated, Rosier took a $5 bill out of his wallet, held it in his hand and said: "If I write a message, will you take it in to him?"

At last the girls were prepared to co-operate. "Oh, yes, certainly," one of them said. Rosier started to write a brief message telling Tittemore it was urgent he see him, but privately. As he was folding the paper, out of the Price conference came "Jeep" Neal, a senior vice-president, and one of the few people in Price whom

Rosier knew personally, and he greeted Rosier warmly.

Rosier said: "I need to talk to Charlie in the worst way, Jeep. Can you get him out of that meeting?"

"Sure, no problem," said Neal, who went back into the room. A moment later, out came Tittemore with a smile on his face and an extended hand for this unexpected visit from an old friend. Tittemore was too phlegmatic to show surprise at the sudden arrival of a Toronto executive in a Laurentian village — or at Camp Seven in the Himalayas, for that matter.

"Charlie, I need to talk to you in private. Can we go somewhere?" Rosier asked.

"Sure," Tittemore replied. "Let's go up to my room."

At 9:50 they reached Tittemore's room and closed the door. Rosier immediately said: "Charlie, in 10 minutes' time, Abitibi will be making an offer for Price . . ."

Rosier quickly reminded him of the attempt to merge in 1969, and stated warmly that Abitibi had never forgotten the great benefits that would flow from the joining of the two companies.

"We want a position in your company, Charlie," Rosier said euphemistically, "because it will bring us close together and we'll all benefit. So right now we're making an offer of $18 a share for 49% of the stock." Then Rosier told Tittemore: "Your job and the jobs of your people are probably more secure under these conditions than if we weren't doing it. We have great respect for your management team, and both Tom and I have high regard for you, personally, Charlie," Rosier assured him. He was giving Tittemore little chance to say anything back, for the moment.

"So you've nothing to worry about, Charlie, but I wanted to be the first one to tell you what we were doing and why we were doing it, and why we couldn't do it by talking to you before we took the action."

Tittemore, a stocky engineer with a somewhat slavic face, replied quietly: "I understand there are benefits. We considered talking a run at you . . ."

"Under those conditions," Rosier interrupted, too anxious to convince Tittemore, "you can't really be mad at our doing it to you."

His eyes blazed, the only way Tittemore ever showed emotion. "The only difference is, we didn't get around to making the offer."

That was the closest the two men came to saying anything unpleasant. Later, Rosier would give Tittemore "full marks for being a sound, level-headed citizen."

"He didn't get mad and thrash around and kick me or punch my nose or anything," he'd tell a friend.

Part of the truth was that Tittemore had immediate reservations about Abitibi's ability to pull the coup off. "This is fine for them to say," he was telling himself, "but maybe they won't be able to do it." Out loud, he finished the conversation in his room with: "I must do what is in the best interest of the shareholders."

"I guess this is going to change the tone of our planning meeting," Tittemore said, with some understatement. Rosier replied: "As far as we're concerned, all the more reason to do a good job of planning." Tittemore privately thought Rosier was too cocksure by half.

Rosier left Tittemore greatly relieved the Price chief executive had taken the news so well. Back at his own motel, he called Bell to tell him he'd had no problems with Tittemore, and to impart another piece of news. Tittemore had told him: "The greatest trouble you're going to have is with the Brits. They don't want to take their money out of Canada. To make a deal with them, you'll have to find some way besides cash." Rosier wanted to tell Bell as soon as possible, so McGibbon could alert LeMesurier. But he was too late. LeMesurier was already on his way to Harmsworth.

When Rosier left him, Tittemore returned to the bay-windowed room and broke the news to the vice-presidents still working there. The meeting broke for coffee, and Tittemore made his way hurriedly to Montreal. When the planning meeting reconvened, the consultant in attendance organized an amusing competitive nickel auction for half an hour to take their minds off the news and illustrate his philosophy that unfortunate confrontations like an auction or a takeover should be elevated into a both-sides-win situation. Then he swung the session into a discussion of how everybody could be made to win in an Abitibi-Price takeover. A strong camaraderie developed among the Price executives, based on a feeling that they were all under fire in the dark.

That afternoon Tittemore would call together a few directors and hold an almost continuous executive-committee meeting for the rest of the day, that evening and most of Friday until a board meeting could be convened on Saturday to deal with the situation.

Ross LeMesurier's aircraft touched down at London's Heathrow Airport at 8:45 a.m. local time, six hours and 45 minutes, plus a five-hour time difference, after its departure from Toronto. LeMesurier, a tall man of distinguished bearing who lost a leg in a wartime action for which he was decorated, walked from the aircraft, went through the Nothing-to-Declare gate and caught a cab to the Montcalm Hotel on Great Cumberland Street, where a room had been booked for him. He showered, freshened up and caught another cab over to Wood Gundy's London office, where he walked in on Trevor Spurgen, the Number Two there. (Ian Steers, known as both a jovial host and a sharp investment dealer, was away talking investments with the Arabs. Steers once had run a Wood Gundy office in the Bahamas, but when he'd discovered how often the firm was asked to do what was illegal he'd recommended that the office be closed.)

LeMesurier's visit had two purposes. He was to make a courtesy call on Hon. Vere Harmsworth, the chairman and chief executive of Associated Newspapers, as an emissary of Tom Bell and to apprise Harmsworth of the offer directly, before he could read about it in a newspaper or on a newswire and act on a false basis. At the same time, the London Stock Exchange would be informed so that a halt-trading order could be placed on Price stock the moment the offer was announced in Canada. Price had large and small shareholders in Britain, but few of both.

Trevor Spurgen had been told what was happening, on a confidential basis. Somebody in London had to know, to make the preparations. At 11:30 a.m., a Wood Gundy man called at the London Stock Exchange and briefed an official, who was miffed that the offer wouldn't be made jointly on the Canadian *and London* exchanges. (In fact, the British takeover rules are much too stringent for a takeover to be entered into on British soil lightly.)

At 12:30, Spurgen and LeMesurier took lunch in a nearby restaurant, then made their leisurely way to the Embankment, alongside the Thames. By 2:25, they were installed at a sidewalk phone booth, 100 yards from the head office of Associated Newspapers.

Spurgen dialed the Wood Gundy office and was told a telephone link had been established with Ian McGibbon and they were awaiting news. To be absolutely sure of getting through, McGibbon had instructed his secretary to place a transAtlantic call to Wood Gundy at 8:30 a.m., and she'd got through immediately to one of the secretaries in London. The two girls chatted for an hour to keep the telephone connection open at a cost that would finally reach $73.83. A month later, the two girls would keep their friendship warm by exchanging Christmas cards.

Carmelite House, Associated's head office, stands on the corner of the Embankment and a short side-street running down from Fleet Street, the home and heart of British journalism. The district presents both the antiseptic hauteur of modern buildings and the romantic squalor of the old City of London. Just below Fleet Street, off the hill down to the Thames, a short, ugly lane runs between a pub and a nondescript building. It's usually filled with overflowing garbage cans, but rejoices to the ringing name of Hanging Sword Alley. Farther down is a tortuous concrete street running crookedly nowhere, with the inappropriate but lovely name of Primrose Hill. Closer to Carmelite House, row upon row of newspaper delivery trucks hide in side streets like beetles in the woodwork.

Spurgen kept the line open to Wood Gundy by stuffing heavy 10p coins from the load in his sagging pockets into the phone box whenever the harsh British "time-up" signal came on the line. LeMesurier kept the phone booth door open by leaning against it. He was tired after his all-night flight.

A few minutes before three, British time, word came through that the bid was on the stock-exchange tickers. Spurgen hung up, and he and LeMesurier walked along the Embankment to Carmelite House.

Like so many British office buildings built before the era of glass and high steel, Carmelite House carried a faint atmosphere of austerity, as if Britain were always at war. The exterior was imposing enough, standing tall in stone over the street, modern by comparison with some of its neighbors. But the impression changed immediately inside the front door. The visitor entered a tiny vestibule and a narrow elevator that would take him to the higher reaches of the building, where there was some room to walk and work. But

98

even on the top story, the executive floor, the rooms were linked by narrow, warren-like passages, walled by partitions with glass panes that let light into the corridor from the window-lit offices but, as was only seemly, prevented any visibility the other way.

LeMesurier and Spurgen had no appointment, but they explained to the commissionaire they were calling on the chairman about "an important matter" and identified themselves. Mrs. White, Harmsworth's motherly secretary, said over the phone they were to "come up." Wood Gundy was well known in the office as a joint underwriter on Price Co. financings from time to time. When the two Wood Gundy men reached the top floor, Mrs. White explained that Harmsworth was out, but she showed them to a dark little room opposite his office where they could wait.

At about 3:10 Hon. Vere Harmsworth returned and received them immediately in his office. It was raining outside, a steady, cold, miserable, London rain pelting down from a lead-grey November sky. And, at just this time, another floor was being added to the top of Carmelite House, to house the business editor of the Daily Mail. In the middle of the long conference table in Harmsworth's office was a big vase, which collected water from one of the many holes upstairs in a steady drip, drip, drip. Other half-full vases, cannisters and buckets were distributed throughout the executive suite. As the dismal afternoon lengthened into the early British winter evening, the room would darken until Harmsworth had no choice but to consume energy by putting on the light.

Vere Harmsworth was an aristocrat for modern times. He was a gentle, sensitive, shy man in his early 50s who tried to act the part in photographs by thrusting out a bulldog chin under smiling eyes, in a playful attempt at the hauteur expected of the son of a viscount, Lord Rothermere. The only clue in Harmsworth's appearance that his name might be found in Burke's Peerage was a full hairstyle vaguely reminiscent of a George III wig.

Harmsworth greeted his guests cordially and seated them around the conference table, exchanging pleasantries across the drips. When a decent interval had passed, LeMesurier was about to get down to business when the telephone rang, and Harmsworth went across to his desk to take the call.

"Oh, it's on the Dow-Jones is it," he said into the phone, surprised. "Well, I do think it could have been done another way," he added, obviously peeved, and hung up. It was the Daily Mail's business editor telling Harmsworth about the bid. Harmsworth came back to the table smiling, and asked LeMesurier if he'd enjoyed his trip across the Atlantic. He was so pleasant that LeMesurier didn't realize he'd been beaten at the post.

LeMesurier broke the news as gently as he could. After a moment, Harmsworth got up quickly and went into the next room for R. M. P. (Mick) Shields, Associated's managing director, who looked after the day-to-day operations of the company. Shields was busy on the telephone, but Harmsworth waited at the door until he could come in. LeMesurier reviewed the bid in full again for both of them: It was $18, for 49% of the stock; it was firm (couldn't be withdrawn); shares would be taken up pro rata; there was no minimum to the number of shares Abitibi would buy; trading was halted, and wouldn't resume until 9:45 a.m. Tuesday. LeMesurier also told Harmsworth he had Bell's and Rosier's authority to say they thought highly of Price management and had no intention of making any changes. This was a compliment to Harmsworth, and it would soothe his sense of responsibility to Price management.

Harmsworth listened politely to LeMesurier, then replied quickly: "The stock is worth $10 more." Events would prove him right, but this alarmed Shields, who quickly cautioned Harmsworth that this wasn't the group for a discussion. "Why don't we thank these people and discuss it among ourselves?" Mick Shields suggested, anxious that Associated keep its cards hidden. LeMesurier eased the strain by explaining again this was merely a courtesy visit and that he believed "the deal" (meaning the $18 price) would be very attractive to individual and institutional investors.

As he was showing LeMesurier to the elevator, Harmsworth asked him where he was staying.

"At the Montcalm," LeMesurier replied.

Harmsworth's eyes twinkled. "Oh, he didn't do too well, did he?"

LeMesurier thought of replying that Wolfe didn't make it on the Plains of Abraham either, but, like a good ambassador, he kept his mouth shut.

At the Abitibi offices in Toronto, the remainder of the morning was busy but uneventful. At about 10 a.m. the adjourned board meeting resumed, and dealt with several mundane matters in a desultory manner. Nobody could generate much interest in Haire's report on Abitibi's financial performance in October. At about 10:30 the meeting terminated. Bell then started a presentation of the Price project to senior management, but he had to hand over to McGibbon in the middle of it. Bell was too tired to continue.

During the morning, press releases were distributed to the news media by both the Tory law firm (to make sure that prompt-disclosure rules were obeyed) and the Abitibi public relations department. Jack Haire was appointed the company's only spokesman on the bid, when newspapers and analysts called, and he was to say as little as possible.

At about noon, Bell, Haire and McGibbon and the two dozen directors and executives drifting around went to the Toronto Club and lunched on Sole Bonne Femme, which had been ordered beforehand. Three or four senior Abitibi executives belong to the Toronto Club, one of the six most exclusive in Canada.

At another of Canada's half-dozen élite clubs, the St. James's in Montreal, Harry Rosier was lunching with Richard Arnold Irwin, chairman of Consolidated-Bathurst Ltd., another major Canadian paper company, and William Ian Mackenzie Turner Jr., Consolidated's president and chief executive officer. Rosier had been proposed for membership in the club by Irwin and had promised Irwin to buy him lunch on his first visit as a member. Irwin had brought along Turner and they told Rosier it was a "fine thing" Abitibi had done.

"We're deep enough in the newsprint business not to want any part of it," one of them said, meaning Price rather than newsprint, "but we can see how Price fits into Abitibi and we wish you well." The next Turner-Rosier conversation would reflect much less camaraderie.

After lunch, Rosier called on Alec Hamilton, president of Domtar, to inform him formally about Abitibi's bid and encourage him to sell Domtar's stock. Hamilton's eyes lit up — with greed at the price being offered, and with ideas of what Domtar might do in retaliation. But he said little.

Abitibi's telephones in Toronto rang all afternoon with calls from analysts and journalists. Jack Haire gave out the bare facts of the bid and whatever financial details about Abitibi he was confident were public anyway. What intrigued callers most was why Abitibi was going for 49% rather than 51%, but Haire didn't explain. The choice of Haire as spokesman had been a master stroke. He didn't like information leaving the company at the best of times. Today he was like a clam with lockjaw. He did disclose to one caller, though, that Abitibi held no stock of Price, and, for want of more exciting information, that fact was reported prominently the following day.

Late in the afternoon, an analyst told Haire over the phone: "It's robbery if you get away with it at $18." In his respectful, thoughtful way, Haire replied: "You're right, the replacement value of the assets is so much greater than the market price. But at $18 we're offering the Price shareholders a significant premium over the market." In a few days time the premium would become even more "significant."

At about the same time, Tom Bell made courtesy calls to Alastair Gillespie, the federal Minister of Industry, Trade & Commerce, and Ontario cabinet ministers to inform them of Abitibi's action and purpose.

Then, toward evening, he telephoned his wife at their second home in Barbados to say he wouldn't be down for the weekend after all.

Day Sixteen

Friday, November 15
"Word came that Alec Hamilton
had taken a plane at noon . . ."

The phones started ringing early at Abitibi and went on all day.

At 10:15 a.m., a supervisor at Abitibi Provincial's fine-paper order desk called Ian McGibbon to report a conversation with an Abitibi alumnus, now with Price. McGibbon's informant at Provincial had called to enquire about Provincial's leasing temporary warehouse space from Price.

The Price man had told him, in passing, that he was "very busy today." "I've been assigned a list of 250 Toronto-area Price shareholders to phone — advising against acceptance of the $18 bid on the grounds it's too low a price," the Price man had said. He'd been told to say that Price's book value would be $19 a share by year-end and earnings were going to be $5 a share. The Price man had been instructed to tell shareholders that a more reasonable bid price would be $24 a share.

This $24 would be five times Price's earnings estimate of $5 a share, just as Abitibi's $18 bid was about five times *Abitibi's* earnings estimate for Price of about $3.20 a share. But that $5 estimate was way too high, McGibbon thought. There must be a mistake somewhere. (Informed later about the conversation, the Wood Gundy people would be delighted that Price was flailing around this way.)

"Keep after that fellow with all sorts of normal business. Try to distract him from phoning shareholders," McGibbon told his caller.

Later in the morning, McGibbon received a call from Jean Pouliot, a contact in the Quebec Department of Lands & Forests, to ask on behalf of the minister, Kevin Drummond, whether Abitibi was Canadian-controlled. McGibbon assured Pouliot, off the cuff, that Abitibi was more than 95% owned by Canadians. He then reminded Pouliot of Abitibi's long involvement in Quebec at its Beaupre mill, and asked: "Is there any special concern in the Quebec government about our bid?" Pouliot replied, "No."

McGibbon immediately informed Rosier of the call, and Rosier vainly tried to reach Drummond by telephone. A day or two later, Rosier would reach Drummond, and would get an impression that Drummond might prefer the control of Price passing to Abitibi rather than to a Quebec-based company. There was concern, it seemed, about problems of concentration that might be created in Quebec — concentration similar to the Irving family's incestuous domination of the New Brunswick economy. Was Rosier's impression reliable? He and his colleagues still felt that nationalist elements in Quebec might make much of Ontario-based control of a company as big as Price.

All morning, rumors came in from Abitibi's friends that Domtar was about to make a counterbid, but nobody could pin them down, though Chuck Rathgeb's warning on November 4 was not forgotten.

At noon, the Abitibi bid team, the Tory twins and Wood Gundy people lunched at the Toronto Club again. John Abell, a senior Wood Gundy vice-president, was asked how the market was reacting to the bid. Very well, he said. Lots of shareholders would tender. Nevertheless, it was agreed that Abitibi's advertising agency, Cockfield Brown, would place ads in all major newspapers in Toronto, Montreal and Quebec City on Saturday and Monday.

The advertisement would be a bald statement of the bid's details, addressed simply to "The Holders of Common Shares of The Price Company Limited," and merely explain: "To accept . . . you should contact your investment dealer or broker." It would be all very restrained and proper, but in the eyes of at least one shareholder it would carry insufficient explanation.

Early in the afternoon, news came over the Dow-Jones wire

that Charles Tittemore had told Price shareholders not to leap at the bid but sit tight. There would be a Price directors' meeting on Saturday and an announcement would be made then.

Realizing the importance of newswires, the bid team asked Paul Masterson, deputy head of Abitibi public relations, and, oddly enough, a forester, to keep an eye on the Dow-Jones and Canadian Press wires over the weekend and phone any one of the people on the team if anything important came over.

All afternoon the telephone calls from analysts, journalists and friends continued unabated. Now and then a flurry of excitement would be caused by this or that rumor, like one that Dominion Securities-Harris & Partners was preparing a counterbid by Price for Abitibi.

If Price could raise the money quickly enough — perhaps $135 million in two working days — there was nothing in the law or the exchange rules to prevent a bid for Abitibi. Wood Gundy hurriedly contacted friends in the brokerage and paper industries to try to find out where the Price board meeting would be held Saturday — in Montreal or Quebec City. The plan was to station outside someone who'd recognize Dominion Securities people. If any went in, the rumor was probably true. But nobody could find out where the board meeting would be. If Price did make a bid for Abitibi, the possibilities were too horrible to contemplate, but Bell sternly dismissed the speculation. The exchanges would never allow such a thing to happen, he said.

The preceding week, Jim Tory had asked a friendly Montreal law firm to have a junior lawyer buy five Price shares and register them in his name. No reason had been given. On Thursday morning, when the bid had become public knowledge, the lawyer had gone to Montreal Trust Co., Price's transfer agent, presented his share certificate, and asked to see the shareholders' list, the right of every registered shareholder. Once granted access, he'd brought in 20 Wood Gundy people to copy the names and addresses of Price's principal shareholders. The lists, by now typed, were starting to arrive at Wood Gundy's head office in Toronto. If, for any reason, the exchange bid ran into trouble Abitibi wanted to know where the stock was, so it could call the shareholders.

Towards 4 p.m., word came through that Alec Hamilton, chief executive of Domtar, had taken a plane at noon from Montreal to

Toronto to discuss a Domtar counterbid with Argus Corp. For 10 or 15 minutes tension rose at Abitibi as Bell, Haire and the others speculated on Domtar's strategy and at what price the bid would come in.

But at 4:07 p.m. an announcement came over the Dow-Jones wire: "Argus Corp . . . is studying the current $18 a share offer for 49% of Price shares by Abitibi and will decide whether to launch a counterbid over the weekend, A. Bruce Matthews, Argus executive vice-president, told Dow-Jones." Perhaps Domtar wasn't going to bid after all. Maybe it was all happening at the Argus level.

At 5 p.m. the Abitibi team began leaving the office, one by one, for the weekend. By 7 p.m., the executive suite looked deserted.

Day Seventeen

Saturday, November 16
**"Bud McDougald was pacing the
heavy royal schedule . . ."**

The Price board meeting began at 2 p.m. in the company's Montreal office. Present from England was Mick Shields, the managing director of Associated Newspapers and Harmsworth's right-hand man, who'd dropped everything and caught the first flight from London on Friday. Also there was ex-fighter pilot Bob Morrow, the vice-chairman of Price, and long-time Montreal counsel to the Harmsworth interests. The other Price directors were either drawn from management or were outsiders chosen for expertise in various fields. Price was basically a company run by management, with little interference from Britain other than approval of major expenditures. Harmsworth himself, and a third director from Associated Newspapers, P. J. Saunders, Associated's corporate secretary, weren't in attendance. Harmsworth was still in England hastily collecting documents — and legal opinions as to what he could and couldn't do.

The Price board examined, one by one, six defensive courses of action.

Have Price or a subsidiary buy up its own stock until there was less than 49% remaining in the market. The purchases would have to be by private arrangement with each shareholder, before the Abitibi bid closed Tuesday morning. Purchases couldn't be made on the exchange because of the cease-trade in effect. The cost would be about $70 million (say, 3.5 million shares, a 35% block to place beside Associated's 18%, bought at $20 a share to outprice Abitibi). Price could probably raise that much money quickly, but would there be time to contact the shareholders? How about Price making a counterbid on the exchange for its own stock against Abitibi? But would a company be allowed to compete for control of itself? Could Price or a subsidiary *vote* Price stock once it was purchased or did bought stock have to be canceled? If it had to be canceled that would strengthen Abitibi's control, rather than weakening it. Were Quebec companies *allowed* to buy their own shares? This was allowed in Ontario, but wasn't in Quebec. On checking with the Quebec government, it was discovered enabling legislation was envisaged, but it wasn't yet on the books.

Find a new group to become a partner with Associated Newspapers in control of Price. Only five Canadian groups were big enough and able to quickly buy control within the restrictions of the Foreign Investment Review Act: MacMillan Bloedel, Argus, Cemp, Canadian Pacific Investments and Power Corp. MacMillan Bloedel was deeply enough into newsprint to want, probably, no more. Argus already had Domtar and wasn't a likely prospect. [This was the view at Price, quite contrary to the one at Abitibi.] Cemp preferred more speculative ventures, but was worth a try. The question there was whether it was better to be controlled by Cemp which had no involvement in the paper industry or by Abitibi which knew the business. Power Corp. had Consolidated-Bathurst, and surely that was a big enough newsprint commitment.

Power Corp? Maybe Power Corp. *could* be interested. The thought was tucked away for a day or two. In the meantime, Price's vice-chairman Bob Morrow would call major Price shareholders, and ascertain that they'd sell a good 50% of the stock to a Harmsworth partnership if the Abitibi bid were bettered.

(The wheeling and dealing fell to Bob Morrow, partly because he was good at it, partly because his responsibility was dual — to Price and the English. Tittemore, Price's chief executive, whose responsibility was to all shareholders, worked hard bringing directors together and advising the shareholders publicly. As an operating man, his forte wasn't in motivating outside blocks of capital. He didn't have the contacts or the temperament.)

The main difficulty in attracting a partner to Associated was that Associated was asking for the money but wanted to keep or share control. Who'd go for that kind of a proposition?

Get the Quebec government to buy control of Price, with Associ-ated as a senior minority shareholder. An approach would be made to the province suggesting that a provincial Crown corporation might initially buy 25% of Price stock, new from the Price treasury, put directors on the Price board, then later move into absolute control. That would also involve, presumably, a government order preventing Abitibi from taking control. The Quebec government would give two reasons for not acting. The first: "There's no logical reason to do so. The way it is, Ontario control will be substituted for English control, which is good for Canada." Later Premier Robert Bourassa would explain in the National Assembly: "We examined all the facts and concluded it was not in the interest of the government and the people of Quebec to invest such a considerable sum in enterprises that created no new jobs, and that could affect us in other decisions about enterprises that did create new jobs."

Ask Associated Newspapers to make a competing bid alone. Even if Associated could raise the money in Britain at a time when most national daily newspapers were in trouble, it was doubtful whether the Bank of England would permit the investment abroad or permit it in time. There was also the question of the Canadian Foreign Investment Review Act. Nobody was quite sure how that would affect a strengthening of control by Associated.

Make a rights issue to enable present shareholders to buy new stock which they could sell to Abitibi at a profit. A rights issue would generate funds for Price and could frustrate the takeover, because Abitibi would either buy the same number of shares bid for, and that would become much less than 49%, or consider raising the number of shares bid for, and face financing troubles.

Say Price sold each shareholder at $2 apiece rights to buy treasury stock for $12 a share. The company was authorized to issue another five million shares above the almost 10 million outstanding, so each shareholder's holdings could increase by up to one third. Abitibi had bid for nearly five million shares. One of two things would happen. Abitibi would stick to five million and the Price shareholders would merely offload to Abitibi at a profit of $4 a share the shares bought under the new rights, at the same time ceding to Abitibi only about 33% of the enlarged capitalization of the company. Alternatively, Abitibi would have to increase the number of shares bid for to 7.5 million (for 49%) at a cost of $135 million, which might prove prohibitive.

But was there time to issue the rights before Abitibi's bid closed? The answer was clearly negative. One business day wasn't long enough.

What *might* have been done was to have the Price board approve a rights issue to be made later. And, if Abitibi failed to gain control of the Price board in time to cancel the rights issue, the takeover would be seriously set back. But the trouble with this course of action was that it was mainly spiteful.

Another defensive act that would occur to Vere Harmsworth when he arrived in Canada later was to pay out all of Price's cash as an immediate extra dividend to shareholders. That would sharply reduce the value of the company to Abitibi. In the days to come, Harmsworth would actually make this threat to Bell, but not seriously. It would be spiteful rather than effective (Abitibi couldn't change its bid anyway), impracticable (not enough time), and carry the appearance of threatening a manipulation of Price to get a better deal for Associated. Another problem was that Abitibi would probably be a shareholder of record (entitled to dividends) by the time the dividend was payable.

Have Price make a bid for control of Abitibi. This would be possible under the Foreign Investment Review Act, providing both takeovers succeeded at the same time. Price would become a Canadian company (because Abitibi held 49% of the stock) and could take over Abitibi. But if each company won control of the other, how could the stalemate be ended? Well, Price would have to make damn sure it gained control of the Abitibi board by the appointment of enough "Price" directors, before Abitibi gained control of Price's board by the appointment of "Abitibi" directors. The Price board would then control: Price directly, Price indirectly (through its control of Abitibi) and Abitibi. It would all be very easy really. Later on the two companies could be merged.

This plan was dismissed as irresponsible. The two companies would be plunged into $230 million of debt: $145 million for Price to buy nine million (50%) of Abitibi's shares at, say, $16 a share, and $85 million for Abitibi to buy control of Price. And all that would be achieved would be the same merger that might flow from

Abitibi's bid anyway. Besides, despite the best-laid plans, chaos could ensue.

The Price board meeting was adjourned *sine die* without any firm plan surfacing. Telegrams were sent to every Price shareholder advising against acceptance of the bid because the price was too low. The board remained on continuous standby.[1]

The morning meal at the Toronto home of John Angus (Bud) McDougald, chairman and president of Argus Corp., was kidneys and bacon; kedgeree, made English-style with rice, hard-boiled eggs and haddock; and coffee or tea. The meal was served at a Queen Anne table covered with a blue linen-and-lace cloth. At breakfast with Bud and Maude McDougald were Princess Anne and Capt. Mark Phillips, married about a year. They'd come to Toronto to open the day before, the Royal Agricultural Winter Fair, whose honorary president was Bud McDougald.

McDougald was reputed to be one of the 10 wealthiest men in Canada, with a fortune of $250 million. He held an office or a directorship in nearly 40 companies, was a trustee of the Ontario Jockey Club and a governor of the Good Samaritan Hospital in Palm Beach, Florida, near his second home. But McDougald's main business connection was as president, and owner with associates, of Ravelston Corp., a private company that owned 51% of Argus, which in turn held about $200 million of the stocks of other major companies, including Domtar.

Argus had been built up in the 1950s by the Canadian financier E. P. Taylor, who still owned 10% of Argus voting stock through Windfields Farm Ltd., the company that owned his thoroughbred breeding farm near Oshawa, Ontario.

When Maude McDougald had been interviewed earlier in the week by the Toronto Star about the entertaining of the royal couple, she'd said she planned to ignore the formal instructions received from Buckingham Palace. All guests at Green Meadows receive the same warmth, courtesy and etiquette. Besides, she'd said, the rules of protocol are "simple things we know anyway . . . We are quite aware of things like that, and my husband doesn't like to be told what to do."

Business associates of Bud McDougald would have understood her last remark only too well. "He treats everybody like an office boy," associates have been known to complain. One company president was "treated as if he's an adolescent who has sat down at the dinner table with dirty fingernails; there's that kind of connotation to it," according to another president who has observed them.

The fiercely independent McDougald was very busy over the weekend. Maude McDougald had told the Star she was worried about the heavy schedule arranged for the royal couple. They'd have time to eat dinner at Green Meadows only once — on the Monday evening, just before they left Canada. ("We'll have loin of lamb cooked until it is crisp and brown," Maude McDougald promised, "new peas if we could find them, roast potatoes, and some awfully good crepes with orange sauce, which are the cook's specialty.") Bud McDougald was pacing the heavy royal schedule — squiring Princess Anne and her husband about town. How much time would he have to study a counterbid for Price by Argus? And if McDougald were preoccupied, who'd dare even partially to take the complicated decision out of his hands? A heightened affection for the royal family developed among the Abitibi takeover team.

Bud McDougald may have been preoccupied, but Ian Sinclair, chairman and chief executive officer of Canadian Pacific Investments Ltd. (and of the railway that controlled it), was certainly not. Abitibi's raid had signaled Price as a good, cash-rich, long-term investment, a takeover prize. Canadian Pacific was one of the few major pools of capital in Canada that could act within the Foreign Investment Review Act. It already had assets of more than $2 billion, including companies in mining, coal, logging, real estate, paper and aviation.

Sinclair now wanted to add Price to the list. He called together his staff to put together a bid that would compete with Abitibi's. That was easy enough to do — $18 could easily be topped without paying too much for Price. But what would happen if Price shareholders tendered to both Canadian Pacific and Abitibi? Was there

112

any guarantee a bidder wouldn't get a bloody nose? There were no exchange rules covering competing bids.

Sinclair and his staff decided the prize was worth winning, but the risks were unclear. Better stay away from Price.

Day Eighteen

Sunday, November 17
**"Harmsworth looked disconsolately
around the lounge . . ."**

Hon. Vere Harmsworth, chairman and chief executive of Associated Newspapers Group, arrived at Heathrow Airport early this Sunday morning in his chauffeur-driven Jaguar. With him was Peter J. Saunders, the corporate secretary, who'd accompany Harmsworth to Canada. They held first-class tickets, but Harmsworth's secretary, Mrs. White, hadn't been able to make bookings when she'd tried on Friday and Saturday. All flights to Canada were full. It wasn't even possible to travel via New York.

In the last three days, Harmsworth had developed a sour expression on what was usually a carefree face. Mick Shields, Associated's managing director, had gone on ahead to give support to Bob Morrow, the vice-chairman of Price, and Tittemore, who were holding the Price board together and working on strategies. Harmsworth had stayed behind to clarify the nature of his company's investment in Price and throw a few papers together.

"Those blasted Canadians. It's like playing poker with a lot of cowboys. They certainly know how to play rough," Harmsworth mused. What if he couldn't get a flight to Canada? What if all the information he needed hadn't arrived by Tuesday morning when the bid closed? The Bank of England was slow in these matters. What would he do then?

Harmsworth dealt with Baring Bros., a London firm of investment bankers, one of whose partners, Lord Cromer, an ex-governor of the Bank of England, was married to a Harmsworth. On Friday, first thing, Vere Harmsworth had asked Baring Bros. to request a ruling from the Bank of England (by letter; the bank wouldn't give a ruling by phone) as to whether the Associated Newspapers investment in Price¹ was "direct" or "portfolio." The type of investment was crucial to Harmsworth's decision whether to accept the Abitibi bid.

Some time after World War II, to support the troubled pound, Britain had started to restrict British investment abroad, and the government made a distinction between investments that were beneficial to the nation and those that were a mere drain on Britain's reserves of foreign currency.

Classified as direct investments were British corporations' holdings in foreign companies with which they also enjoyed beneficial commercial links, such as the sale of their products to the foreign subsidiary or favorable arrangements to purchase raw materials for British industry. Direct investments could be made in the normal way: the British company simply bought foreign currency and purchased the shares. When direct investments were liquidated, the proceeds had to be returned to Britain and any new investment had to be re-classified and approved by the Bank of England²

All other investments by corporations or individuals were classified as portfolio investments, and had to be made with "premium currency" purchased by the investor from a special pool at a high price. On Day Sixteen (Friday), the premium was 62⅝%. An investor would have to pay £1.63 for every pound purchased to invest abroad. When a portfolio investment was liquidated, the investor could either roll most of it over into another foreign investment or repatriate the proceeds, selling back most of the "investment currency" into the special market and retrieving the premium prevailing at the time. (It can vary widely.)

Vere Harmsworth wasn't sure how Associated's investment in Price would finally be classified. The original investment had been made way back when a predecessor of Price had been created to provide the Harmsworth papers with newsprint. That had been long before the foreign investment rules were written. And the investment didn't seem to be clearly of one type or the other. True, Associated bought newsprint from Price, but at the going price; there was no great economic benefit for Britain in that. True, holdings of 20% and more, if there were effective control and trade, were commonly classified as direct, but what about 17% in a company that was run day-to-day by its own Canadian management? Associated had effective control but did little more than approve major Price expenditures. Only holdings of less than 10% were sure to be classified as portfolio, but some greater than 10% were also so classified.

The whole question was difficult. Associated had never known for sure the category of its Price investment, but had leaned toward the opinion it was portfolio. Although the Price shares were carried in Associated's accounts at cost, there was a note giving the "market value . . . on the basis of the Canadian Stock Exchange quotation *excluding London premium . . .*" That was a hint the premium probably applied. What's more, there was confirmation of this assumption. Harmsworth had received verbal assurance from the Baring firm, which had contacted somebody at the Bank of England after the Abitibi bid, that the investment would probably be classified portfolio.

This classification when it came in writing would be crucial to Harmsworth's decision. It would determine whether Abitibi's $18 bid was a good price.[3] If Associated held a portfolio investment, the proceeds could be freely rolled over into another Canadian or American stock and protected from the falling pound, or sold into the investment-currency market at the prevailing premium — probably still close to 62%. If that were done, Abitibi's $18 bid price would mean more than $26 a share (before capital-gains tax) in pounds in Britain. The pound would have to fall a long way before it wiped out that gain from the market. Harmsworth had told LeMesurier, Bell's emissary, that the stock was worth $28 a share. Well, by George, that was almost what he'd get for the 49% he could sell. That was, of course, if the Bank of England did classify the investment as portfolio. They usually took two to three weeks to give a ruling. Would they be able to come through in time?

Harmsworth was angry, worried and sad. He might get a reasonable price for the Price shares, but, under one name or another, they'd been in the family for half a century. The hardest man couldn't avoid a sentimental attachment, especially if his grandfather had built the company's first mill. And Harmsworth wasn't a money-grasping tycoon. In the fiscal year 1975 he'd take only $26,000 out of Associated as his personal salary — less than in 1974 and less than nine other directors. He was a sensitive man, conscious of dynasty in the company, a reader, a painter who spent much of his leisure at the canvas. But sentiment alone didn't rule his feelings.

The Price shares were carried in Associated's accounts at a historic cost of about $2.50 a share, which bore little relationship to the current market price. Valuing the shares at $15 each (because Abitibi was offering $18 a share for 49% of what had been trading at $12), the block was worth about $24 million. That was equivalent to almost a third of the Associated's net worth of about $80 million.

Harmsworth was pondering in the British Airways first-class lounge when he realized that he and Saunders hadn't been called for a flight. He began to wonder if he'd get to Canada before the bid closed. He looked disconsolately around the lounge at the travel-weary wealthy of many nations. Suddenly: "Oh, there's Sir David Nicolson. He might be able to do something for us." Harmsworth walked over to greet Sir David, who'd just entered the lounge. Harmsworth explained his problem, and Nicolson, the chairman of British Airways, reassured him: "We'll be able to arrange something, Vere, but I'm afraid you'll have to travel economy."

On arrival in Montreal, Harmsworth and Saunders went straight to Price's offices, but nobody was there. Late that afternoon they checked into the Ritz-Carlton Hotel, Harmsworth's favorite in Montreal. After a quick dinner, they went through the ritual of holding an Associated Newspapers board meeting, since Harmsworth, Saunders and Mick Shields, the Associated managing director who'd arrived in Montreal earlier, formed a quorum. And the board troika gave Harmsworth power to negotiate on the company's behalf.

The Abitibi executives had tried hard to relax over the weekend. The day before, Saturday, Bell had gone into the office and read press releases, but decided he'd rather get away from it all. In the afternoon, he'd driven up to open his ski lodge at Blue Mountain near Collingwood, Ontario, for the imminent start of the season. But he came back today, afraid to be away from the office too long.

McGibbon had had more success. He'd enjoyed a Saturday of hard physical labor on his Caledon Hills property. He gave the children some of his time this afternoon, then returned to Toronto. On arrival, he immediately reported in to Rosier, who'd been trying to reach him both at his farm and at his Forest Hill home in Toronto.

The news was good. Vere Harmsworth was coming in tomorrow to see Bell and would probably tender his stock. The Domtar board meeting scheduled for tomorrow had been canceled, Rosier had heard, and the Price board meeting had dragged on for two days with little result other than a communique to shareholders not to sell, the price was too low. On balance it looked fine. Most Price shareholders would probably disregard their board's advice when they could get a 50% premium on market. Besides, the Price board didn't seem to have much fight in it. For the first time, Bell and Rosier felt certain of success.

Day Nineteen

Monday, November 18
**"Can we reach all the clients
in time, Norman . . .?"**

John P. S. Mackenzie, the stylish vice-president (investments) of Canada Permanent Trust Co., was angry. Those damned exchange takeovers were getting out of hand. There'd been that White Pass & Yukon takeover in June 1973, when Federal Industries got away with buying out the control block holus-bolus, then taking out only a third of the small shareholders' holdings. Then there'd been that dreadful Noranda episode — and now Abitibi was trying to stampede the market. It really was too much. Mackenzie picked up the phone and dialed his capable aide, Norman Halford, assistant vice-president (portfolio management).

When the Abitibi bid had been announced the previous Thursday, Mackenzie had been in Montreal at a meeting of the Canadian investment committee of Prudential Assurance Co. At 10:15, when told of the bid, Mackenzie had immediately phoned his head office and given instructions for all of Canada Permanent's 52 branches across Canada that administered trust accounts (about 22 of them) to call a broker and accept Abitibi's bid — but not irrevocably, in case a better one came along. (Binding commitments to sell wouldn't be made until Tuesday morning, when the sellers' brokers would walk across the floor of the exchange between 9 a.m. and 9:45 a.m. to tender their clients stock to the stock-exchange official "filling the book" with a record of each parcel of stock tendered under the bid.)

Where Canada Permanent had discretion over an account, the bid could be tentatively accepted the same day (Thursday) or Friday, but with some accounts a co-trustee or executor had to be consulted. Canada Permanent would have to work hard to contact all the co-trustees before Tuesday when the bid closed, Mackenzie had figured. Canada Permanent didn't hold much of Price's stock in trust — 128,000 shares (less than 2%) in accounts belonging to 157 clients. (Montreal Trust held a lot more — about 5% of the stock.) But it would be a chore for Canada Permanent nevertheless, and there'd probably be some co-trustees still unreached by Tuesday.

On Thursday at 3 p.m., Jack Mackenzie had flown back from Montreal to Toronto, met an investment-dealer friend, and traveled with him to Griffith Island, in Georgian Bay, for some pheasant shooting. They'd arrived at dinner and been regaled all evening with business tales and anecdotes by former Ontario Premier John Robarts and railway chieftain Norman MacMillan, the only two Abitibi directors who'd chosen shooting after the Thursday board meeting that had given the takeover the okay. Mackenzie hadn't realized they were Abitibi directors, and the bid hadn't been discussed.

This Monday morning, Mackenzie looked cool, even conservatively festive, in a dark-grey pin-stripe business suit set off with a bright pink handkerchief bushing elegantly out of the top pocket and a merry polka-dot tie. But it was Monday morning and he was irritated.

"Can we reach all the clients in time, Norman?" he asked over the telephone. Halford thought it unlikely. He didn't like this takeover either. The salesman over at Wood Gundy kept pestering him to tender Canada Permanent's stock through Wood Gundy so Wood Gundy would receive the sell commission from Canada Permanent as well as the arranged fee from Abitibi. (When Price shareholders tendered stock through other brokers, Wood Gundy would receive only the Abitibi fee.)

It was bad enough that there were only three business days to reach all the accounts, and now there was this salesman fellow making a pest of himself as well. Besides, $18 wasn't much. It was high enough above market to call for a "sell" rather than a "hold," but the stock should fetch more than that in a takeover. There just might be a counterbid. Argus had announced Friday it was considering one, but would there be enough time? Halford and Mackenzie talked a while longer before they hung up.

A few moments later, Halford picked up the telephone again and registered a firm protest with Bill Somerville, executive vice-president of the Toronto Stock Exchange, over the brief open time of the Abitibi bid, and the difficulty of reaching clients. "We need a week," Halford told him bluntly.

Somerville, who was close to retirement and seldom seemed to get excited about anything, told Halford mildly: "There's no need for an extension."

That annoyed Halford, and he telephoned Harry Bray, the quick-thinking vice-chairman of the Ontario Securities Commission. Halford made the same pitch to Bray but much more religiously. Bray's initial reaction was the same as Somerville's. But Halford persisted. Why should all the trust companies have to work like beavers over the weekend just to accommodate Abitibi? What about the little shareholders who were bound to be left out? Perhaps a light went on in Harry Bray's mind. He didn't like this kind of thing either. It made a mockery of the securities laws that he and others had so carefully drawn up. Bray softened and promised to talk to Arthur Pattillo, the new Securities Commission chairman. He asked Halford to spell out his complaint in a letter as soon as possible.

At 11:45 Halford placed a draft letter in the hands of Mackenzie's secretary, and Mackenzie signed it at 1:30 when he returned from lunch. By 2 p.m. the letter was at the Ontario Securities Commission.[1]

At 3 p.m., Maj.-Gen. A. Bruce Matthews, C.B.E., D.S.O., C.D., E.D., chairman of Canada Permanent, executive vice-president of Argus Corp., the man who'd made Friday's announcement about Argus looking at Price, and Mackenzie's and Halford's boss, walked down the wide corridor outside Mackenzie's office and looked in the door. Mackenzie hadn't seen Matthews for a week, and he felt he should let him know what he and Halford had done.

Bruce Matthews' connection with Canada Permanent arose out of shareholdings of his family's investment company, which he'd joined after the war. (Matthews had been in command of the Second Canadian Division during World War II.) Matthews was not only chairman of Canada Permanent and high in Argus, but he was also a director of 14 other companies, including Domtar, which Argus effectively controlled. These multiple connections tended to hobble Matthews at Canada Permanent. Whenever the trust company's investment committee talked about placing money in stocks with which Matthews was involved, which was unavoidable if the portfolio were to be properly balanced, Matthews would have to fall silent to avoid any conflict of interest.

Matthews remained at Mackenzie's door and read the letter handed to him. He handed it back and grunted: "Reasonable thing to do. Got to protect the clients." Then he walked off.

When he was sure the letter had arrived at the Ontario Securities Commission, Norman Halford telephoned Wood Gundy and told the salesman, not without satisfaction, what he'd done. The salesman went on the defensive. "Wood Gundy are only representing their clients," he told Halford.

Later in the day Halford was needled from more than one quarter about "Gen. Matthews' involvement." Harsh language was used about Matthews and Argus, implying that Mackenzie's letter was motivated by a desire to give Argus more time for a counterbid, an accusation that would be heard on Bay Street for months to come, and that Mackenzie would always strenuously deny. Gen. Matthews hadn't known about the letter before it was delivered, he'd always point out. But the cost of the Canada Permanent letter to Abitibi would be reckoned in the tens of millions of dollars.

After rising refreshed from Sunday night's sojourn in the opulent comfort of the Ritz Carlton Hotel, Hon. Vere Harmsworth went out to Montreal International Airport and boarded Price's BH125 executive aircraft to fly to Toronto for a confrontation with Thomas Bell, that energetic antagonist who'd exploded into Harmsworth's affairs. Traveling with Harmsworth were Bob Morrow, vice-chairman of Price and the Harmsworths' Canadian counsel, Peter Saunders, secretary of Associated Newspapers, and Jack Cole, Wood Gundy's vice-chairman, who was based in Montreal. Harmsworth still didn't know the official status of Associated

Newspapers' investment in Price, but he'd steeled himself, not against the worst, but for the best.

On arrival at Toronto, Harmsworth and entourage drove downtown to the Royal Trust Tower to call on Charles Gundy, the senior to their original contact, Ross LeMesurier, and the chairman of Abitibi's fiscal agent. Rushing straight to Bell would have been unseemly.

At Abitibi, Tom Bell, Ian McGibbon, Harry Rosier and Charles Gundy had held a hurried meeting to enable Gundy to straighten out what might have become a false impression. Wood Gundy had always been the second-echelon underwriter for Price and that was why Cole was traveling with Harmsworth. Cole was there merely to bridge the protocol' gap in the progression of Harmsworth's contacts: Associated Newspapers, Price, Price's number-two underwriter. Associated's contact over the bid. Abitibi's agent, Abitibi, finally Tom Bell. But it did look odd. *Here* was Wood Gundy acting for Abitibi, and *there* seemed to be a Wood Gundy man in the other camp. Charles Gundy clarified the picture for the Abitibi executives and reassured them before the party arrived. Then Gundy returned to Wood Gundy to receive Harmsworth.

While they were waiting, Bell and the others read press reports and releases by the Price directors. Over the weekend, to add fiction to the excitement, Bell had read Richard Rohmer's novel *Exoneration*, in which a Canadian company takes over Exxon, the huge American-owned petroleum corporation. Now, Bell noted, the Price press releases contrasted sharply with the fictional fight put up by Exxon management when most Exxon shareholders wanted to sell their stock.

In his own takeover, Bell was pleased to see that Price management could do little better than say the stock was worth more than $18 and advise shareholders to watch for a better offer. It would be hazardous for the Price board to come out strongly against the Abitibi bid. If enough shareholders tendered to Abitibi despite the board's advice, they could yield Abitibi effective control — and that was possible with only the 18% controlled by Harmsworth. And, later, if the market fell back to $12 at the close of the $18 bid, shareholders who'd taken the Price board's advice possibly could sue the board for $6 a share.

At 11 a.m. Tom Bell and Harry Rosier made a friendly call to Alec Hamilton, Domtar's chief executive, on a conference phone and asked him if Domtar would tender its stock. Yes, Hamilton said.[2] So, Domtar wasn't preparing a counterbid after all. That was one peril out of their path. But then, when you thought about it, Domtar would be ill-advised to take over Price. Domtar was a balanced conglomerate with only 12% of its sales in newsprint. To finance a Price acquisition, Domtar would have to rob borrowing power from the building materials and chemical divisions and would become lopsided with newsprint capacity. It was well known too that Domtar was less optimistic about newsprint than Abitibi, despite access to the same Arthur D. Little study. For Abitibi, on the other hand, the alternatives to newsprint, board and fine paper, were less attractive for one reason or another, and a heavy move into newsprint offered some degree of price leadership to offset the effects of having so many eggs in one basket.

But why had Domtar been studying Price financial information a week or two ago? It must have just been a yearly updater —or something like that.

There was still Argus to worry about, but that quarter had been quiet since Friday. Besides, Tom Bell had never thought Argus a likely bidder anyway (partly through optimistic self-delusion). The other possibles — Canadian Pacific, MacMillan Bloedel, Cemp Investments — didn't seem to be planning anything. By now, possibly 75% of the Price stock already had been set aside for Wood Gundy. The Price shareholders obviously liked the bid, and it was getting wide publicity. The worst of this battle was surely over.

The Harmsworth group, with Charles Gundy and Ted Medland, president of Wood Gundy, arrived at the Abitibi office about noon. At first, the meeting wasn't pleasant. Bob Morrow, the Harmsworth lawyer, acting as spokesman, banged the table and talked about the lousy way the English had been treated, and how unfair Abitibi had been. For quarter of an hour, Morrow, the ex-fighter-pilot, strafed Bell, the lieutenant-colonel of artillery.

"Look, we've got all sorts of people who can team up with us against you, and all we've got to say is, 'Come in.' " Morrow boasted vaguely, while Harmsworth sat quietly in the background, above this kind of thing. "We think this is an underhanded business," Morrow continued acidly. "Do you know we studied the acquisition of Abitibi, but we turned it down at the executive-committee level because we didn't think it was cricket," he told Bell. The Price takeover of Abitibi had been abandoned ultimately because of difficulties created by the Foreign Investment Review Act, but at an earlier stage Price's executive committee could well have dismissed a stock-exchange raid as the route to use in any possible attempt. "We feel pretty badly you've done this to us when we went through the same thing and decided not to do it to you," Morrow said.

"Anyway," Morrow said at last. "We're here to discuss this matter frankly with you and see if we can't do a deal. We've got tax problems in England, the problem of repatriating the money, and the problem of capital-gains tax if we don't roll it over," he explained. "We would like to sell our whole interest. This is our major objective." (If Associated sold only 49% of its 17% Price block, it would be left with less than 10% of Price. This would have serious tax consequences — loss of double-taxation relief in Britain on dividends from the remaining holdings.)[3]

The Canadians and the British talked about this proposal for half an hour, then Bell said firmly: "We've made a bid on the exchange, and there's no way we could extend a bid to one shareholder that was any different from the bid made to every other shareholder. There's no way to do it." He was recalling Jim Tory's advice and his own earlier inclinations. Besides, Wood Gundy had informed him that a large proportion of Price's shareholders were going to tender their stock. So the British 17% was important but not vital.

Bell's firmness quieted Morrow, and he and Harmsworth began to consider avenues of compromise. After some discussion, one of them said: "Maybe we'd like to do this deal. What we'd need to end up with is 10% of Abitibi [to avoid the tax problems below 10%] and a seat on the board."

Behind this approach lay the hint of a forceful nutcracker play in the future: one that, on the face of it, looked deadly to Abitibi. Wood Gundy was confident by now that most of the Price stock would have been tendered when the bid closed on Tuesday, so Abitibi would take up about 49% of the holdings of each tendering shareholder. (In a stock-exchange takeover, if more stock is tendered than bid for, the bidder takes up whatever proportion of the stock tendered that will give him the quantity bid for.)

If Harmsworth tendered, say, one million shares, and Abitibi took up 49%, that would leave Associated with more than 10% of Price (7% kept and 5% "returned" from what was tendered to Abitibi), and therefore no British tax problem. With the $18 per share proceeds from the Price shares it sold, Associated could buy a position of 5% or 6% in Abitibi (capitalization 18 million shares; market price $9 per share) and wait. Harmsworth didn't need Abitibi's approval for that; the Abitibi stock could simply be bought on the market. If Abitibi later on wanted to merge with Price, then Associated could make Bell pay dearly for the privilege of removing Associated's 12% of Price stock out of the way of a merger. (A merger cannot be forced unless the parent holds 90% of the stock.) With the proceeds from this second sale of Price stock, Associated could then buy more Abitibi stock (perhaps even force Abitibi to make a share exchange) and, in effect, move from more than 10% of Price to more than 10% of Abitibi without triggering British tax problems. A seat on the Abitibi board would ensure that Associated wasn't just a big investor out in the cold but an associate of the control group, which might help when a newsprint contract was being negotiated.

The great danger to Abitibi in this potential train of events was that a foreign company would end up with more than 5% of Abitibi's shares, which might destroy Abitibi's "Canadian" status under the Foreign Investment Review Act. But Bell needed Harmsworth to tender his stock — that was today's worry. The other problem mightn't be as bad as it appeared. Better deal with that later when it arose out of what was now only a hypothetical merger. At this stage Abitibi couldn't control any market purchases of Abitibi stock by Associated, so why bother about them? Besides, wasn't there something in the Foreign Investment Review Act that would prevent Associated doing that? (The act requires any non-resident planning to buy more than 5% of a Canadian public company to give notice beforehand. The Canadian government then reviews the proposal and decides, on the basis of whether it is beneficial to Canada, whether to allow the purchase or not.)[4]

Vere Harmsworth's new tack was discussed in a desultory way with no promises made on either side, except one seat on the Abitibi board if Harmsworth tendered a good quantity of shares. That couldn't be regarded as a special consideration to one shareholder. A seat on the board isn't a payment; it's a recognition. Just what the seat would be recognition of — Associated's remaining position in Price, or its future position in Abitibi, or Harmsworth's ability as a businessman — wasn't certain at this stage.

At 1:30 the Harmsworth group left for lunch and a private powwow. Harmsworth's decision involved a complexity of factors that would be difficult enough to evaluate at leisure after the event. But he had to act within an hour or two of being advised of Abitibi's position and without the benefit of all the facts. The Bank of England hadn't yet spoken, the effects of the Foreign Investment Review Act weren't fully understood. The only assurance of what the rest of the Price shareholders would do was Wood Gundy's informal assessment of their intentions, and, after all, Wood Gundy was Abitibi's agent. Most important of all, Harmsworth was completely unaware of what was going on between Canada Permanent and the Ontario Securities Commission.

Harmsworth, Morrow and Saunders returned from lunch and agreed to tender one million of their Price shares, to accept a seat on the Abitibi board, and to entertain the hope that Abitibi and Associated Newspapers would be "good partners" in the future operations of the two companies. By 3:30 p.m., Tom Bell and Bob Morrow, and Vere Harmsworth and Tom Bell, and Harmsworth and Gundy and Medland, had all shaken hands twice and Bell had pronounced: "Now we're partners and we'll make this thing work together." One of the Harmsworth group replied: "Yes, we're with you. We'll tender the stock and we'll go with you." The next day, Bell would remind Harmsworth of the handshake and say: "You know, in this country, that's a deal."[5] But Bell didn't fully appreciate the difficulty of Harmsworth's position.[6]

When Harmsworth had left, Bell and his advisers wrote the first of what would become a series of eight or nine press releases announcing the success of the takeover. This draft release read: " 'Abitibi Paper Co. Ltd. will purchase — percent of the common shares of Price Company Ltd. as a result of the $18 per share offer to shareholders of Price,' according to T. J. Bell, chairman and chief executive officer of Abitibi . . . 'We are very pleased and proud of this new and close association with the Price Company,' said Bell . . ." But this was too restrained and the release was rewritten: "Abitibi Paper Co. was successful in its $18/share bid for a maximum of 4,830,000 common shares of Price Company Ltd. . . . 'We are pleased and proud,' said Bell . . ." But this version seemed to crow too much, so third, and fourth and fifth drafts were written.

At about 3:30 p.m., Arthur Pattillo, chairman of the Ontario Securities Commission, telephoned Abitibi's lawyer Jim Tory and told him: "You better come up here and bring Kimber with you." He'd also telephoned Kimber, president of the Toronto Stock Exchange, in the same peremptory way. Relations between Pattillo and Kimber were less than cordial, because of the tension that can easily develop between the exchange and the commission that regulates it.

Within half an hour Tory and Kimber were at the commission offices on Yonge Street, and were told that Pattillo intended to hold a meeting to adjudicate between Abitibi and Canada Permanent, whose letter he explained. Kimber had brought along Bill Somerville, the exchange's executive vice-president. And Jim Tory had brought along Ted Medland, Ross LeMesurier, Bob Morgan and Don Bean — all the Wood Gundy people except Charles Gundy who were involved in the bid in any way. Kimber made it clear that Bob Morgan, the stock exchange's chairman, was there only as a Wood Gundy vice-president.

The man sternly facing the Abitibi delegation, Arthur Pattillo, was, among other things an able lawyer, a good administrator and a long-time Progressive Conservative. On a sideboard in Pattillo's office, to emphasize the point, was a large, stand-mounted portrait of William Davis, the Progressive Conservative Premier of Ontario. This display of political loyalty was surprising in a civil servant, heading as he did a quasi-judicial body, supposedly above politics. Davis wasn't in any sense the head of state of Ontario.

Pattillo had started vigorously to reorganize the Securities Commission, replacing some of the dead wood, activating sleepy departments, unwinding bad appointments and building a staff that wasn't too dependent on an indispensable Harry Bray. Pattillo was also building a reputation as a fighter where there was no battle, a wise and merciful judge of congenital stock touts, but a tough and uncompromising regulator of big brokerage firms and corporations — fearful they might get away with something.

Today, Pattillo was probably a little out of his depth, even though his self-confidence would never allow it to show. He'd been the commission's chairman for only a few months, and here was this huge takeover roaring through an exemption in the law. The securities market is so hedged about with complex, counterbalancing rights, and regulations to protect this and that group, it usually takes a new chairman a couple of years to master it all and develop a firm philosophy of regulation. Arthur Pattillo had been given only a few days to decide whether this bid was equitable to all parties — and some would say that wasn't the *prime* consideration — in the midst of a months-long controversy in the investment industry, and against a background of intended new legislation. What the hell should he do? He must have yearned for time to sort out his tangled reactions.

The hearing began and Kimber argued strenuously against any extension of the bid. The exchanges had agreed on a three-day period even before the Abitibi bid had turned up, and this was five days with the weekend. And the commission hadn't indicated in advance any preference for the length of time bids should be open. Why change while the bid was in progress? Someone at the meeting even pointed out bitterly to Pattillo that the Securities Commission was always saying the institutions were white knights and the brokers crooks, well here was the brokerage community outperforming an institution. "I bet if you gave Canada Permanent's list to a good broker, he'd contact them all within two hours," was the challenge thrown to Pattillo in disgust. Of course no argument was given as to *why* the trust companies should be forced to act quickly. It was also suggested that Canada Permanent had an ulterior motive (Jack Mackenzie and Norman Halford of Canada Permanent weren't present). But it was to no avail. Arthur Pattillo decided an extension was necessary to enable all Price shareholders to be contacted.

"If Abitibi doesn't act," Pattillo told the meeting, "and I have to act, I'll suspend trading in the Price stock, and my interpretation of the act is that I can only do that for a minimum of 15 days." Pattillo was referring to a section of the Ontario Securities Act that some other lawyers interpreted as setting a 15-day *maximum* on any suspension.[7]

A 15-day suspension of Price trading would be disastrous for Abitibi. If Abitibi decided to close the bid as announced on Tuesday morning at 9:45, it would be able to buy no stock at that time because of the suspension of trading in Price shares. If Abitibi wanted to stay with the bid until it could buy stock, the bid would have to remain open for a total of about 20 days (the original five plus 15), and that would be almost the 21 days required by law when a bid is made by mailed circular. All the advantages of the exchange route (principally speed) would be lost and all the disadvantages retained (cash-only offer, no withdrawal if too little stock offered, and so forth). The 21-day circular bid did have certain compensations if you had to go that route. A 20-day exchange bid would be the worst of all possible worlds. Pattillo stood up and ended the meeting, leaving the matter hanging. James Tory remained behind, thinking hard.

After the others had gone, Pattillo softened and asked Tory what Abitibi suggested as an appropriate extension. But Tory wasn't fazed by that kind of pressure. "I believe Abitibi could agree to a 24-hour extension," he suggested, as if that would be extremely generous of his client. "If it were a two-day extension, I could accept that now," Pattillo bargained, much more reasonably than his opening remarks would have suggested, and out of keeping with his image on Bay Street of a man who doesn't compromise.

Tory reminded Pattillo of the huge sum of money Abitibi had hanging out there in the market, of the need to protect Abitibi's shareholders as well as Price's, and of the lack of adequate procedures to deal with a counterbid if one were to come in. The exchange still didn't know how it would regulate competitive bidding. He also pointed out that, if Pattillo suspended trading, Abitibi wouldn't be able to take up on Tuesday the shares tendered under the bid. The result would be to deny the Price shareholders a price that was 50% over the market — and *that responsibility* would be Pattillo's.

Pattillo suggested that Tory go talk to Abitibi, which he did. At about 5 p.m. after several phone calls back and forth, Tory told

Pattillo: "A one-day extension is all Abitibi could reasonably go for, certainly without calling another board meeting. With the big liability Abitibi has incurred, we couldn't give you an answer quickly on anything longer than a day." As chairman and chief executive officer, Tom Bell was allowed some initiative in such a matter, but he chose (because so much was at stake) to take the position that any extension longer than a day would require board approval. Bell reasoned that a two-day extension could possibly generate bid competition, and, considering the lack of rules, Abitibi might win less than control — which would be much worse than winning nothing.

In the end Pattillo agreed to a one-day extension, with the bid to close on Wednesday morning at 9:45. The alternative was to leave the whole thing up in the air 'while Abitibi held a board meeting that, in the end, mightn't approve any extension at all.

The irony of Pattillo's concern for the minority shareholders in this takeover was that he had, in the past, also fought vigorously against their rights. In 1963, Pattillo was counsel for Union Gas Co. of Canada which wanted to wind up a subsidiary, United Fuel Investments Ltd., over the protests of aggrieved minority shareholders. Pattillo took the case to the Supreme Court of Canada and won. At one stage in that case, a ruling by the Supreme Court of Ontario was interpreted by The Financial Post as proving that "majority shareholders rule the roost and minority protections and rights are worth very little."

At Abitibi, once Pattillo's decision was known, a press release was written for dissemination immediately, as well as through the stock exchange and the daily newspapers the following day. It began: "At the request of the Ontario and Quebec Securities Commissions, Abitibi Paper Co. Ltd. announces it will extend . . ." But when Jack Kimber called Robert Demers, chairman of the Quebec Securities Commission, to read the release for his approval, Demers said: "Strike out Quebec Securities Commission. We're not asking for any extension." And that would be the beginning of what, over the next year or so, would become one of the biggest policy differences the Ontario and Quebec commissions had ever had.

Robert Demers, a slight man in his late 30s, was the youngest securities commissioner in North America ever to hold office for any length of time, and his appointment by Premier Robert Bourassa in 1971 was far removed from the Ontario tradition of putting old, mature men into that office. Demers belonged to no clubs, didn't even like them, and would entertain friends and visiting commissioners alike in restaurants — which led at least one elderly Ontario commissioner to sniff loudly. Demers' thinking was a refreshing ferment of radical views on ways of cleaning up the darker side of the securities industry among the mines and junior industrials, but his official policies so far had been cautious and gradual. Like Pattillo, he was a political appointment. Demers had first gained attention as the Quebec government's courageous negotiator with the Front de Libération Québecois (FLQ) terrorists who kidnapped British diplomat James Cross and murdered Pierre Laporte in 1970. But, in contrast to Pattillo's Premier-portrait, Demers' office displayed a picture of Japanese fish. He'd once said he found it more soothing than the picture of his Minister.

Demers and Pattillo had discussed the Canada Permanent letter over the telephone and Demers held it in low regard. "You can't change the rules in the middle of the game," he'd argued with his Ontario counterpart, "all because one trust company isn't quick enough to reach all its clients in time." Demers, unlike anybody senior at the Ontario Securities Commission, had worked in a stock exchange (the Montreal exchange). He understood how fundamental the speed at which transactions occur was to the liquidity of the market.

Demers also believed that takeovers can be valuable to society, because they tend to concentrate productive assets in the most capable hands. "If we react to Canada Permanent," he told Pattillo, "the liquidity of the market will be reduced to its lowest common denominator." Perhaps it had been this viewpoint from a seasoned commissioner that softened Pattillo's position on a 15-day suspension.

In early evening, Vere Harmsworth arrived back in Montreal to find a nasty surprise awaiting him at the Price office. The Bank of England had ruled that the Associated Newspapers investment in Price was deemed to be direct not portfolio. Harmsworth fully realized what that meant: the investment wasn't in premium currency, only ordinary currency; and once liquidated the proceeds had to be repatriated to Britain, and the Bank of England had to give its permission before the funds could be re-invested abroad in Abitibi or any other company.

(The author's calculations show that that Abitibi's $18 bid was now worth only $15 a share to Associated — even as little as $10, if Associated tendered all its stock and lost double-taxation relief.) Several other disadvantages had sprung into being. The intricate manoeuvre of moving from 10% of Price to 10% of Abitibi looked now only remotely possible. It all depended on whether the purchase of Abitibi stock would be approved by both the Bank of England and possibly the Canadian government administering the Foreign Investment Review Act. Harmsworth believed there were only a few hours of darkness left before the bid closed, and it looked as if he'd nothing but bad options open to him. All he could do would be to take a beating and go home.

That evening was not a happy one for Vere Harmsworth[8] —until he learned of Abitibi's one-day extension.

At 8:15 p.m., after writing the press release, Bell, Rosier, Haire, McGibbon and Jim Flintoft, the company's secretary and general counsel, went out to celebrate at the York Club. Flintoft had delayed a trip to South America to support the team during this crucial period. Now, the British were going to tender, and so was Domtar. There was a one-day extension — so what? No bids were in sight. What could go wrong? Flintoft would leave the next day to join his family and friends already on vacation. To celebrate the occasion, Bell selected a fine wine to go with dinner and, for the first time, nobody ordered sole.

Day Twenty

Tuesday, November 19
"Harmsworth remembered with regret, but what else could he do . . .?"

At about 11 a.m., the silver clouds at Abitibi started to mass into thunderheads, gradually obscuring the sun. First, lawyer John Tory, Jim Tory's twin brother, called from West Palm Beach, where he was on vacation, to say he'd heard, and confirmed by his own calculations, that the English would have acute tax problems if they tendered their stock. They must surely be having second thoughts now that there was an extension.

Then, towards noon, Vere Harmsworth telephoned Tom Bell and warned him vaguely he might soon find there was "competition for control of Price." (A possible bidder had approached Bob Morrow that morning and started nibbling at Associated's block of stock, though Harmsworth didn't explain that to Bell.) Harmsworth remembered with regret he'd made a verbal agreement with Bell, but what else could he do? It was *their* fault for riding into town with six-guns blazing. When he was able, he'd explain to Bell he'd been acting on bad advice.

"There's a one-day extension, and there may be a counterbid coming up," was all he could tell Bell at this time. Bell felt troubled, but he dismissed the call and went out to lunch.

While Bell was at lunch, Harmsworth called again and Jack Haire took the call. "I'm trying to reach Mr. Bell," Harmsworth told him. "We're going to have some tax problems." At about 3:30 p.m., Harmsworth telephoned a third time, and told Bell person-

134

ally that Associated was faced with "*severe* tax problems," using that blanket expression to cover all the intricate difficulties created by the Bank of England's ruling. But once again Harmsworth gave no indication what he was going to do about it. To start with, he couldn't. No plans were settled and, in any case, it would be foolish to show his hand now.

Somewhat later in the afternoon, the news started to reach Wood Gundy through friends and salesmen in the field, that somebody "out there" was calling the portfolio managers of institutions — banks, insurance companies and so forth — about their Price stock. But it was hard to pin down who was doing it and for what purpose.

Thoroughly alarmed by now, Tom Bell called Harry Rosier into an emergency session with Charles Gundy, Ted Medland and Jim Tory, who hurried over from their offices. Later Jack Haire and Ian McGibbon were called in. The atmosphere was tense and solemn. All kinds of imaginary possibilities were examined and counterplays conceived of, but it was a waste of time. Nobody knew what was going on. It must all somehow hinge on Associated's tax problems. But what were they doing? The fog was even thicker because Wood Gundy had studied the possible legal and tax problems of the British before the bid, but hadn't drawn the right conclusions, perhaps the firm's only important slipup. But even if the tax tangle had been correctly forecast, how could the firm have known in advance what the Bank of England would rule?

At 6 p.m. — after much futile speculation — Ian McGibbon volunteered to go downstairs for sandwiches and milk in case the team had to remain in the office well into the evening. Most of the people present placed an order, but Ted Medland said: "No, thank you. We won't be here too long. I'd rather wait until I get home and have a good dinner with a bottle of wine." He couldn't have been more wrong.

A little after six, Vere Harmsworth phoned Bell again to inform him that Associated Newspapers and the Harmsworth family interests had formed a consortium with Power Corp., which would buy more Price shares to add to the English group's holdings placed in a voting trust. (The two groups would sign an agreement to vote the stock-in-trust jointly.) Based in Montreal, Power Corp.

was a $500-million investment and management company with holdings in major transportation, paper and financial companies. Quite justifiably stunned by this announcement, Bell hid his feelings and said: "Well, ah, when the offer comes out, we'll have a chance to respond." Harmsworth replied non-committally: "Yes, I suppose you will."

Harmsworth elaborated on the consortium's plans only so far as to tell Bell the bid would be $20 per share, and it would be for all the holders' shares, not just a percentage. The consortium's bid looked far superior to Abitibi's for those lucky shareholders who'd be presented with the offer, though it wasn't clear how the consortium would go about that.

"What do we have to do to maintain the agreement we had with you yesterday?" Bell asked lamely.

"You'll have to meet that," Harmsworth answered, seemingly illogically. His description of the consortium's plans seemed to indicate the new stock bought would be *added to* the English group's holdings-in-trust, and Associated and Power Corp. would exercise control of Price jointly from a much wider base than before. If that were the case, Associated wasn't receiving anything for its stock, so how could Abitibi "meet that" and win Associated back to its side?

Bell was too distraught to think the question right through immediately. "Well, there's no way we can meet that," he protested. "We have a stock-exchange offer and we . . . we just can't do that."

"I'll give you an hour to come up with some sort of a deal and, if you want to call me back, well that will be fine," Harmsworth said. When Harmsworth hung up, Bell felt betrayed, told too late Harmsworth was going to break their agreement. In fact he was being told too early. Harmsworth's new deal hadn't yet jelled.

Bell and his advisers thrashed around for half an hour looking for a way out of this corner, then Bell called Harmsworth back and pleaded: "We're finding it very difficult to manoeuvre." Harmsworth, now exercising the whip hand, told Bell: "Please conduct any further conversations with our Mr. Saunders." He gave a telephone number. Throughout the negotiations of the day before, Harmsworth had exposed himself directly, leading his delegation about, sitting in on and lending authority to delicate negotiations conducted by his advisers, and even holding out his hand to be shaken over what was now a broken deal. He'd surely have had a deeper line of defence if he'd remained in the background, in constant touch, certainly, but free to modify or reject whatever his advisers (if they were capable) rightly or wrongly committed him to. But Harmsworth was a man in a hurry, not by choice but because he'd been stampeded, and he felt that his responsibility to himself, his family and Associated's public shareholders called for his direct personal involvement. That is, until now, when he had negotiations with two groups to think of.

At about the same time as Harmsworth's call, Doug Gardiner of the Royal Bank, which also had a heavy stake in Abitibi's bid, phoned to shed some light on the enemy troop movements. The bank's pension-fund manager had been telephoned after the market closed that day and asked not to tender the bank's Price stock to Abitibi, but to wait for an offer of $20 *for the bank's entire holdings.* The pattern was beginning to emerge: the Power Corp. consortium was going to buy control privately from a few banks and trust companies that held large blocks of stock.

Doug Gardiner didn't know who was making the bid, except he thought it might have been a particular broker that had a long association with Price. Whoever did the calling couldn't have realized the Royal was bankrolling Abitibi's bid, or such a revealing call wouldn't have been made so early. It would have come eventually, of course, because the Royal Bank had as much responsibility to get the best price for its Price stock as anybody else.

A few fast telephone calls by Wood Gundy people soon established that several institutional portfolio managers had been called at home that evening with news of the same imminent bid: "$20 for all your stock." Jack Kimber, the Toronto Stock Exchange president, was informed and he immediately called somebody on the opposite side to say: "If the purchases bring the buyer's holdings to more than 20% of Price, the bid had better be to fewer than 15 shareholders or it will be in violation of the Ontario and Quebec Securities Acts."

A little later, McGibbon came back, having hunted down some sandwiches. Bell had ordered a chicken on white, but the distant restaurant to which McGibbon had been forced to go didn't have it. Bell was so absorbed he didn't notice he'd been handed a ham on rye with mustard and a slice of pickle. All Bell's attention was now absorbed in a great fear: that Power Corp. would buy control of Price through the back door (privately from less than 15 shareholders) and leave Abitibi with a bid hanging out on the exchange — which could only bring in perhaps 30% or 40% of Price's stock. It was probably possible for Power Corp. to rustle up 50% of the stock from 14 shareholders when it could start with Associated's 18%. Associated didn't have to be counted as one of the "less-than-15" shareholders because it was a joint principal, not a seller. Bell reminded everybody tartly that the Abitibi board hadn't authorized him to spend $30 million to $40 million on a simple investment in Price, with no representation on Price's board and no option to go forward to merger, and with somebody else in control.

Jack Haire summed up Abitibi's plight eloquently: "If the Price shareholders tendered only 25% of the stock to our bid, we'd have to eat it." And if that happened, the consequences for Bell's and perhaps others' employment might well be terminal.

The lights burned late into the night at Abitibi, and so did the incoming telephone wires. Each call brought the news of yet another portfolio manager being called at home, presumably on behalf of Power Corp., whose chairman, Paul Desmarais, had proved many times that he was a Bobby Fischer at this kind of corporate chess. And now there were two brokers involved. C. J. Hodgson was also calling portfolio managers, the team was told. (Hodgson would later claim it was the only brokerage firm making calls. Who made the earlier calls remained a mystery.)

By 9 p.m., under pressure of the fear that Power Corp. would buy Price through the back door, the Abitibi team worked out an alternative offer for the British, and obtained approval for it from Jack Kimber and Arthur Pattillo. It seemed years since Jim Tory had shot down Ian McGibbon's question path containing the notion, on Day Eleven, that Abitibi might make a special offer to Associated. The team had agreed that all shareholders had to be treated the same. But this special offer to Associated was no more generous than the general bid to other shareholders — it was only different — and that's why Kimber and Pattillo approved it.

The special offer worked out this way: Abitibi assigned a value of $10 a share to its own shares (which was their market value at that time) and an $18 value to Price shares (exactly the same value as the Abitibi bid on the exchange). Under the offer Abitibi would take up 65% (1.11 million) of Associated's holdings in Price and, by

138

paying for these shares with two million newly issued Abitibi treasury shares, give Associated 10% of Abitibi (two million new as a percentage of 18 million old, plus two million new) and enable Associated to avoid its British tax problems. Those problems would be triggered if its holdings in whatever company fell below 10%. The beauty of the offer was that if Abitibi bought 1.1 million Price shares from Associated (65% of its holdings), that would leave about 8.6 million Price shares still out in the market. If Abitibi purchased 4.9 million in the market as originally planned, Abitibi would be taking up about 60% to 65% of the holdings of all the other shareholders, too (assuming Associated didn't tender again). This elegant offer to Associated would be at the same price and for the same proportion of stock as the bid now on the exchange. The only difference was that Associated would receive Abitibi stock rather than cash. To Abitibi, the cost was dilution of its common stock and the taking up of more Price shares (about 60%) than it really needed for control.[1]

The spokesman chosen to sell the deal to the British was lawyer Jim Tory. Bell couldn't make the call, because the man on the other end was Peter Saunders, Associated's secretary, not Harmsworth. In the early investigation stage of the takeover, Tory had been quiet and cautious, playing the devil's advocate to keep the enthusiasm within bounds and the obstacles in view. Now, he proved to have a silver tongue. In the midst of the surrounding gloom, he sat back expansively in Bell's chair, smoked a cigar, and actually joked with Saunders over the phone, as if this new offer were just a throwaway concession to the British to help them, in a friendly way, out of their difficulties. The Foreign Investment Review Act? That would be no problem, Tory believed sincerely. Ever since Abitibi had come out of receivership in 1946, with the help of J. H. Gundy and other powerful groups, the company had been controlled by its board and management. A British group taking 10% of the stock wasn't going to upset that arrangement, even though the foreign-investment act drew the line at 5%. Abitibi would still be firmly controlled by Canadians.

But the British were as concerned about the Foreign Investment Review Act as Abitibi's executives, because the act makes provision for declaring a transaction "nugatory" if it goes ahead and is later discovered to involve the giving of control to a foreigner.[2] ("Nugatory" means that a transaction can be deemed to be retroactively non-occurring — and therefore must be taken apart.) Associated's Montreal counsel, who was nearby, concurred with Jim Tory's opinion about control of Abitibi. As a parting shot, to sweeten the deal, Tory told Saunders the British could have two seats on the board, not just one. At 9:45 p.m. Saunders agreed to discuss the offer with Harmsworth and promised "to be back to you shortly." For 45 minutes everybody breathed more easily, highly impressed by Jim Tory's performance at one end of the telephone. But no call came.

As 10:30 came and went, Bell and his crew sat around the office, morosely chewing cigars, and worrying more and more. But the British didn't bite. What ways were there out of this trap now? Two perhaps. Well, they could tough it out and assume that nothing adverse would happen, but nobody was prepared to take the risk. Or they could withdraw the bid and lay Abitibi open to a class-action lawsuit from Price shareholders, and, in the bargain, destroy their company's credibility and reputation. Were there really no other alternatives? No one could think of any and, horrifying through it was to contemplate, the decision was tentatively made to withdraw the bid. Abitibi's responsibility, legally and morally, was to its own shareholders not to Price, or the public, even in these circumstances. From time to time during this depressing period, Jack Kimber would telephone from his office at the exchange to discuss procedures to be applied in the event of a competing bid. When he did, he was closely and intensely questioned about what did and didn't constitute a valid bid, which made him very nervous.

As night deepened, Bell's office filled with the crushing tension of a submarine evading depth charges from an unseen destroyer. All they'd worked for was slipping away, and the company would either lose $30 million or be totally discredited. And what a bitter choice that would be. At one point, Ian McGibbon had the temerity to offer advice from the background, through the heavy, acrid cigar smoke. Bell turned on him and shouted: *"Don't tell your grandmother how to suck eggs!"* Then he slumped back in his chair again, morosely. The outburst should have helped Bell, but it didn't. As for McGibbon, he was demolished.

Oh, come on, maybe the British will call back after all, later in

140

the evening, somebody suggested with the mournful gaiety found at wakes and funerals. But how would we close the deal with them? was the reply. You couldn't trust their word, so we'd have to have it in writing. What about the Telex? "Ian, call the office manager at home and have him send a Telex girl up here, pronto." The girl arrived, was installed in the corporate secretary's office, with the leftover sandwiches and a copy of Time magazine, then given her cab fare and sent home again — because the English didn't call.

All the while, Harry Rosier dully worked on the phone, trying to reach Harmsworth at the Ritz-Carlton, Bob Morrow at his home, and Bill Turner, the president of Consolidated-Bathurst (the Power Corp. paper subsidiary), at several places — without luck. Rosier wanted to remind Turner that, at luncheon in the St. James's Club, the previous Thursday, Turner had said Consolidated wasn't interested in Price. Was it now on behalf of Consolidated that Power Corp. was calling pension-fund managers in the middle of the night to wrest control of Price away from Abitibi? Consolidated was a newsprint company, so that seemed to be the most logical explanation. But Turner wasn't at home and the switchboard at Consolidated was dead. Rosier did eventually manage to raise the night watchman at Consolidated, but he answered grumpily that there was no big meeting going on in the board room or anywhere else for that matter. Rosier continued dialing the other numbers mechanically in the midst of the surrounding depression.

By 11 p.m., Tom Bell could bear the suspense no longer, so he called Earle McLaughlin, the Royal Bank's chairman, who was also on the executive committee of Power Corp. The Royal provided banking services to Power Corp. jointly with the Bank of Montreal. As Bell waited for the telephone in McLaughlin's home to answer, he wondered whether the Royal was bankrolling both Abitibi's and Power Corp.'s takeovers. It would only have to provide the money to one; *both* takeovers couldn't succeed. But then surely Earle wouldn't . . . McLaughlin picked up the phone.

"Earle, what in the hell are Power Corp. doing, sticking their nose into this field?" Bell exploded. "And they're doing it in a highly unethical manner. Even to the Royal Bank they're making an offer for *all* of the stock [that really hurt Bell]. They're trying to corral the whole goddam deal."

McLaughlin replied soothingly: "I don't know anything about

it, Tom." It was true that McLaughlin had been with Power Corp. executives in Winnipeg the day before at a board meeting, but the matter hadn't been discussed. McLaughlin had brought back his Power Corp. confreres in the Royal Bank plane, but the conversation had been primly confined to the federal budget, because the Royal's involvement in the Abitibi takeover was well known.

"I can hardly believe that," Bell said rudely. "Would you get hold of Desmarais and try to confirm what they're doing and . . . ah . . . what they've done because, you know, it's upsetting for me. What's more, they're making an offer for blocks of stock and I think, because there's an offer on the exchange, it's highly unethical. Can you . . . confirm it?" he asked, cooling off a little.

"Well, I'll do my best," McLaughlin promised, sympathetically ignoring Tom Bell's impulsive lack of courtesy. He was sorry that his old friend was in such a tight spot.

Within the hour Bell had called McLaughlin back twice, but was told the banker hadn't been able to reach Paul Desmarais, chairman of Power Corp., who must be working somewhere behind Power Corp.'s closed switchboard.

At 12:30 a.m., Tom Bell, who was by now emotionally exhausted, decided to go home and rest. You could worry just as easily in bed as out of it, and he'd given instructions for the others to telephone him immediately, at any time of the night, if news came through. Harry Rosier also started for home, after leaving the Abitibi telephone number at every conceivable place the Montrealers might be. Ian McGibbon remained alone in the office, hoping there might still be a call bringing enlightenment.

At 1 a.m., Bell's ambassador at large, Ross LeMesurier, his searching, detailed mind at work even at this late hour, phoned McGibbon to point out that if the bid had to be pulled by nine o'clock in the morning, every minute between 8 a.m. and 9 a.m. had to be plotted, because there weren't many people they'd be able to raise at that time of day. For instance, Arthur Pattillo, chairman of the Ontario Securities Commission, had said they were free to call him up to midnight but, after that, not until 8:45 a.m. at his office. That wouldn't leave much time to work everything out, LeMesurier pointed out. And there was another important question that had to be thought through: What was the latest time Abitibi could withdraw the bid?

The "opening and closing of the book" was a simple enough procedure. In the morning at nine o'clock, exchange officials would walk out on to the floor and accept verbally from each broker a commitment to tender so much stock. (The certificates would change hands later.) The amounts tendered would be written by the exchange official against the broker's name on an alphabetical list, and at 9:45 a.m., when the "book" closed, the list would be totaled, and the success or failure of the bid announced.

LeMesurier asked McGibbon, as part of his own thinking process: Could Abitibi safely go ahead with the bid if it hadn't received the news by 9 a.m. that Power Corp. had bought control of Price? Could brokers tender stock to Abitibi during the 45 minutes the book was open, and the stock still be pulled out again and sold privately to Power Corp? A broker was bound by his word given on the exchange, but was the broker's client? The danger was that if Abitibi went ahead with the bid at nine, not having heard Power Corp. had bought control of Price, and stock were pulled out for Power Corp. during the tendering period, then Abitibi would be truly "mousetrapped." Abitibi's bid couldn't be withdrawn while tendering was in process. Obviously, the decision to withdraw the bid would have to be made by 9 a.m. at the latest. LeMesurier and McGibbon talked over these problems for a while, then the other phone rang and McGibbon switched calls. It was Harry Rosier reporting he was home. McGibbon wearily made a mental note and hung up. As the night dragged on to 2 a.m., McGibbon dozed on Bell's chesterfield, which had been pulled close to the telephone.

The day before, Monday, Paul Desmarais, chairman of Power Corp., and William Ian Mackenzie Turner Jr., president and chief executive officer of Consolidated-Bathurst, had been in Winnipeg for a board meeting of the Investors Group (also a Power subsidiary) along with Earle McLaughlin, chairman of the Royal Bank and a director of Investors Group. Desmarais and Turner hadn't been able to give much thought to a bid for Price that day, even though there'd been distant attempts to interest them in one by Bob Morrow, hunting for a way out of Associated's dilemma. In any case, Turner and Desmarais had believed the Abitibi bid was to close on Tuesday morning, giving them no time to act.

But early this morning, on learning of the extension of the Abitibi bid, Desmarais and Turner met and drew together a 10-man task force to discuss whether to make a lightning bid for Price, whether there was time to raise the money. Present were lawyers, executives and financial men from both Power Corp. and Consolidated-Bathurst.

Early in the day, the task force called in Bob Morrow of Associated Newspapers and Price's chairman, Ross Moore, to explore a bid springing off a base of Associated's stock. "You have nearly two million shares. Place them in a voting trust* with us, and we'll pay $20 for another three million shares. You've got the shareholders' list. You must know where the stock is." That was the gist of Desmarais' offer to Associated. Control of Price would link up nicely with Consolidated-Bathurst's million-ton newsprint operation, which accounted for 20% to 25% of the company's sales. Unlike Domtar, Consolidated was basically a wood-products company (pulp, packaging and so forth) and had only 16% to 20% in other products (mainly glass).

Once Associated had shown interest in the proposal, it would be up to Bill Turner to pull the deal together. One of the most capable chief executives in Canada, though not widely recognized as such, Bill Turner might one day match his mentor, Paul Desmarais, in the high skills of corporate chess for which Desmarais was renowned, and in whose shadow Turner stood. Desmarais was an instant legend in the popular press — to the point where even his mistakes were believed to be successes that hadn't yet been understood. Turner was eclipsed by all this. But, to those who saw beyond Desmarais, Turner even looked the part of a comer: tall, youthful, clean-cut, contemptuous of people who take martini lunches. He was tirelessly dedicated to acquiring profit for Consolidated-Bathurst, a cumbersome conglomerate.

Early in the afternoon, Turner telephoned Arnold Hart, chairman of the Bank of Montreal, pulling him out of a board meeting.

"We need $80 million this week, Arnold," Turner told him.

---

* A voting trust is an agreement to place stock in a trust and vote it as a block by joint agreement.

144

"Geez, that's a lot of money, Bill," Hart replied. "But, well, yes, we can manage it. No problem."

By now, the looser-money trends of the previous week had been confirmed, and Hart also knew that Consolidated was backed by its parent, Power Corp. Joint assets of the two companies were greater than $1 billion, almost three times Abitibi's. Obviously, it was easier for a bank to lend $80 million to Consolidated than to Abitibi. After the initial commitment by the Bank of Montreal, Canada's third largest, about 40% of the $80 million loan would be laid off to either the Royal Bank, if it wanted, or to Power Corp.

Once the money had been arranged, Turner and Desmarais discussed alternative strategies again, and an approach was made systematically to fewer than 15 trust companies and other institutions to test an offer of "$20 for all your stock." These were the first calls reported to Abitibi in the late afternoon and early evening. The point of calling fewer than 15 shareholders was that, at that number, Consolidated could buy as much stock as it wanted without the purchases coming under the provisions of securities law (21-day circulars and so on). Abitibi similarly was dodging the provisions by using a different exemption — going through the stock exchange.

By mid-evening though, it became apparent to Turner that Consolidated would have to change its tactics. One of the company's legal advisers pointed out that the fewer than 15 institutions telephoned didn't *own* the stock spoken for; they were merely holding it for customers. Those big juicy blocks were really hundreds of parcels beneficially owned by small shareholders. Consolidated's lawyers quickly advised Turner that buying those shares without sending out a 21-day information circular wasn't permitted under the securities acts. Turner had been having second thoughts anyway, but for other reasons. "If we went that route," he thought, "Abitibi would be stuck with a bid on the exchange it couldn't withdraw. Why make Abitibi and Wood Gundy look silly? You can't use a company in which there's a huge irate minority shareholder. When we want to put Consolidated and Price together, they'd hold out and get what they'd lost out of our hide."

Consolidated's people telephoned the portfolio managers back again and said: "Sorry, we can't take out all your stock after all." This was the second series of calls Abitibi heard about, but the distinction between it and the first wasn't explained, adding to the confusion. Despite Turner's compassion over egg stains that might be left on Wood Gundy's face, Consolidated-Bathurst had no choice but to back out of its original plan. It was illegal, and that was that.

At 8 p.m. the British group arrived at Consolidated-Bathurst's offices for the first face-to-face encounter with Turner and Desmarais.

"What was suggested earlier [the voting trust] won't work," Bob Morrow of Associated stated immediately. "If you make the bid, we'll be seen by [British] Inland Revenue to have lost control. So what we want to do is swap our stock for some of yours in such a way that we move from the control block of Price into the control block of Consolidated-Bathurst." Associated didn't realistically expect to buy part-control of Consolidated in this way. What Morrow was talking about was a friendly association with the controlling shareholder, Power Corp., so that the investment would be classified as "direct" (beneficial to Britain) by the Bank of England. (The bank would probably permit a rollover from a direct investment in Price to a direct investment in Consolidated, but would probably reject a switch from a "direct" to a "portfolio" investment with all the intrusion of premium currency and repatriation of the proceeds.)

Before he could agree to such an arrangement, Turner had to make sure he wasn't falling into the same trap as Abitibi. What if Wood Gundy had also sewn up large blocks of stock off the exchange, as Consolidated was going to try to do? Even more institutional portfolio managers (over and above the fewer than 15) were telephoned during the late evening to ascertain whether stock would be available if a counterbid were made at $20. This last series of calls was also reported to Tom Bell by his friends, adding even more to his alarm.

At 2:30 a.m. the telephone close to McGibbon's ear rang again, waking him. It was Bill Turner of Consolidated-Bathurst. "Harry?" Turner asked. Rosier had left messages at both Turner's and Morrow's homes for them to call as soon as they got in. "No, it's Ian," McGibbon replied sleepily, then apologized for the lateness of the hour and for possibly upsetting Turner's wife. Turner had been expected home that evening but had phoned from the office at the last moment to say he'd be late. Turner wasn't the kind of husband who stayed out and, when McGibbon telephoned, his wife had said she hadn't expected he'd be *this* late.

"Harry really wants to talk to you," McGibbon told Turner. No, Turner wouldn't have any of that. "No point in getting anybody out of bed at this time of night," he stated flatly and, perhaps, defensively. McGibbon had agreed with Rosier earlier that his role would be to re-direct any calls and not enter any discussions. But when Turner refused to be re-routed, McGibbon said: "I know what Harry wants to talk to you about, but if you won't call him, I'll have to do it. What we're trying to figure out is this: Are Abitibi and Con-Bath being played off one against the other by some Englishmen?" McGibbon didn't want to let on how much he knew about the evening's events. Turner answered: "There's a little of that going on, but I'm not going to say any more now. I'll call Harry first thing in the morning bright and early." Turner was friendly. He apologized for the lateness of the call, and hung up.

McGibbon immediately called Rosier to report Turner's conversation for whatever comfort it might bring. While they were talking, McGibbon's other phone rang.

"Harry?" Bob Morrow asked.

"Harry's trying to reach you," McGibbon told him. "Will you call him at home?" He gave Morrow Rosier's home number.

A little later McGibbon's phone rang again. It was Morrow, checking the number McGibbon had given him. He hadn't been able to write it down. McGibbon gave him the number again, hung up, sat back and waited 15 minutes for Morrow to get through. Then he telephoned Rosier to see if the connection had been made. The line was busy, so presumably it had.

Tom Bell slid into his bed at about 2 a.m. as taut as a wooden puppet, and quite unable to sleep. Bed was merely a gesture toward habit. At 2:45 the telephone rang; he sat up in bed and eagerly grabbed the receiver from the night-table.

A slurred voice at the other end of the line said: "What's the number?"

Bell recited his telephone number and asked: "What number are you calling?"

"Oh, that's the number," the caller replied, obviously drunk. "Who's this?"

"It's Tom Bell."

"Oh!" said the caller, who belched and hung up.

At 3 a.m. Rosier called Bell with good news. Morrow had told him the English had sold all their Price shares to Consolidated-Bathurst in exchange for Consolidated stock. In the morning Consolidated would make a bid for more Price stock on the exchange.[3]

"I shouldn't be telling you this," Bob Morrow had said. "The Brits would shoot me if they knew, but we did have a handshake and I feel I should tell you the whole deal has now been done and Abitibi is out." Morrow was dramatizing this generous gesture to Abitibi. By informing Rosier at three in the morning of what he'd learn anyway at sunup, he'd betrayed nobody, and had succeeded in giving everybody a fairly peaceful night.

Ironically, after all the fatigue and tension and worry that Bell had experienced over the previous two and a half weeks of pushing the Price takeover forward, he now felt immensely relieved. Abitibi wouldn't be left exposed on the exchange for $30 million to $40 million. And there'd be no humiliating withdrawal of a firm bid. Abitibi was out clean. Thank heaven.

Rosier ended the call to Bell and placed one to McGibbon to tell him to go home, which he did, arriving at his front door at 3:30 a.m.

Charles Tittemore, Price's president, didn't join the British-Desmarais-Turner group until late in the evening. Tittemore wasn't asked to be party to any of the negotiations and spent most of the time in an outside office talking to Spike Irwin, Consolidated-Bathurst's chairman. On one occasion, though, he was asked to answer specific questions about Price's operations and value. Later, after the signing of a three-page agreement between Associated and Consolidated, Tittemore was asked (perhaps a little unfairly) how Price's management would probably react. Ever the loyal soldier, Tittemore replied that his people were all professional managers and their principal concern was to do a good job of managing, regardless of who owned the shares (an overstatement, perhaps, but understandable in the tight spot Tittemore was in).

In the early hours of the morning, when the meetings were over, Tittemore went alone to Ben's Delicatessen ("We're Open 24 Hours") for a smoked-meat sandwich and perhaps a sad reverie. But his thoughts were interrupted by an accidental meeting with two of the British group, and one of Paul Desmarais' right-hand men. The four enjoyed their sandwiches together. When the bill arrived, Tittemore, who'd just lost "management control" of his company, discovered that none of the others had the ready cash, and he picked up the bill.

Day Twenty-One

Wednesday, November 20
"There wasn't an ounce of fight left in the Abitibi team . . ."

The phone rang in Harry Rosier's home at 7 a.m. It was Bill Turner in Montreal to tell Rosier officially what Bob Morrow had reported during the night. Consolidated had exchanged its own treasury stock for all the British group's Price shares and would make a bid on the exchange by 9 a.m., just before Abitibi's book opened.

In the early grey of morning, just up from bed, Rosier didn't react properly. "Oh, look, Bill, is there no way we can go partners on this thing?" he asked impulsively and with melancholy.

"No, there isn't," Turner replied firmly, and Rosier realized it had been a foolish thing to say.

Soon after the call, Rosier drove to the office where the others were assembling for an 8 a.m. council of war. What happened now? What was Abitibi's position vis-à-vis the counterbid? One had never before been made on the exchange.

After a little thought, Jim Tory came up with the answer. At 9:45 a.m., when Abitibi's bid was due to terminate, it would vanish. The bid was for five days extended to six, Tory pointed out. When the Consolidated-Bathurst bid was announced, the exchange would have to extend the suspension of trading in Price stock for the duration of Consolidated's bid. Consequently, no Price shareholder could sell his stock to Abitibi by 9:45, because that would constitute a "trade" and trading was suspended. If no

150

shares could be sold to Abitibi, the bid would terminate at 9:45 and Abitibi would be released without obligation. The company could either make a new bid or bow out.

By 8:30 a.m. the Consolidated bid was publicly announced and the details could be read on the tickers and newswires: $20 a share for four million shares, almost a million fewer than Abitibi's.[1] But the proportion of each shareholder's stock that would be taken up under either Abitibi's or Consolidated's bid was the same. Consolidated already held Associated's 1.7 million shares,[2] which left about 8.2 million out in the market, and the four million bid for by Consolidated was about 49% of that remaining amount. (Abitibi also wanted 49% of the entire 9.8 million. If Abitibi won, it was possible Consolidated would tender the 1.7 million.)

There wasn't an ounce of fight left in the Abitibi team, but nevertheless the men made an attempt to answer certain questions. Would Abitibi's board approve another bid? Would the Royal Bank supply the extra funds necessary? What was the maximum Abitibi could raise internally and borrow to put into a new bid? What was the most Abitibi could pay and still benefit from the acquisition? What was the best way to compete: by little increases in the bid price or big ones? Did any downside ("mousetrap") risk remain?

Chairman Tom Bell and his executives and the legal and fiscal advisers spent most of the morning in talks, telephoning here and there, and exploring these questions. The exchanges and the Securities Commission also had to find a few answers about the competitive bidding regulations. Jack Kimber telephoned Michel Bélanger, president of the Montreal exchange, and Arthur Pattillo. Bélanger telephoned Jack Kimber and Robert Demers and each of the four held conference calls with various combinations of the others plus their own staff members, to work out a counterbid procedure that would be acceptable in both Toronto and Montreal. Later they'd enjoy the luxury of radical disagreement about the exchange route, but that couldn't be allowed to happen while a bid was in progress. Afterward, the only person who'd remark that he'd enjoyed the process was Robert Demers, and he'd say: "I expect the chairman of the Quebec Securities Commission to be called any time of the day or night for a quick decision on an important matter. It keeps your mind active."

151

At Abitibi, a high-level study group had been put together around the chief financial officer, Jack Haire, to tackle the question of how much more money could be raised. But even before that was settled, the target percentage had to be changed from 49% to 51% for a good reason: 49% was a whisker off absolute control, which might be dangerous in a close fight. The number of shares to be bid for, therefore, was raised from 4.83 million (49%) to five million (51%.) Now, how much could be raised to buy that many shares? The first answer that came up, throwing in every possible source of financing, was $150 million, which made possible a very attractive bid price of $30 a share. But Tom Bell didn't like the inclusion of some of the money sources the study group had lumped in to find this ceiling.

Could Abitibi sell anything to Price after the acquisition to cause a flow of cash from Price to Abitibi that would help pay off the bank loans? Yes, there was the Abitibi newsprint mill at Beaupre (capacity 161,600 tons), which was in Price's territory, the province of Quebec. That could surely be sold for $25 million.

It might be worth $25 million, but Bell disliked the idea of selling the mill to Price after a takeover; it would amount to a non-arm's-length transaction. It would appear to be oppressing the minority shareholders of Price even if the value of the mill were independently appraised — even, indeed, if the value of the mill were determined by the directors of Price. Bell thought it would still look fishy, and the sale of the Beaupre mill became a point of controversy within the study group. [There was another reason why the sale was unpalatable. The effect of the sale would be to swap Beaupre's newsprint capacity (161,000 tons) for less than 1/10th of Price's stock (830,000 shares at $30 equals $25 million), and that was equivalent to buying less than 1/10th of Price's overall newsprint capacity (110,000 tons). So 161,000 tons would be paid to get 110,000 tons. The only advantage was that the Beaupre sale would facilitate the whole takeover, which *was* profitable to Abitibi.]

Could Abitibi, once in control, cause Price to declare a special year-end dividend, the proceeds of which, in Abitibi's case, would help pay off the bank? Yes, Price held cash and short-term investments (which could easily be liquidated) worth $33 million at the end of 1973, which would enable a special dividend of up to $3.30 a share to be paid. Abitibi's share of such a dividend would be

152

about $17 million, though there might be a problem with designated-surplus tax now that Abitibi was going for 51% rather than 49%. At a $3 level a special dividend would be equitable to all parties because it was much less than the premium over market ($18) Abitibi was paying to "half the shareholders" to part with their stock. But once again Bell didn't like this idea. A $3 dividend would strip Price of all its liquid assets, and Price needed cash for the big expansions planned.

What was the maximum Abitibi could raise internally? At the end of 1973 Abitibi's liquid assets totaled about $35 million, but during 1974 there'd been a heavy drain on cash and the company could now expect to raise only about $15 million.

What was the maximum long-term debt Abitibi could service? After taking the most restrictive covenants into account, and the present long-term debt, the answer came to about $110 million.

If all four wells of cash were plumbed, Abitibi could easily raise enough capital to take the bidding up to $30 a share. But Bell insisted that ceiling wasn't valid, because he didn't like two of the sources of funds. The argument was temporarily left open.

The next question was to define bidding risks, and that was a job for Jim Tory and Ross LeMesurier. In the seven days since it had been announced, Abitibi's lucrative bid had been very well publicized. (The night before, Robert Demers, the chairman of the Quebec Securities Commission, had been questioned closely about it by his taxi driver on the way home.) Almost all the Price shares outstanding were waiting to be tendered to one bidder or the other (or even, it was thought at that stage, possibly both).

While one bid ($20) was clearly better than the other ($18) there seemed little danger that shareholders would tender stock to both Consolidated and Abitibi. But a danger lay in the number of shares for which Consolidated was bidding. Four million shares would give Consolidated (with the 1.7 million it already held) about 58% of Price, more than it needed for control. By reducing the number of shares bid for (to, say, 3.3 million), Consolidated could reduce its cash requirements at higher bidding prices and still be aiming at 51% of Price. If Consolidated did reduce its share target and cash requirements, it could bid higher with the same amount of money and perhaps reach a point where it *appeared* to be offering a higher price than Abitibi. Such a bid would actually be worth *less* to the Price shareholders, because fewer of their shares would be taken up.[3] Then there'd really be confusion. Less astute Price shareholders might tender to Consolidated, while the pros might go for Abitibi's bid — and both companies would end up with less than control.

Tom Bell laid down a clear condition: there was to be no Abitibi counterbid unless the exchange devised rules that would prevent this from happening. Jim Tory spent most of the rest of the day telephoning Montreal and calling at the Toronto Stock Exchange to help work out ways to circumvent this difficulty.

Earlier in the morning, Bell had called a directors' meeting for noon. Many of the directors were still in town watching the progress of the takeover, so it was an easy matter. After very little discussion, the board approved an expenditure of $125 million on Price, as long as there was no danger of Abitibi getting stuck with a minority position. The directors didn't like the notion of special dividends and a Beaupre sale either.

While the directors' meeting was in progress, Jack Kimber, president of the Toronto Stock Exchange, relayed a requirement to both Abitibi and Consolidated for an affidavit declaring their exact holdings in Price. Kimber wanted to know if there had been any back-door buying so far and to be able to calculate any from this point on.

In the afternoon, Bell telephoned the Royal Bank to ask for more money. Rowlie Frazee, executive vice-president and chief general manager, told Bell: "I'll have to call you back." McLaughlin and Gardiner were both in New York for the day. A little later, Frazee called Bell back and told him: "The bank will stand behind Abitibi." Once the loan to Abitibi reached $100 million, it would become the biggest in the history of Canada for such a purpose.

By mid-afternoon, the newswires started reporting sickening, depressing statements by Bill Turner in Montreal. "Until the next annual meeting we are in de facto control of the [Price] company," Turner crowed. "To consolidate our position, we are offering to buy more than 50% . . . We think we know where 50% of the shares are." Abitibi also knew where the shares were. It too had the shareholders' list. Turner must mean that, through its effective control of Price, Consolidated would cause Price to issue to Consolidated

154

five million treasury shares, giving it an uncatchable lead. (Five million plus 1.7 million came to 6.7 million, almost 50% of the 15 million Price shares that would then be outstanding.) So that was how Consolidated was going to gain control of Price! This fear held currency for a while, but was soon dismissed as fanciful.

Turner publicly rubbed salt into Abitibi's wound. "I think it is evident from the fact they came to us where their preferences lie," he told the press. If Consolidated kept control of Price, he pointed out, the resulting firm would be the largest newsprint producer in the world with annual capacity of more than two million tons. Turner added that the Quebec government was "very, very concerned" about the Abitibi bid, but was glad it hadn't intervened because Consolidated-Bathurst might some day want to bid for an Ontario company. (Did he mean *Abitibi*?) This Turner talk left everybody tired and despondent, except lawyer Jim Tory and Ted Medland of Wood Gundy, who insisted they didn't think Abitibi had lost its position. Throughout the last couple of days Medland, the financial firm's president, had proved himself a man of clear vision, unclouded by the emotional valleys and peaks of the chase.

At the exchanges the bidding procedures were gradually being settled. Jack Kimber and his officials didn't want the bidding to go on day after day, up 25¢ a time, stringing out the Price cease-trade indefinitely until one competitor gave up. Liquidity had to be restored as soon as possible. Price shareholders might need to sell stock on the exchange to buy groceries or whatever. The only alternative, in Kimber's mind, was just one bidding, with both bids submitted by sealed tender. Abitibi prepared a draft statement: "T. J. Bell announced this morning [the next day] . . . Abitibi has submitted a sealed bid . . . with the contents to be made public at 4 p.m. today . . ." But the sealed-tender idea was soon dropped by the exchanges. Robert Demers, for one, felt nervous about changing the rules of the game at half-time.

At 4 p.m., Tom Bell called a second board meeting, and informed the directors the money for a counterbid would be available. The board gave no ringing endorsation of a counterbid, but joylessly confirmed the authorization it had given at noon — pointing out to Bell, who was tired and despondent, that it was all his responsibility. After the board meeting, the council of war — Jim Tory, Medland and Bell — wearily resumed its deliberations. But

155

at 6 p.m., Ted Medland suddenly said: "To hell with this! Everybody go home and get a good night's sleep. There's nothing we can do tonight, anyway. We can figure out what our bid will be in the morning when the ground rules are finalized."

Everybody did as he suggested.

Day Twenty-Two

Thursday, November 21
"He lit up like a torch,
and realized fully that it
was all over . . ."

Harry Rosier stepped out of his office and met Ian McGibbon striding toward him across the color-of-gold broadloom.

"I'm fighting mad and I've got my fighting tie on!" McGibbon announced, sporting a vivid, red woollen tie, chosen that morning to express his mood. It was 8 a.m.

"Come on into Bell's office," Rosier replied, in the same vigorous tone, extending a friendly arm to shepherd McGibbon along.

Harry Rosier had also come into the office determined to save Abitibi's takeover. He was incensed at a gloating "nice-guy" Bill Turner, saying in the morning's Globe & Mail he didn't "believe in these kinds of takeovers, which don't give enough time to shareholders to react properly." He'd loftily exonerated himself: "But we were brought into the middle of this one and we have to play by the rules." Then Turner had turned the knife in the wound: "Whatever happens now, Consolidated-Bathurst will at least have been responsible for bringing control of Price to Canada." That kind of talk from Turner infuriated Rosier.

On arrival at the office, Rosier had gone straight into Bell's office and said: "Come on, Tom! Let's make our counterbid." Bell had arrived in the same frame of mind. He'd telephoned Ted Medland of Wood Gundy at 6:30 and thought aloud to him, drawing on Medland's unshakable resolve: "We'll fight — and we'll get it."

157

By 9 a.m. the Wood Gundy people were over, also raring to go, and reinforcing the infectious fighting mood. When they arrived, Bell told everybody: "Get into the board room." Then he started handling out assignments. The first was: "All right, Ian, your job, and get at it, is to start writing press releases. We're going to do exactly what that goddam Turner is doing. I want to be ready to flood the Dow-Jones with the kind of garbage they're putting out." Ian McGibbon left for his own office deflated at having to do the joe-job of writing press releases when there was a council of war going on. But it was an important task. Somehow the Price shareholders had to be influenced to favor an Abitibi bid in the imminent competition, just in case there was any confusion as to which was of greater value. "Mr. Shareholder," McGibbon scribbled, ". . . carefully examine the relative values . . . It's not only the price per share, but the number of shares you're going to be taken out for." He returned to the board room towards 10 with a long, aggressive press release, but it was hacked down to a brief announcement that would go out with the counterbid. On second thought, they decided Abitibi really wasn't the kind of company that wanted to put out a flock of loud-mouth propaganda.

In the board room, Tom Bell, Ted Medland and Jack Haire had been deciding what to bid. Bell was determined to "blow it all in one bolt and scare the ass off these people." So a decision was made: Abitibi would bid $25 a share for five million shares (51%), which would cost $125 million, the maximum authorized by the board.[1] Bell took McGibbon's truncated press release and added one razor-edged paragraph: ". . . [Mr. Bell] noted that the Price operations complemented those of Abitibi in a way that makes that company of greater value to Abitibi than to any other paper company." They hoped Turner would think "greater value" meant that Abitibi was determined to go one higher no matter what Consolidated came up with. Bell also decided to table Abitibi's bid only a few minutes before the deadline to give Consolidated the least amount of time to recover from the shock and come back with another bid. A heavy snow storm was raging in Montreal; that also might disrupt Consolidated's communications and slow the company's reactions.

Tom Bell didn't realize — so anxious was he to win the contest — that by going to his limit ($25) in one crack he may have been doing exactly what Consolidated hoped he would. Bill Turner well understood Bell's fighting spirit and he'd claim afterward that he'd deliberately goaded Bell into this reaction.

As the morning progressed the exchanges started to lay down the counterbidding procedure. The day before, it had been decided that Consolidated's bid would remain open one day — until 9 a.m. today. But, because the regulations weren't ready in time, the bid was extended until noon and Abitibi was given until 2 p.m. to make a counterbid. After that, successive counterbids would be spaced two hours apart: Abitibi at 2 p.m.; Consolidated at 4 p.m.; Abitibi at 9 a.m. the next morning, and so on.[2]

Rules had also been devised to ensure that one bidder would come out clean with clear control of Price. After each counterbid, the other bidder had the right to withdraw his bid, confirm it (let it stand) or raise it. If at the end of the contest there were two bids standing, the book for the higher bid (according to price per share) would be opened for half an hour, the number of shares tendered would be counted, and the total announced. The second bidder would have an hour either to withdraw, which he'd probably choose to do if the higher bidder had close to 50% — or confirm his bid, which would be the proper strategy if the higher bidder had met with a disappointing response and the lower bid was more appealing because of a greater amount of stock to be taken up. If the lower bidder chose to proceed, the higher bidder could turn in to the lower bid any shares owned before the bidding or acquired when his book was opened. The lower bidder's bid was then unconditional and he had to accept all shares tendered, including the higher bidder's. Considering that almost every Price shareholder in the world was waiting out there to tender his stock, there was absolutely no downside risk, Wood Gundy advised Bell.

Towards noon, Tom Bell, Jim Tory, Ted Medland and Ross LeMesurier walked over to the exchange to conduct a final discussion on counterbid procedure with Kimber and tell him confidentially what Abitibi would bid. Jim Tory said playfully to Kimber: "You write what you think our bid is on a piece of paper." Kimber did and folded the paper over. Tory then handed Kimber a note disclosing Abitibi's new bid. When he read it, Kimber crumpled his own piece of paper and threw it away, refusing to say what he'd speculated Abitibi's bid would be.

Back at Abitibi, Jack Haire, Ian McGibbon, Don Bean of Wood Gundy and a couple of secretaries speculated on what Consolidated-Bathurst would do. Jack Haire, confident in his financial wisdom, bet Ian McGibbon $10 that Consolidated would throw in the sponge as soon as Abitibi's bid was announced. McGibbon argued, between sandwich bites: "There's no way they'll give up. If we were Con-Bath with one million seven shares, we wouldn't need another three million to do the work." McGibbon also reminded Haire that Con-Bath could easily counterbid against Abitibi's next bid by putting up the price per share and reducing the number of shares to be purchased. That way Con-Bath could bid higher than Abitibi with less money. Yes, that was true, Haire said with characteristic patience, but let's wait and see.

A little after noon, word came through from Montreal that the early editions of the French-language afternoon newspaper La Presse had carried a public threat by Paul Desmarais, chairman of Power Corp.: "If Abitibi makes a counter-offer superior to our offer to take control of the Price company, we will make an offer to gain control of Abitibi." Power Corp. was one company that could easily do that. It would only cost about $135 million, and Power Corp. had more than $40 million in liquid assets and a net worth of more than $300 million. When Jim Tory was told of what Desmarais had said, he grew angry: "How can the securities commissions allow him to make such a statement without ordering a cease-trade in Abitibi's stock and demanding that he explain Power Corp's intentions — if they really have any?"

Despite the Desmarais threat, Abitibi made a public announcement on the exchange and the Dow-Jones newswire that a counterbid would be forthcoming. At 1:50 p.m., only 10 minutes before the exchange's deadline, the press release was sent out announcing the $25 a share bid and carrying the "we'll beat you" warning to Turner.

In Montreal, at that moment, Bob Morrow, Harmsworth's lawyer and Price's vice-chairman, was stuck in his car in a traffic jam on the Champlain Bridge caused by the heavy fall of snow. Morrow was forced to keep in touch with the Consolidated bidding team through the radio of a taxi that was caught in the same traffic jam.

At 3:45 p.m., the great moment arrived. Consolidated-Bathurst announced it would withdraw from bidding and tender all its shares — so recently purchased from Associated Newspapers — to Abitibi.

It would be easy to jump to the conclusion that Consolidated-Bathurst had made a profit of more than $10 million in two days. After all, the company had exchanged one treasury share (when the market was $24-$26) for two Price shares which were suspended at about $12 a share. It was tempting to say that, therefore, the shares were exchanged on the basis of their market value (about $25 per share for the Consolidated treasury stock). And, later, many people would fall into this line of thinking. Associated Newspapers entered the Consolidated stock it received into its books at the market price ($26), and a few financial writers published the idea that Consolidated had made a handsome $10-million profit by selling half its Price stock to Abitibi (at $25 when it had supposedly been purchased at $12) and retaining half its original Price holdings. But Consolidated officials later on would recall those articles with anger, because they ignored the careful accounting procedures Consolidated adopted for that transaction.

According to Consolidated's books, the company would suffer losses — not profits — as a result of the overall Price transaction, and therefore pay no taxes. In fact, the transaction would generate a tax loss.

In its books Consolidated has assigned a value of $50 per share to the treasury stock issued to the British, possibly based on the notion that the agreement was only substantiated when it was approved by the Consolidated board on Day Twenty-Two, and at the time there was a bid of $25 per share on the exchange for the Price stock. (Therefore, one Consolidated share was worth two $25 shares, or $50.)

On that basis, Consolidated only broke even when it sold half its Price stock to Abitibi, and would make a loss whenever it sold any of the remaining half-parcel for less than $25 a share, which it would do. (During 1975, the trading range of Price stock would be: high $18½, low $12¼.) Obviously the accounting procedure adopted for the Price-shares transactions would bring Consolidated considerable tax benefits. It would eliminate any "profit" that might be taxable from the transactions, even though the company had made considerable financial growth during these transactions. (Consolidated's assets rose by $45 million, and the shareholders' equity rose by the same amount.)

Convenient though Consolidated's accounting approach may be, the basis of it is open to other interpretations. The British, for instance, obviously regard the market values of the Consolidated and Price stocks as the basis for the exchange. And there's another way of determining when the agreement was substantiated other than the time of the Price directors' meeting. The agreement was made in the early hours of Day Twenty-One, while there was still an Abitibi bid of $18 a share on the exchange. That morning before nine o'clock, Consolidated entered a competing bid of $20 a share for more Price stock to complement what it would receive from the British. Surely, the agreement with the British must be regarded as firm at that point? Otherwise Consolidated had made its $20 bid without knowing with certainty what Price stock it already held. (Besides, Bill Turner stated at the time that the $20 offer to the remaining shareholders was better than the deal given the British — the most telling point of all.) If the agreement had been firm at that time, then wasn't the Price stock worth only $18 a share for half of Consolidated's holdings? And by later selling half for $25 didn't Consolidated make a considerable profit? Despite these and other questions raised by Consolidated's accounting procedures, the firm's auditors, Touche Ross & Co., felt able to give a clear opinion on the 1974 accounts.[3]

To maximize the sale price, Consolidated had become publicly arrogant and needling deliberately to excite Bell, whose determination they knew so well, into raising the bidding as high and as fast as he could to drive them out of the contest. The $25 price was so high that it prompted one American investment house to ask if Abitibi had a new accounting wrinkle to pass it through its books. [It hadn't. And the price was still profitable to Abitibi.]

A moment or two after the Consolidated announcement, Tom Bell emerged quietly from his office and turned to face Harry Rosier who was walking towards him. For two hours everybody in the executive suite had kept their heads down, trying to work, but listening and watching for any signs of what might be happening. As Rosier reached him, Bell spoke with a smile.

"You've got yourself a company," he told Rosier.

Ian McGibbon had been standing outside his office, watching and listening. When he heard those words, he gave a loud whoop, rushed up to Bell and put his arms around him.

"Well done, sir!" McGibbon boomed. The company's expert in acquisitions became the first to congratulate the grand acquisitioner.

Bell lit up like a torch, and realized fully that it was all over, and what he'd achieved. Following McGibbon's cry, a shout went up in the offices of conservative old Abitibi, rolling out from the executive suite even to the floor below. Company officers came out of doors grinning, watching the elder statesman Bell. A group gathered around him and somebody was heard to say: "We've won!" Bell turned and corrected him sternly.

"No, sir. We're going to wait until we're told by Jack Kimber. There are to be no phone calls to anybody. Not even to directors. We're going to wait until we can see a slip of paper in our hands," he said. Bell had learned his lesson about celebrating too early.

Within a few minutes the Wood Gundy people arrived. With a troop of Abitibi executives, they walked over to the exchange. When the Abitibi book closed at 4:45 p.m., it was discovered that more than 95% of Price's stock had been tendered. Weeks later, this figure would be revised downwards a little, because a few people had tendered stock they didn't have. Nevertheless it was a tribute to the successful dissemination of the bid information and the generosity of the $18-$25 prices.

At 5 p.m. photographs were taken on the exchange floor: a smiling Tom Bell being handed a slip of paper by exchange vice-president Lester Lowe and Jack Kimber; a radiant Tom Bell surrounded by Ted Medland, Ross LeMesurier and Jack Haire; a proud Tom Bell with the same people standing in different places. Throughout, Ted Medland, president of Wood Gundy, maintained an air that said: "These takeovers are all in a day's work. We'll probably find another one when we get back to the office."[4]

163

Everybody then drifted back to Harry Rosier's office at Abitibi, where he brought out three or four bottles he keeps in a cabinet of books, and three or four secretaries were called in. At 6:30 p.m., after a couple of drinks, everybody went home. Abitibi Paper Co. was never the scene of boisterous celebration, no matter what the occasion.

Aftermath

About a week after the takeover, a small British shareholder of Price — Joe Dixon,* a single man in his forties — wrote from his London home, which he shared with his mother, angry letters about the lightning speed of the takeover to: the London, Montreal and Toronto stock exchanges; the Ontario and Quebec Securities Commissions; Wood Gundy; the London Takeover Panel; Associated Newspapers; his bank; several British and Canadian newspapers; and the Canadian High Commissioner in London. Many of these august institutions, believing Dixon's letter to be significant, photocopied it and sent it to a few of the others, so that, for a while, there must have been a stream of Dixon's letters passing around among the various authorities.

Dixon, a senior accountant with a big British manufacturer, felt that he and his mother had been trodden upon. Dixon's mother held 56 shares of Price which had been in the family for a long time. A larger parcel owned by Dixon's grandmother had been divided among that woman's children on her death, and in Joe Dixon's branch of the family at least, the shares seem to have taken on the character of a family heirloom.

In keeping with British regulations about foreign securities

* Not his real name.

held by British investors, the Dixon shares were kept in an "authorized depository" — a London bank. (If British residents were allowed to hold their own foreign share certificates, they might spirit them out of the country and sell them, avoiding the Bank of England's portfolio-investment rules.)

On Day Seventeen, a Saturday and the third day after Abitibi's bid had been announced, Joe Dixon received at 9 a.m. a letter from the bank explaining the bid. It was his first notification. The letter stated he would have to inform the bank by Monday morning if he wished to accept the bid, because of the chain of connections through which instructions to sell would have to pass back to a Canadian stock exchange. In effect Dixon was given two days to make up his mind (and his mother's). And it wasn't an easy matter. "I was feeling ill that morning," he said later. "Mother's stockbroker had lost his wife that week and his firm had just been absorbed into another, so I didn't know who to call. I could have called my broker at home but I didn't want to do that if his wife had just died." Dixon needed somebody to help him assess the effect of Britain's overseas investment regulations on the acceptance of an $18 bid.

On Monday morning, instead of accepting the bid, Dixon decided to fight and, from his bed (he still wasn't feeling in top form) called "every national newspaper in the country." Dixon now considered himself an experienced corporate activist, after a set-to earlier in the year with British Leyland. He'd written a series of letters to British Leyland management telling them how to pull the company out of its difficulties. They'd ignored him, but new management had been appointed and, by George, seemed to be doing exactly as he'd advised. Only a little before the Abitibi bid, Dixon had written a letter to British Leyland management commending them for doing the right thing. Now he was determined to get some publicity against this miserable Abitibi business.

Unfortunately, Dixon soon discovered that most newspapers weren't interested in his views. Finally, he telephoned Vere Harmsworth's Daily Mail and was told abruptly: "We're involved. We can't write about it." Despondently he sank back into his bed.

The next day, up and about, and feeling chipper, Dixon went bustling into Wood Gundy's London office to give the firm a piece of his mind. The staff there were polite but reserved. When Dixon said pointedly that Bob Morgan was *also chairman of the Toronto Stock Exchange*, they stared at him blankly waiting for the significance to be explained.

Late Wednesday afternoon — Britain being five hours ahead of central Canada — the bank phoned Dixon to tell him there'd been a second bid. He didn't advise the bank to accept because all week (he said later) the newspapers had predicted a battle between Domtar, Abitibi and Consolidated-Bathurst which might push up the price. Abitibi's final $25 bid was made at about 7 p.m. British time (2 p.m. on Day Twenty-Two in Toronto) well after bank employees had gone home, so Dixon received no telephone call. He read about the bid the following morning in the newspapers, phoned his bank to say he wanted to tender, but was told, "It's too late." Eccentric Dixon fired off his letters, but he was the only British shareholder to do so. He planned to use his savings and his vacation to buy one share of Abitibi and fly to Canada for the 1975 annual meeting to "beaver away at them — try to make them uncomfortable — in a civilized manner."

Ian Steers, head of Wood Gundy's London branch, had also had a trying week. It was bad enough having Dixon storm around the office, but Steers also had to contend with the London Takeover Panel, a body formed by the financial community to draw up and administer a code of proper takeover conduct. The takeover panel had no powers, but was mighty in its influence. A leading financial man has, on occasion, been forced to resign after the panel had publicly denounced him as a bounder. Now, here was this Abitibi takeover — a travesty of the takeover principles underlying the panel's very strict code, which has never been adopted in Canada. Ian Steers was called to account, and he explained quite simply that he'd no control over the matter — he was merely the bidder's agent's London representative.

Steers was called a second time when the Consolidated-Bathurst-Associated Newspapers share exchange became news, and asked why the same offer wasn't made available to all the Price shareholders, which probably left him considerably puzzled.

Finally, Steers told the panel that if it turned out that any British small shareholders had lost during the bid, "somebody would probably dip into his pocket and help them out."

In Canada, a highly educated, accomplished Price shareholder, Jonathan L. Meakins, M.D., D.Sc., F.R.C.S.(C), assistant professor of surgery and microbiology at McGill University, and a surgeon at Royal Victoria Hospital, also wrote letters of complaint when the dust had settled — to the Quebec Securities Commission and the Montreal Stock Exchange. Meakins wrote to Robert Demers, chairman of the Quebec Securities Commission:

"I am indeed a small shareholder in Price, holding 45 shares . . . I followed the details in the newspaper of the Price takeover by Abitibi with great interest. The interest I had, of course, was the expectation of receiving $18 and then $20 and finally $25 per share for my shares in Price. At no time while reading about this takeover bid was it made clear that one had to declare the intention of submitting shares for purchase by Abitibi. In fact I interpreted one article to mean that all shareholders would receive some benefit from this takeover bid and that approximately half of each individual's shares would be purchased for $25 and, therefore, did not pursue the matter . . . One of my friends who works in the investment business informed me that no monies would be forthcoming because I had not turned the shares in . . ."

Robert Demers wrote Meakins a courteous, sympathetic reply asking for further information. But Michel Bélanger, president of the Montreal Stock Exchange, had difficulty taking Meakins seriously. He wrote: "Your letter . . . did perplex me. Frankly, I could not believe that a person who had followed [the bid] closely . . . would not realize that he had to call his broker . . . I did not consequently quite know what to answer. I had a vision of a person once told by a physician that he required an operation and who would just do nothing with this advice. Having taken no decision and not asked his physician to proceed I should think that person would later on have a very poor case to complain that nobody came forward to perform the operation . . ."

Bélanger who was hurriedly dictating the letter in his office at the exchange suddenly realized he was being ungracious, and continued: "Upon further reflection, I realized that you have indeed a very clear problem . . ." and explained cordially Meakins should always seek "proper professional advice." But Meakins remains disillusioned about the securities market.

An elderly lady living in a small Quebec city also fired off a letter to Robert Demers after the takeover: "I was very perturbed to read in the papers of the proposed purchase of the Price Company (Common Stock) by Abitibi with overtones by Argus Corporation Limited, and finally a bid from Consolidated-Bathurst. As a small shareholder (30 shares), and am very sure there are many, [I was] utterly bewildered at the turn of events . . . I sincerely wish to make representation to you that . . . a Notice should have been forwarded to shareholders to assist them in a decision, and not to have to depend on news media. It is reasonable to assume that holders of large blocks of stocks have an advantage over the minority group. I am a widow. It is very difficult to budget on a fixed income — dividends and interest are important . . ."

Demers replied: "I am very happy that you took the time to express your opinion. So few small shareholders advise us of the difficulties which they sometimes face . . . This whole matter . . . will be the object of review . . ." Demers and the widow — who did tender to Abitibi and benefit from the takeover — then exchanged a series of friendly letters about her case and the "turbulence and anxiety that takeovers cause."

About a month after the takeover, John Mackenzie and Norman Halford of Canada Permanent Trust Co. felt maybe some thanks were due to Arthur Pattillo and Harry Bray for having Abitibi's bid extended [at a cost of about $40 million to Abitibi], and enabling Canada Permanent to reach most of its clients in time. Halford wrote to Pattillo:

"My reasons for . . . [telephoning Bray the day before] were twofold: first to express . . . our company's appreciation to the Commission for its prompt response to our request for a delay in implementing Abitibi's initial offer, then to describe the final results of this transaction as applied to our trust clients . . ." Halford then explained that of 116,000 shares of Price held for clients, Canada Permanent had "70,000 shares held on behalf of individual trusts, which in nearly all cases required client consent before any investment action could be taken. By the time the issue was settled we were able to tender all but some 5,000 shares, those owned for clients we were unable to reach before the offer expired. We have no way of documenting how many shares would not have been tendered had Abitibi's original deadline remained in effect, but informal talks with some of our branches satisfied us that the action taken by your commission did allow us time to reach some additional clients."

Halford stated once again: ". . . we are particularly grateful . . ." But he didn't mention the jump in price from $18 to $25 that had sprung out of the commission's action. Perhaps that would have seemed crass.

When trading in Price Co. stock resumed on the exchanges about noon on Day Twenty-Three (November 22), there was a flurry of hectic buying and selling. About 2.5 million Price shares changed hands at $11.75 to $12.73, an extraordinarily high volume of trading. Immediately, exchange officials suspected short selling to the bid.

(A sale of stock is "short" when the seller doesn't own the stock, but intends to buy it for delivery to the buyer, later, when he hopes the price will be lower. In a free-moving market, short selling involves a gamble by both buyer and seller. One hopes the price will fall; the other that it's rising. But an exchange takeover is a sure thing; the price of the target stock is almost bound to drop when the bid is over. So the exchanges ban short selling during takeovers. Otherwise everybody would want to short and chaos would ensue.)

In the Price takeover, another indicator that there may have been short selling was the high acceptance of Abitibi's bid — about 97% of the outstanding Price stock was tendered. Surely some of those tenders must have been shorts, newspapers exclaimed. Acceptance of the bid had seemed unbelievably high.

The exchanges instituted investigations and hearings that would still be going on in February 1976. At that time it would be believed that about 200,000 shares out of the total of 9.4 million tendered may have been shorts, or tendered in violation of some other exchange rules in effect during the bid.

Those other rules banned sales by house accounts and brokers' employees, and padding (an investor tendering more than he owned so that more than 50% of his real holdings would be taken up). Hearings were necessary because in some cases padding had been unintentional. A typical case arose when an investor had shares held by his bank and gave instructions to tender to both his broker *and* his bank, with the result that twice as many shares as were owned were tendered.

By February 1976 it would be thought there'd been only 20 cases in which the rules might have been broken, and that about 95% of the Price stock had been legitimately tendered. That was still a very high proportion.

The most flagrant case of short selling involved two American brothers who, through a California investment house, by way of Gordon Securities Ltd. of Montreal, tendered 160,000 shares they didn't own to Abitibi, and had 79,955 purchased for about $2 million. On Day Twenty-Three another Montreal broker had been given a big order to purchase by an American broker with instructions to deliver quickly. Successive orders came through to deliver more quickly, then even more quickly, until finally the broker was asked to deliver not in the United States as initially requested, but to a Montreal bank. The Americans' ruse was soon discovered by Montreal Stock Exchange investigators.

Others accused of short selling included a Toronto lawyer, who, on the basis of a defense that he held an *option* to the stock he tendered, was acquitted by an Ontario provincial judge. (Some thought it an odd legal decision, because it might mean that, in future, blocks of shares could be tendered twice if an option were held on them, once by the owner, once by the optionee.) A Bay Street mining engineer and promoter was also charged by the Ontario Securities Commission, and an officer of a Swiss investment corporation in Montreal had his securities licence revoked after allegedly tendering short stock. The street believed the Swiss was a scapegoat for bigger fish behind the shorts.

To unwind the effect of the short selling, the short sellers (in particular the American brothers who made about $1 million in profit) were pressed to return the difference between the $25 received and the $12 spent buying the stock eventually delivered to Abitibi. Funds, which may reach $1.5 million, have been earmarked for reimbursement of legitimate Price shareholders who, as a result of the shorts, had less stock taken up than they otherwise would have. Ironically, one fifth of the fund will be disbursed to Consolidated-Bathurst.

A little while after the takeover was completed, Washington and Ottawa initiated investigations into the anti-trust and anti-combines possibilities. The Canadian investigation seemed most concerned with the possibility of Abitibi, Consolidated-Bathurst and Domtar, which all held Price stock after the takeover, operating the company together by joint agreement, an arrangement that Abitibi would be unlikely to accept. In early 1976 there had been no announcement as to whether either investigation was still in progress.

Soon after the Abitibi takeover, the stock exchanges and the securities commissions reviewed the method. Exchange takeovers were outlawed until the exchanges could work out new rules that would satisfy themselves and the securities commissions. In Montreal, new rules initiated the following changes:

— The bidder must make positive, direct contact with the shareholders of the target company. Use of the news media isn't sufficient for dissemination of the details of the bid.

— The bid must be open for 11 clear business days, and that, of course, includes two weekends, making the open time a total of 15 days, almost as long as the 21 days required for a circular.

— The directors of the target company must disclose their views of the takeover.

The proposals of the Montreal Stock Exchange on the new rules were accepted — by the Quebec Securities Commission — and the exchange route was open again in Montreal.

The Ontario Securities Commission, however, firmly blocked

the exchange route in the draft of the revised Ontario Securities Act, which was due to appear before the Ontario legislature.

Because most large companies have many shareholders in Ontario, it was doubtful any big takeovers would be able to go ahead through the Montreal Stock Exchange alone. So the 22-day adventure that led to the takeover of Price might well have been the last, great financial drama of its kind in Canada.

Reference
notes

DAY ONE

Note 1:

The Canadian pulp and paper industry is made up of about 75 companies, which are relatively small by international standards. The industry is Canada's largest industrial employer and its biggest exporter of manufactured goods. In 1974 the industry employed 140,000 people who produced over 23 million tons of product valued at about $6 billion. About 75% of production, made up principally of newsprint and pulp, was exported to the United States and offshore markets, and these sales, valued at about $4 billion, accounted for close to 13% of Canada's total exports for the year.

For 50 years newsprint has been the most important product of the industry, and the industry has been the leading supplier of newsprint to the American market. In 1974, newsprint accounted for 41% of the industry's output; more than 90% of the industry's newsprint was exported to the United States and to offshore markets; and Canadian-based mills supplied about 66% of the total American newsprint requirements. In 1974, the Canadian newsprint industry was made up of 22 companies operating 43 mills, with a combined capacity close to 40% of the world's total. The industry was largely concentrated in Eastern Canada (85%), mostly in Ontario and Quebec, and close to 50% of its capacity was owned or controlled by non-Canadian companies, including some publishers. Abitibi was the newsprint industry's third largest producer (with 10% of the industry's total capacity).

Since the late 1950s, the Canadian newsprint industry had experienced a sharp decline in its share of world supply (from 46% to 38%); an erosion of its once dominant position in its traditionally largest and most profitable market in the United States (from 74% to 63%); a gradual deterioration in its earnings that for a time had been masked by a favorable Canadian dollar exchange rate.

At the same time there has been an emergence of a strong American newsprint industry. Over a period of 15 years, the American industry, centred largely in the southern states, had doubled both its capacity and its share of the United States mar-

DAY ONE

ket. Cost advantages over the average Eastern Canadian producer were roughly 15%, principally because of lower wood, transportation and labor costs. The southern American industry has also been able to live with a newsprint price that eventually provided only marginal earnings to most of its Canadian-based competitors.

This situation had reached a critical stage in the early 1970s coincident with the freeing of the Canadian dollar, which occurred in the midst of a soft market resulting from over-capacity in the Canadian industry. The operating levels of mills in Canada had been depressed to about 83%, and Canadian-owned producers carried a somewhat greater burden of slack mill time than companies controlled by foreign publishers. Many producers experienced after-tax returns on sales of 3% or less.

The seriousness of the situation had prompted Canada's federal and provincial governments to inquire into the matter. A report prepared by a federal/provincial group, *A Working Paper Concerning the Canadian Pulp and Paper Industry With Implications for Other Forest-Based Industries* (August 24, 1973), had suggested that the Canadian presence in the industry should be strengthened, that merger of some Canadian companies might be desirable to develop stronger corporations better able to compete against foreign-owned firms.

In late 1973, because of normal growth in demand coupled with mill closures and curtailed expansion plans, there had been a strengthening in world newsprint markets. This had led to full-capacity operations in the industry throughout 1974, newsprint price increases and a strong improvement in industry earnings.

At the same time, the pressures of the energy crisis and double-digit inflation were playing havoc with costs — including those related to building new plant. Hence, although newsprint operating levels and prices and earnings had improved, they hadn't reached a level that supported any significant expansion in the industry's capacity.

Note 2:

Abitibi Pulp & Paper Co. was founded in 1913 by Frank H. Anson, an American, born in 1859 in Niles, Michigan, who'd been a railroad passenger agent, a rubber prospector in South America, an export sales manager of a New York flour mill and general superintendent of Ogilvie Flour Mills, in Montreal.

In the summer of 1909, when in his late 40s, Anson grubstaked two McGill University students with $1,000 to look for minerals in northern Ontario. The students returned in the fall with nothing to offer Anson but the conviction that the trees and rivers "up there" would support a paper mill.

Anson obtained water and timber rights from the province of Ontario, and built a mill on the raging Abitibi River at Iroquois Falls, helped in the financing by Shirley Ogilvie, a son of the Ogilvie Flour Mills family. The mill was designed for groundwood, but soon switched to newsprint production and changed its name to Abitibi Power & Paper Co., reflecting ownership of its own power plant nearby.

By 1927, Abitibi had purchased a sulphite pulp mill at Smooth Rock Falls, Ontario, to provide raw material for the manufacture of fine paper. It also had purchased a substantial interest in Manitoba Paper Co. and Ste. Anne Paper Co.

In the 1920s the newsprint industry was overconfident, still basing its outlook on the high prices and growing demand of the years immediately following the Great War. By 1928, the price had fallen to $68 a ton from $80 a few years earlier, but it was thought that consolidation in the industry through merger, takeovers, and joint ownership of mills would reduce price competition in the industry.

In 1928 Abitibi took over three other Canadian newsprint companies, some of them with high-cost mills that wouldn't be profitable if prices fell any further, as they certainly did. The amount of the industry's capacity used to fill dwindling orders also shrank, but Abitibi continued to expand with further purchases through 1930.

DAY ONE

By 1932, in the midst of the Great Depression, the price of newsprint had fallen to the uneconomic level of $48 a ton, and only 28% of Abitibi's merger-swollen capacity was in use.

On June 1, 1932, Abitibi defaulted on payment of interest on its first mortgage gold bonds, and a month later a power subsidiary defaulted on its bonds. The bondholders foreclosed and a receiver and manager were appointed. At the time, The Financial Post calculated that Abitibi's $50 million of bonds accounted for the bulk of the industrial securities then in default in Canada.

The receivership would last for 14 years and would be described as "the longest and largest in Canadian industrial history." The memory of receivership and the disastrous expansions that preceded it would make Abitibi a defensive, conservative company for a quarter of a century.

At the time of the takeover, inflation and heavy demand for newsprint had pushed Abitibi's earnings to a quarter-century high — 1974's would be 50% higher than 1973's. This table shows earnings per share before extraordinary items, adjusted for stock splits in 1951 and 1963.

1950	$0.73	1962	$0.80
1951	$0.77	1963	$0.93
1952	$0.50	1964	$1.01
1953	$0.57	1965	$0.96
1954	$0.62	1966	$0.92
1955	$0.80	1967	$0.72
1956	$0.89	1968	$0.55
1957	$0.71	1969	$0.64
1958	$0.55	1970	$0.24
1959	$0.68	1971	$0.19
1960	$0.71	1972	$0.44
1961	$0.79	1973	$1.66
		1974	$2.50

Note 3:

If the company tried to make a takeover in the United States, Abitibi would likely offer cash for control (50%-plus) of the American company, but would like the option of offering stock at a later date to buy in the remaining shares (to 100%). (Cash has much better alternative uses in the later stages.) Offering stock to Americans would create three problems:

— Abitibi's stock would have to be relisted on the New York Stock Exchange (it was listed there until receivership in the 1930s), and all the NYSE reporting and administrative procedures complied with.

— Abitibi stock would have to be registered with the Securities & Exchange Commission in Washington, which would involve a certain expense and compliance with SEC regulations concerning reporting of financial information and accounting procedures. These regulations are often at variance with the requirements of the Ontario Securities Commission and the Quebec Securities Commission.

— Offering stock to Americans might destroy Abitibi's Canadian status under the Foreign Investment Review Act, which classifies corporations as Canadian or non-resident, and permits the federal cabinet to block the purchase of a Canadian company by non-residents. Generally speaking, a non-resident public company was one that had more than 5% of its stock in the hands of a non-resident. The biggest shareholding in Abitibi, foreign or otherwise, was the 2% belonging to the Cox family of Augusta, Georgia. That stock was paid to the Coxes in part exchange for Cox Newsprint Inc., which Abitibi had bought in 1968.

Note 4:

In 1970, newsprint manufacture by existing mills had returned only 3% to 4% after tax on the capital invested — one of the lowest returns ever experienced by the industry. In 1971 that return had

DAY ONE

tripled, and in 1974 it had almost doubled again, all in response to growing demand and higher prices. For one brief year the industry had enjoyed returns close to 20%, but in 1975 strikes and declining demand would reduce the return once more.

Returns from new mills showed a different pattern. In 1975 new mills would be expected to give only an 8% to 10% return, because the cost of construction had risen faster than newsprint prices. The 1975 newsprint prices would give a good return from mills built at construction costs prevailing say 10 years previously, but wouldn't give a good return from mills built in 1975. The return on newsprint made by new mills wasn't expected to rise to 15% for several years, because the upward drift in newsprint prices probably wouldn't be any faster than the rise in construction costs.

In May 1975, when the New York selling price of newsprint would be $260 a ton, Abitibi would calculate that a 15% return on the capital invested in a new mill demanded a price of $380 a ton. For a mill started in 1975 and completed in 1978, the price in 1978 would have to be $440 a ton, almost 70% higher than in 1975 — an unlikely price increase.

Why did Abitibi want a 15% return from new mills?

First, profit had to be made on the *value* (purchasing power) of the money invested, not merely on the number of dollars, otherwise it wasn't entirely profit. (If a company made a 5% "profit" in a year when the value of money fell 10%, it hadn't truly profited.) In 1975, inflation would be eroding the Canadian dollar at a rate of about 10% a year. Therefore Abitibi wanted to make 10% a year from its new investment just to keep up, plus a true profit of 5% on top of that. The 8% return expected from new mills at the time wouldn't even cover inflation.

Second, the greater the risk taken by an investor or lender, the greater the return should be. In 1974 the prime lending rate of the chartered banks was about 10%. A company investing in a mill takes more risk than a bank does in lending money for the mill (the bank is a secured lender), therefore the company should get a

184

return on investment greater than the interest rate of 10%.

Note 5:
The $65-million extension would have a capacity of 500 tons a day. The smallest economical newsprint mill in the mid-1970s would have to have a capacity of about 1,000 tons a day.

Note 6:
Great Lakes Paper Co. was building a $163-million expansion at its site at Thunder Bay, Ontario. It involved a kraft pulp mill, a board plant and other items, all of which would be completed by mid-1976. The project had been planned in early 1973, before the worst inflation effects had become obvious.

Note 7:
Wage inflation in the Canadian pulp and paper mills was outpacing that in manufacturing as a whole at the time.

	Average hourly earnings at the end of August					
	1970	1971	1972	1973	1974	1975
All manufacturing	$3.02	$3.28	$3.56	$3.83	$4.44	$5.08
		8.6%	8.5%	7.6%	15.9%	14.4%

(August 1970 to August 1975: 68.2%)

Pulp and paper mills	$3.71	$4.32	$4.69	$4.79	$5.79	$6.28
		16.4%	8.6%	2.1%	20.9%	8.5%

(August 1970 to August 1975: 69.3%)

DAY ONE

Note 8:

A company's assets, less what it owes (its liabilities) to lenders, is *book value*. The book value represents the value in the company belonging to the shareholders. Divided by the number of shares, this becomes *book value per share*, which can provide a reference point against which to judge the market price of the stock. As a company makes a profit each year and that profit goes into retained earnings, so the book value increases. In 1974, Price's book value rose from about $18.10 to close to $20 as a result of its earning $3.22 a share and paying out dividends of $1.15.

Note 9:

Profits had risen sharply for most corporations in 1974, but so had inflation. A company with an apparently high return on investment of 15% was in fact making a real profit of only 5% because of the 10% inflation.

The earnings per share of the companies that comprised the Toronto Stock Exchange Industrial Index told dramatically how profits had soared:

	For the month of September					
	1970	1971	1972	1973	1974	1975
Earnings per share	$1.44	$1.28	$1.46	$1.75	$2.41	$2.35

At the same time, the prices of the shares had plummeted — as the price-earnings ratio of the TSE Industrial Index showed:

	For the month of September					
	1970	1971	1972	1973	1974	1975
Price-earnings ratio	15.29	16.44	17.71	14.34	6.90	8.22

As a hedge against inflation, Canadians had been rushing into real estate. The demand for real estate (and, of course, real estate prices) had soared, as the sales statistics of the Multiple Listing Service* showed clearly:

	Dollar volume by region (in thousands)			
	1971	1972	1973	1974
Canada.........	2,118,607	2,507,504	3,460,454	4,556,785
B.C.	458,200	507,585	694,819	795,994
Alberta.........	199,343	248,378	358,892	479,699
Saskatchewan	47,646	62,758	81,246	116,933
Manitoba.....	93,443	110,183	138,705	194,077
Ontario.........	1,137,533	1,348,035	1,881,879	2,512,213
Quebec.........	153,178	195,700	254,826	386,958
Maritimes	29,264	34,865	50,087	70,911

	Average sale price by region (in dollars)			
	1971	1972	1973	1974
Canada.........	24,548	26,851	32,315	41,114
B.C.	22,813	25,741	31,665	43,169
Alberta.........	23,549	25,056	30,144	37,293
Saskatchewan	15,856	16,718	19,225	24,970
Manitoba.....	18,358	19,488	21,441	27,619
Ontario.........	27,249	29,217	36,853	46,774
Quebec.........	23,834	25,713	26,790	32,826
Maritimes	21,533	22,566	25,490	30,539

*From the Real Estate Development Annual, 1975.

DAY ONE

And the impact of inflation could be read from a comparison of Canada's Gross National Product expressed in current dollars with the figures adjusted to "constant" dollars:

Billions of dollars

	1970	1971	1972	1973	1974	1975
GNP in current dollars	85.7	93.5	103.9	120.4	140.9	155.0*
GNP in 1971 dollars	88.4	93.5	99.1	105.9	108.9	108.7*

Note 10:
Jack Haire's rough calculation of the bid price looked liks this:

Ball-park estimate of what would be a successful bid = $20 a share. This consisted of the market price ($13 a share) plus a $7 premium as an incentive for the Price shareholders to sell. It was hoped that enough Price shareholders would be attracted by the $7 premium to enable Abitibi to buy 50% of the stock.

Cost of buying 50% of the Price stock = $100 million. Price had 9.8 million shares outstanding.

Capacity of Price's "five" newsprint mills = 3,400 tons per day. Price actually owned six mills — four completely and two 50%. Five were devoted to newsprint (one was a paperboard mill).

Cost of building newsprint mills in 1974 = $200,000 per daily ton.

Cost of building Price's mills in 1974 = $680 million.

Cost of building "50%" of Price's mills in 1974 = $340 million. If Abitibi owned 50% of Price's stock, it could be considered to own "50%" of Price's mills.

* Estimated

188

The depreciated 1974 cost of 50% of Price's mills = $250 million. Ten-year-old mills like Price's couldn't be realistically compared with the cost of building new mills, because the old mills would be "worn down" and less efficient. Price's mills had been regularly modernized and were worth about 80% of new mills of the same size.

Abitibi's saving by buying into Price instead of building = $150 million. By buying into Price, Abitibi would be paying $100 million for what would cost $250 million to replace at 1974 costs.

Note 11:
Price and Abitibi would have combined. Price and Abitibi shares would have been exchanged for stock of a new company, so that agreement on the relative value of the two stocks had been vital to any merger. Valuation is always difficult: price-earnings ratios and book values per share had been similar, but Price had been trading at about 50% higher than Abitibi. Abitibi had disputed Price's valuation of its stock, claiming it was too high.

Note 12:
At the time of the takeover investigation, this was how various important characteristics of the two companies compared:

Financial Highlights	**Price**	**Abitibi**
Net sales, 1974 ($ millions)	335	510
Net earnings, 1974 ($ millions)	35	44

Ownership	**Price**	**Abitibi**
Common shares		
authorized for issue (millions)	15	24
Common shares issued (millions)	9.8	18.1

DAY ONE

Shareholders	Price	Abitibi
Number..	9,464	25,674
Key blocks (in 1968):		
Associated Newspapers Group (%)	16.4	—
Domtar (%)	6.7	—

Common-share statistics	Price	Abitibi
Market Price,		
Nov. 13, 1974 ($)	12	9¾
1964-1974 high ($)	18	16
1964-1974 low ($)......................................	5	5
Estimated 1974		
earnings/share ($)	3.50	2.45
Estimated 1974		
equity/share ($)	20-21	14
Indicated dividend rate ($)......................	1.00	.80
Actual earnings		
per share ($)	3.22	2.50

Principal operations	Price	Abitibi
Newsprint:		
Capacity (tons per year)	1,187,000	1,300,000
Mills (number)	5	7
Mills on tidewater* (number)	2	1
Market proportion:		
North America/offshore	65/35	90/10

The Price newsprint operation had important plus factors:
Relatively good plant.
Five new machines, since 1962.
Manufacturing costs slightly lower than Abitibi's.
Know-how in the area of lightweight newsprint and chip

---

*Ocean transportation offers lower freight costs and access to foreign markets.

190

groundwood. (Conventional technology was to make groundwood
— the main component of newsprint — by grinding logs against
grindstones. Price had developed a method of making groundwood
from the chips produced as waste in sawmills, with obvious economies.)

Good management.

Price had newsprint output at five sites in Canada and the
United States:

Location:	Ownership:	Capacity (annual tons):
Alma, Que.	100% Price................	367,000
Kenogami, Que.	100% Price................	230,000
Chandler, Que.	51% Price/49% New York Times..	237,000
Grand Falls, Nfld. ..	99.8% Price...............	338,000
De Ridder, La.	50% Price, 50% Boise Cascade.....	75,000 (Price's share)

	Price	Abitibi
Kraft paper and board:		
Mills (number)...	2	2
Paper and board production (tons/year)...	110,000	70,000
Market-pulp production (tons/year)...	11,000	115,000
Building-materials (hardboard) plants (one in Canada, rest in U.S.) (number)	—	7

	Price	Abitibi
Lumber:		
Sawmills (number).................................	4	4
Capacity (1976) (millions of board feet)......................................	320	250

DAY ONE

	Price	Abitibi
Fine paper:		
Mills (number)..	—	3
Capacity (tons per year)	—	200,000

	Price	Abitibi
Converting and retail operations		
Type of papers	Coarse	Fine and corrugated
Name of company	Price-Wilson	Several

	Price	Abitibi
Mining (base metals):		
Location	Buchans	Mattabi
Partner	American Smelters	Mattagami
Earnings/share, 1974 (millions)..............	4.5 (pre-tax)	9.0

Price also owned 50% of Plastal Manufacturing Ltd., Granby, Quebec, which made acrylic cockpit canopies for aircraft and Boeing 747 flight simulators. The Price group also distributed laundry and dry-cleaning equipment in Western Canada, was a wholesaler of disinfectant soap, and operated a janitorial service in Toronto. Price also had interests in tungsten and copper deposits in Newfoundland, and minority shareholdings in four mineral and oil exploration companies.

Price's wood base was substantial. In Quebec: 18,000 square miles of forest leased from the province; and in Newfoundland: 7,500 square miles leased from the province. (Abitibi had 24,700 square miles, of which 1,000 square miles were freehold, giving Abitibi wood at no stumpage cost.)

Price's newsprint markets were split about 65%/35% between North America/Europe. In the United States, Price sold about

600,000 tons a year (6% of the market) in sizable to large accounts mainly in the Middle West. In Canada, Price had about 9% to 12% of the national newsprint market. Offshore markets were principally served by the Grand Falls mill in Newfoundland (which specialized in the lightweight paper popular in Europe).

Note 13:
If the earnings per share of a subsidiary were greater than the earnings per share generated by a new-mill company, it was obviously more profitable to buy in more shares of the subsidiary. (A sophisticated version of Powis' idea might have gone like this: Abitibi should buy its own stock in the market for cancellation, thereby distributing among the remaining shareholders the earnings attributable to the purchased and canceled stock. But only Ontario companies were permitted by law to do this. Abitibi was a federal company.)

Note 14:
Price Co. had a long, colorful history.

In 1810 the Baltic Sea was closed to shipping because of the Napoleonic Wars, and the British navy's supply of masts from Scandinavia dried up. Christopher Idle & Co., London lumber brokers, sent a Welshman, William Price, across the Atlantic to develop a new supply. Idle's manager in Quebec City sent Price up the Ottawa and St. Lawrence Rivers to raft lumber down to Quebec for shipment across to England. But after a while Price went into business for himself and built a series of sawmills along the St. Lawrence. He also bought a sawmill at Ha Ha Bay from a bankrupt group of French-Canadian lumbermen called the "Society of the Twenty-One." William Price died in 1872 and the business was carried on by his sons.

DAY ONE

By 1902, William Price & Sons had 10 sawmills in operation and had branched into the pulp business by buying Jonquiere Pulp Mill Co., a tiny groundwood producer in Jonquiere, Quebec, that had run into difficulties. In 1904 the business was incorporated as Price Bros. & Co.

In 1912, at about the same time Anson was forming Abitibi, Price decided to move into the paper business, and a newsprint mill was built at Kenogami by the same engineer who designed the Abitibi mill at Iroquois Falls. In partnership with J. B. Duke of the American Tobacco Co., a power plant was also built on the Saguenay. It produced so much power the decision was made in 1920 to build another newsprint mill at Alma, Quebec, near the other mills. In 1927, during the period when Abitibi was also expanding vigorously, Price purchased control of Donnacona Paper Co., and in a few years ran into trouble. In the early 1930s, control of Price passed out of the hands of the Price family and into the Royal Bank which was holding the family stock as collateral for a loan. In 1932, Price was declared bankrupt after defaulting on the interest due on the company's first mortgage bonds. It remained under the management of a trustee until 1937.

In 1959, Price took over J. C. Wilson Ltd. (later Price Wilson Ltd.), which manufactured bags, toweling and related products.

In 1961, the company acquired control of Anglo-Newfoundland Development Co. from Associated Newspapers, London, by a share exchange — and the process ended up with Associated Newspapers in effective control of Price. During the 1960s Price expanded its newsprint capacity and bought various other properties, such as a major interest in Plastal Manufacturing. In 1970, jointly with Boise Southern Co., Price incorporated Boise-Price Southern Newsprint Corp. and brought into production a newsprint mill at de Ridder, Louisiana.

At the time of the takeover, Price's earnings had been cyclical over the previous quarter-century — high in the early 1950s, low in the mid-1950s, high in the mid-1960s, low in the early 1970s and very high in 1974, as a result of inflation and heavy newsprint demand. With the exception of 1974, Price's earnings pattern had remained basically unchanged for the prior 25 years.

The table below shows Price's earnings per share before extraordinary items. The earnings prior to 1966, when there was a three-for-one stock split, have been adjusted to make them compatible with later figures.

Year	EPS	Year	EPS
1950	$1.37	1962	$0.84
1951	$1.27	1963	$0.89
1952	$0.89	1964	$1.32
1953	$0.89	1965	$1.14
1954	$1.20	1966	$1.25
1955	$1.36	1967	$1.10
1956	$1.34	1968	$0.76
1957	$0.97	1969	$0.95
1958	$0.84	1970	$0.41
1959	$0.87	1971	$0.11
1960	$0.79	1972	$0.67
1961	$0.89	1973	$0.78
		1974	$3.22

DAY TWO

Note 1:
Price's new capacity would be added to mills already built, and part of the expansion was a refiner groundwood plant which would enable the manufacture of newsprint from groundwood alone, thereby obviating the need for chemical pulp.

Note 2:
Background to the Arthur D. Little study.

The long-range trend line of world demand for newsprint, which had been interrupted by the economic downturn of 1970-1971, began to resume its upward curve in 1973-1974. The recession expected in 1975 (at the time of the takeover) would likely keep demand static, but the next upward move in world economies would probably produce real shortages in newsprint.

Thomas Bell's long-term view: "A shortage of wood fibre is now evident in industrialized countries where pulp and paper facilities are concentrated. Newsprint demand has increased over 50% in the last 15 years and the future should be no different. As the lead time for new mills is two to three years, and as the economics are [in 1974] not yet viable for new mills, we predict at least 10 years of shortages." *

Highlights of the Arthur D. Little study:

Newspapers

— No basic change in appearance (that would affect newsprint consumption).

— New technology would tend to offset cost increases. (The price of newsprint could rise and still not eat too hard into publishers' profits.)

— No evidence that new communications technology would adversely affect the newspaper market through 1985. (Television

---

* Bell's views were taken from an internal address made during the preliminary stage of the takeover.

196

had done its worst, and in the last decade or so there had been a tendency for advertisers to return to newspapers.)

Newsprint

— Tight supply through 1985 and a price of $490 per ton for 27-pound sheet newsprint. (Abitibi planned to charge $260 a ton on January 1, 1975, for 30-pound paper — more costly to make than 27-pound.) Little was forecasting a 10%-a-year (almost) price increase for a decade. For almost a decade in the 1950s and 1960s, the price had remained unchanged, in the face of publisher antagonism. Little also had forecast inflation of 10% a year to 1985.

— Present technology wouldn't change dramatically.

Bell's perspective: "In 1974 world demand is 25 million tons. World supply is 26.7 million tons, and that's total capacity, not effective capacity. Canada will supply 10.3 million tons in 1974, or 40% of world total, and Abitibi will supply 1.25 million tons, or roughly 5% of world total. We look for world demand by 1980 to be above 30 million tons, and at present there are no major facilities planned worldwide (because of low return on new mills). We have the prospect in this project [the Price takeover] of doubling the newsprint capacity under our control to 10% of world supply, at a low cost, thus improving profitability for our shareholders."

Note 3:
For the nine months of 1973-1974 to September 1, Abitibi had sold its newsprint at least $10 a ton below the prevailing market price (from July 1 until September 1 it had been $20 below market). Industry observers felt Abitibi simply underestimated the strength of the newsprint market when it had announced its pricing policy the previous fall. Considering that mills were running flat out throughout the industry, there was little competitive advantage for Abitibi in its lower pricing, unless perhaps in long-term customer goodwill. The company returned to the fold in September with a $20 price increase.

DAY TWO

Note 4:

About the Wood Gundy connection.

Wood Gundy Ltd. was formed in Toronto in 1905 by G. H. Wood and J. H. Gundy (the father of Charles Gundy). Initially, the firm dealt in government bonds but soon expanded into industrial underwritings. The firm is the biggest of its kind in Canada.

Few records of the connection that developed between Wood Gundy and Abitibi during the latter's receivership are available publicly. The following was taken from a eulogy of Harry Gundy published after his death in 1951:

". . . He took arms in 1937 against very powerful U.S. and Canadian interests that planned a reorganization of Abitibi Power & Paper Co. along lines which he believed would eliminate the preferred and common interests. Mr. Gundy got into this fight and continued in it against all odds because his firm had sold preferred and other securities to clients and he considered it their duty to go to the mat against any plan which did not preserve an opportunity for these holders to benefit if the company's business recovered some day . . . After years of fighting there was a favorable issue which recognized the full rights of all bond and stock issues . . ."

The Gundy family has been influential in Abitibi ever since.

Note 5:

Canada's five major pools of capital that could act within the restrictions of the Foreign Investment Review Act were:

Argus Corp. — "The company is a specialized investment company whose policy is to invest the major portion of its funds in relatively few enterprises which are considered to have long-term growth potential."*

---

*All data for Argus, Canadian Pacific, Macmillan Bloedel, and Power Corp. from Financial Post Corporation Service.

Some of the Argus background:

Fiscal year	Total assets	Securities at market value	Share-holders' equity	Total income	Net income
		(in thousands)			
	$	$	$	$	$
1974	185,491	172,199	168,468	12,649	11,696
1973	116,390	217,589	104,876	7,099	6,251
1972	104,834	214,000	94,132	5,944	5,113

Canadian Pacific Ltd. — "The company operates one of the two transcontinental railway systems in Canada. Other related operations include highway transport, cargo vessels and transportation. A subsidiary engages in non-transportation operations, including natural resources, pulp and paper, iron and steel, real estate, hotels and equipment leasing and has a substantial investment portfolio."

Fiscal year	Total assets	Fixed assets	Share-holders' equity	Net income
		(in thousands)		
	$	$	$	$
1974	5,434,527	3,774,790	1,851,076	181,276
1973	4,358,325	3,003,335	1,766,971	119,876
1972	3,895,579	2,808,655	1,714,370	94,175

Cemp Investments Ltd. — "The company is engaged exclusively in investing for gain over the long term, through income from dividends and through capital appreciation. The company's investments include large positions in both publicly traded and closely held companies, as well as other marketable securities. The holdings represent various degrees of influence, risk and potential in a variety of unrelated businesses."

At the end of that fiscal year, July 31, 1974, Cemp had held in-

DAY TWO

vestments worth $80.5 million at cost. Its total assets at the end of fiscal 1974 had been more than $221.6 million, and it had earned more than $3 million of net profit during the year.*

MacMillan Bloedel Ltd. — "The company, with its subsidiaries, is engaged in timber operations and the manufacture and marketing of pulp, paper and lumber products."

Fiscal year	Total assets	Investments, etc.	Shareholders' equity	Net sales	Net income
		(in thousands)			
	$	$	$	$	$
1974	1,200,063	93,955	513,447	1,396,330	72,299
1973	1,016,092	51,128	472,171	1,215,191	81,752
1972	904,429	37,690	404,043	964,190	35,033

Power Corp. of Canada — "The company is an investment and management company which has as its main operating subsidy, Canada Steamship Lines Ltd."

Fiscal year	Total assets	Investments at book value	Shareholders' equity	Gross income	Net income
		(in thousands)			
	$	$	$	$	$
1974	495,088	288,533	332,689	223,492	37,847
1973	457,791	255,684	296,369	242,767	30,959
1972	422,690	246,699	268,702	170,002	17,545

*All data for Cemp from the company's annual report for the year ended July 31, 1974.

Note 6:

What's a cross?

A broker matches a "buy" order with an identical "sell" order off the exchange, and makes the transaction through the exchange. The transaction is usually arranged privately between the two principals and, for legal reasons or convenience, crossed through the exchange by a broker acting for both sides. If Abitibi had decided to buy out the whole Associated Newspapers block of Price stock first, it might have arranged a price privately with the British, then tried to have the stock crossed by Wood Gundy.

If a cross is at a price above the market, exchange regulations require that the buyer purchase all stock offered at prices ranging from market up to the special price.

On any day, for any stock, the exchange floor traders are likely to have "ask" orders ("sell" orders as opposed to "bid" or "buy" orders) at prices above the market, given by clients hoping the market will rise high enough to enable them to get out of their stock at higher-than-market prices. These "ask" orders must be mopped up with the cross to prevent the public exchange being used entirely for private convenience.

Note 7:

What is a takeover bid? The Ontario Securities Act defined one this way:

" 'Takeover bid' means an offer other than an exempt offer made to shareholders [resident in Ontario] to purchase such number of equity shares of a company that, together with the offeror's presently owned shares, will in the aggregate exceed 20% of the outstanding equity shares of the company."

"The period of time within which shares may be deposited pursuant to a takeover bid shall not be less than 21 days from the date thereof ..."

"A takeover bid shall be sent by prepaid mail to the offerees and shall be deemed conclusively to have been dated as of the date on which it was sent."

"A takeover bid circular shall form part of or accompany a takeover bid."

"Every takeover bid circular shall contain the information prescribed . . ."

What *isn't* a takeover bid? This is what the Ontario Securities Act had to say:

" 'Exempt offer' means:

"(i) an offer to purchase shares by way of private agreement with fewer than 15 shareholders and not made to shareholders generally.

"(ii) an offer to purchase shares to be effected through the facilities of a stock exchange or in the over-the-counter market . . .

"(iii) an offer to purchase shares in a private company, or

"(iv) an offer exempted by order of the Commission . . ."

Note 8:
How to take over a public company in Canada. There are four basic methods.

1. *By stampede*:*

Your broker announces on the floor of the exchange that you'll pay a high premium (perhaps 30% to 50% above the market price) for the target stock, then he stands back and waits for the rush.

---

* At the time this book went to press the "stampede" route was blocked by the Ontario Securities Commission.

2. *The gentleman's way:*

Mail a circular to all shareholders of the target company, declaring your intentions honorable, detailing your credentials and naming a decent price. Then wait 21 days (prescribed by law) to allow the shareholders to carefully consider your offer and to permit anybody else who wants the company to offer them a higher price.

3. *By creeping and pouncing:*

Buy stock slowly and secretly on the exchange until you have enough to exercise control.

4. *By wheeling and dealing:*

Buy enough stock privately from less than 15 people.

There are varying advantages, disadvantages and inconsistencies attached to these takeover methods.

Advantages

For the raider

The stampede is quick; there's no time for competitors to bid. It could be cheap if the market is very depressed.

The gentleman's way: He can withdraw the offer if not enough stock is tendered. Can offer cash or securities.

For the shareholder

The stampede offers a fast sale for a good cash price that's easily understandable. If he tenders stock, he knows some must be bought.

The gentleman's way: He has good time to consider the offer; its purpose is explained in full. There's a legal cooling-off period in which he can withdraw his stock again. Maximum opportunity for competition for his stock.

DAY TWO

Creeping and pouncing: If lucky, he can buy the stock at the market price. Needs little planning. Can change his mind at any time.

Creeping and pouncing: None whatsoever.

Wheeling and dealing: Easier to control; few people to deal with; not covered by regulations.

Wheeling and dealing: The big shareholder can negotiate. But the small shareholder gets no advantage.

Disadvantages

For the raider

For the shareholder

The stampede: Controversial; authorities might intervene and rules might change. He must buy all stock offered, and that could be less than control. Must pay cash — no securities. Once made, offer can't be withdrawn.

The stampede: Competition for his stock is inhibited by the speed.

The gentleman's way: Gives time for competitors to enter the bidding and push up the price.

The gentleman's way: No certainty any of his stock will be sold. It can be confusing, even bewildering, to read one or more complicated circulars.

Creeping and pouncing: He must report new holdings once a month once holdings reach 10% of all shares outstanding, every three days when 20% or more. The only practical use of this route, without alerting competitors, is to buy effective control with less than 20% of the stock.

Wheeling and dealing: Fourteen people may not hold enough stock for absolute control. Then the raider must get the rest by some other method.

Creeping and pouncing: He doesn't know somebody is buying the stock. If he sells, he gets only the market price.

Wheeling and dealing: The big shareholder has none. But the small shareholder is out in the cold.

Criticisms

From securities commissions

The stampede: Makes use of a loophole in the law; not well enough regulated. May not allow enough time for news of the bid to reach all shareholders.

From the exchanges

The stampede: Exchange regulations are still under development.

From small shareholders

The stampede: Too much rush; big shareholders may have an advantage because they get better service and quicker news from brokers. Relies too much on brokers; if the shareholder has no broker, he gets no advice and perhaps no news of the bid.

DAY TWO

The gentleman's way: None. If properly conducted, it conforms fully to the law as drafted.

Creeping and pouncing: Secrecy is undesirable.

Wheeling and dealing: None.

The gentleman's way: Makes no use of brokers; shareholders may receive no advice on what could be a share-exchange offer explained in an arcane circular.

Creeping and pouncing: None.

Wheeling and dealing: Uneasy about fairness to the public.

The gentleman's way: Can be very confusing if two bidders offer him securities that only a sophisticated analyst can evaluate. Any single circular may be difficult to understand.

Creeping and pouncing: Unfair to those not in the know. May wake up one day and find somebody undesirable in control.

Wheeling and dealing: Small shareholders don't receive the premiums paid to the big boys (in fact, the little guys don't even sell their stock). Somebody undesirable may gain control.

There's obviously considerable inconsistency in the regulations governing takeovers. To achieve essentially the same takeover the raider can go any of four different routes and be subject to four different sets of rules and philosophies. The four variables that affect the fairness of the bid to the target-company shareholder are: *time* (the disclosure/dissemination/decision period); *information* (what he's told about the bid); *price* (what he's offered); and *competition* (the possibility or encouragement of other bids).

The stampede. The philosophy of regulation here is very confused.

Time: The Ontario Securities Commission wants a longer period, but not 21 days.

Information: There are no regulations now or contemplated.

Price: There are no regulations now or contemplated. The raider pays market price plus an incentive-to-sell premium.

Competition: The extension of time would permit more competition, but there's no clear policy on the extent to which competition should be encouraged. There's no thinking about the minimum time needed for a competitor to work up his bid.

The gentleman's way: There are some oddities in this area as well.

Time: The legal minimum, 21 days, is a long period. In these days of postal strikes and fast telecommunications, it seems absurd that information has to be *mailed* to shareholders rather than, say, telephoned or delivered by other means.

Information: This is closely regulated. The raider must disclose his identity, corporate details and so forth.

Price: There are no regulations. The raider pays the market price plus an incentive-to-sell premium.

Competition: The 21 days allows any competitor time to work up his bid.

Creeping and pouncing. This area provides a stark contrast to the others.

Time: No takeover bid is made, so there can be no regulations. Nor are there regulations about the length of time over which control may be bought.

Information: There are no regulations about what the shareholder is told about the raider, his purpose, or the price he's paying, but there are strict rules about disclosing how much stock the raider has bought.

Price: There are no regulations. The raider pays the market price.

Competition: Disclosure of raider's holdings tends to alert competition.

Wheeling and dealing. There's no regulation at all now. But the Ontario Securities Commission early in 1975 proposed blocking this route permanently by an amendment to a new draft Securities Act.

Time: None.

Information: None.

Price: None. The raider pays a negotiated price related to market, book value and perhaps asset replacement value, plus a *control* premium.

Competition: None.

The greatest policy confusion is in the area of *price.* The market price of stock is established by public auction on the exchange. In the stampede, the slight encouragement of competition tends to create an auction of the bid premium. Under the gentleman's way, there's full scope for auctioning of the premium (by competitors offering the shareholders a variety of bids). In creeping and pouncing, there's no auction and no premium. And in wheeling and dealing the big shareholders receive a *control* premium for their stock, while the little shareholders can only sell in the market.

The premium offered by the bidder under the various methods has a triple nature.

1. There's *a straight incentive to sell.* The shareholders of the target company are offered a price higher than market to induce them to sell at the time the raider wants to take control.

2. There's *a control premium.* Shareholders of the target company are paid a premium for their individual portions of "control" that the raider acquires by buying their shares. The concept of a

control premium is well accepted where the "raider" actually buys control by private negotiation with a major shareholder, but buys no stock from the others.

3. The premium may be *a dividend.* If the raider gains sufficient control of the target company, he may later pay himself and the remaining minority shareholders a dividend. The raider could use it to help pay off the money borrowed to make the raid. In effect, the cash within the target company can be divided three ways: part to the remaining minority shareholders in the form of the extra dividend; part to the raider now in control; and part, in the form of the premium, to the shareholders who sold their stock. The transaction can be equitable to all parties — for example, when the bid is at or above book value per share of the target company and the dividends paid after control from earnings retained before control are no greater than the premium.

Note 9:
About the troublesome legal question of control.

The success of Abitibi's bid for Price at this stage appeared to depend on the company's being able to skirt the legal definitions of control and yet still gain undisputed control of Price. Here are the many ways in which one company can be controlled. They illustrate the inconsistency of the law and the problems faced by the lawmakers in deriving an adequate universal definition.

1. Absolute control: With more than 50% of a company's stock, control can never be upset, though it's conceivable that Company A could hold 51% of Company B's stock and choose not to exercise effective control because of indifference or the high quality of B's management. Most Canadian law assumes that control occurs above 50%, and various absurdities occasionally occur. In 1972, control of Ontario Trust Co. passed out of Canada in violation of the spirit of the Ontario Loan & Trust Corporations Act, which seeks to prevent this happening. Clear legal control of Ontario

DAY TWO

Trust was held by Hambro Canada (1972) Ltd., but, because Hambro was only effectively (42%) controlled by a British banking group, the Ontario cabinet took the view that control of Ontario Trust did not lie outside Canada.

2. Under normal circumstances, unshakeable control of a widely held public corporation can be maintained with 35%-40% of the stock. Unless management proves itself flagrantly incompetent, it's unlikely the remaining shareholders could be organized into effective opposition.

3. Effective control begins at 20% for the purposes of the takeover provisions of the various provincial securities acts. This is an arbitrary figure. Effective control can be and is exercised in Canadian corporations from 100% down to 0%.

4. The federal Foreign Investment Review Act presumes control can be exercised at 5%, and any public company with a non-Canadian holding 5% of its stock or more must seek federal cabinet approval for any Canadian acquisitions it seeks to make.

5. Non-ownership control can be exercised with few or no shares:

— By option. If the control person holds an option to buy say 50% of the stock, he can say: "Implement my corporate policies or I'll exercise my option and you'll be out of the company altogether."

— Voting others' stock. A small Canadian trust company is believed to be effectively controlled by its management through their voting shares of the company's stock held in the trust accounts. The company's management also, of course, determine the stock-buying policy of the trust accounts.

— Management control. Price and Abitibi were both controlled by their managements. Price management ran the company without much intervention by the "controlling" shareholder, Associated Newspapers. Abitibi was also controlled by management. It would appear easy in such a situation to organize shareholders to vote in a new control group, but, while Abitibi management was performing well, institutions holding the stock would resist change.

210

DAY TWO

For the success of the Price project, Abitibi might have to thread its way around three legal definitions of control: At one point Abitibi would have to avoid being classified as a non-Canadian under the Foreign Investment Review Act, even though there was a possibility more than 5% of its stock would be given to a non-Canadian; the bid had to be exempted from the takeover (20%-plus) provisions of the securities acts; and Abitibi hoped to obtain clear, effective control of Price (with 49%) without triggering designated-surplus tax (at 50%-plus).

Note 10:
About the designated surplus consideration.

Dividends paid from one taxable Canadian public corporation to another owning its shares normally flow free of tax because they're already taxed (that is, they come out of taxed profits). But when the investor corporation acquires *absolute* control (more than 50%) of the dividend-paying corporation, a large part of the subsidiary's retained earnings (profit kept rather than paid out as dividends) may become "designated surplus" under the Income Tax Act. If the parent causes dividends to be paid out of this "designated surplus," the dividends are taxable at a rate varying from 15% to 25%. If dividends annually are less than earnings, no tax is payable.

If the parent has *effective* control rather than *absolute* control, there's no tax on dividends paid. At 49%, the parent would have almost as much effective control over its subsidiary's dividend policy as at 51%. Therefore at 49% the parent has powerful control over the flow of tax-free dividends.

Merger from a 51% position triggers the tax, because the two companies combine and the surplus is deemed to be paid from one to the other. Merger from 49% does not.

DAY FIVE

Note 1:
Thomas J. Bell was born in Southampton, Ontario, on June 26, 1914, and educated at Ridley College and the University of Toronto (B.Comm.). After graduation in 1936, Bell went to work as an accountant with Federal Wire & Cable Co., Guelph, Ontario, which had only 35 employees. "It was a happy little company and it just grew like Topsy," Bell said later. "The thing that I could do well to make it grow was to sell wire and cable. I ended up as executive vice-president."

In 1955 (after war service 1942-1946), a friend of Bell's asked him to go to Toronto and head Fiberglas Canada Ltd. (which was owned by Owens Corning Fiberglas and Duplate Canada). "This company was just beginning to go," Bell said. "It had sales of about $15 million and it was making a breakthrough in the field of insulation and textiles. I came in when they were having a difficult political fight between the two partners and they needed somebody in the middle to fend them off and make it grow independently. That company grew very quickly."

In 1965 Bell was appointed chairman of the board of trustees of the Toronto General Hospital. Earlier, in gratitude for the saving of the life of one of his children, he'd agreed to head a fund-raising campaign for Toronto's Hospital for Sick Children. Charles Gundy was chairman of that hospital and a director. "I got to admire his abilities," Gundy said later. "His big asset is he can get people to work with him."

In 1967 Bell was appointed president and chief executive officer of Abitibi, and in 1973 he became chairman and chief executive officer.

212

DAY SIX

Note 1:

About the development of official thinking on stock-exchange takeovers.

The *Report of the Committee of the Ontario Securities Commission on the Problems of Disclosure Raised for Investors by Business Combinations and Private Placements*, published in 1970, hints that at that time the commission hadn't envisaged a takeover being achieved entirely by a quickie exchange raid. The report stated:

"Market Purchases . . . The second class of exempt offer, purchases in the market place, have been scrutinized not only in the light of the Canadian Breweries takeover but other acquisitions in which the takeover involved both a circular and purchases in the market place. The theory of the exemption is straightforward. No special effort is made to force the offeree shareholder to sell. He bases his decision on the market price of the securities and, when a formal takeover bid is outstanding for part of the shares, may be influenced into taking the lower market price by the fact that he can dispose of all and not merely part of his holdings.

"While the Committee agrees that this exemption should be continued we have concluded that the fact that a material change of control is occurring or is about to occur in the target company is an important item of investment information. It is within the basic objectives of the Commission's 'timely disclosure' policy. We have considered the methods of achieving this at some length. In the United States recent amendments to the '34 Act have barred takeovers in the market place without disclosure. The 'City Code' [in Britain] requires that the offer should first be placed before the board of the offereee company or its advisers. Although trading is permitted through the London Stock Exchange for all the outstanding shares, the purchases must be reported to the Exchange on a daily basis and made public. We are suggesting another solution.

"We have concluded that the 'insider' whose holdings reach 20% as the result of market purchases should be required, as a matter of timely investor information, to report the fact of his pur-

213

DAY SIX

chases within three days of reaching 20%. In this, and in other connections, we have examined the definition in section 108 which, in subsection 1(c) (ii), speaks of anyone who 'beneficially owns, directly or indirectly, equity shares of a corporation carrying more than 10% of the voting rights attached to all equity shares of the corporation for the time being outstanding . . .' We recommend that the excuse for delay in reporting built into the concept of ownership should be removed by deeming the purchaser to own the shares on the day the market order is executed. Any excuse for delaying reporting will be removed. We further recommend that the three-day reporting requirement should continue as each additional 5% is achieved, i.e. 25%, 30%, etc. The question of intention to acquire control was considered and rejected on the basis that purchases, even when effected through far flung nominees, are more certain of compilation than an intent which can only by crystallized with certainty once 50% has been exceeded.

"The question of whether there should be the equivalent of a takeover bid circular available once the purchaser achieved 20% was considered and rejected.

"Uncertainty does arise where the offeror states in the takeover bid circular that it intends contemporaneously to purchase in the market and will reduce the number of shares it will take through the takeover bid by the number it has purchased in the market. This, among other things, led us to consider prohibiting market purchases while a formal takeover bid is outstanding. While recommending against the latter we do recommend that for certainty, where the offeror elects to purchase in the market as well as through a takeover bid, he must announce his intention in the circular and shall be prohibited from reducing the minimum number of shares he will take under the offer by the shares purchased in the market," the report stated.

The 1973 *Report on Mergers, Amalgamations and Certain Related Matters*, by Ontario's Select Committee on Company Law, also failed to realize the potential of the stock-exchange route:

"Market purchases during a takeover bid . . . The Committee

214

can find no compelling reason why an offeror should be prevented from purchasing shares in the market during the course of a takeover bid, particularly if, in the case of a partial bid, the recommendation of the Committee in section 3 of Chapter 12 are implemented."

There's no reference to an exchange raid.

Note 2:

About Price Co.'s book value (net worth) per share.

At the end of 1973, Price's shareholders' equity (net worth) was $182.6 million. To calculate net worth per share: deduct the par value of 37,500 $100-par peference shares ($3.7 million), to get $179 million. Divide that by 9.8 million outstanding common shares, to get $18.27 per share. Price was expected to earn a net profit of about $3 per share (it actually earned $3.22) in 1974. This (less annual dividend rate of $1 per share) would boost retained earnings by about $2 per share and bring the net worth up to about $20 per share. (Precise 1974 earnings and dividend figures weren't known to Abitibi in November.)

Note 3:

About the bid price and price-earnings ratio.

At this stage Haire talked of a bid price of $18 to $20 per share which was about six times 1974 earnings and about 50% above the market price of $13 per share. The price-earnings ratio within Haire's bid price, six, compared well with the industry average of four at the time.

DAY SIX

Note 4:
About a company's many values, and who looks at which.

To a shareholder: If the company has nine million common shares outstanding, each share represents one nine-millionth of the collective ownership of the company. To a small shareholder, however, the value of a share (ignoring dividend payments) is *the price at which other investors will buy or sell it.*

To a potential investor: The *dividend* per share paid annually by the company (compared with return on other investments) and the *anticipated increase* in the value (market price) of his shares.

To a parent company: The company's *earnings*, which can be consolidated into the parent's earnings. Earnings per share is an important measure because (a) it indicates change in the company's ability to pay dividends, (b) it indicates rate of growth of the company's net worth, because some earnings are retained, and (c) it's also the starting-point for highly sophisticated calulations of what value will be placed on the shares in the marketplace. Earnings per share is also the "return on investment" for the price paid for the stock, but this relationship is really arbitrary, because a shareholder with five shares can't participate in the company's earnings the way a corporate parent can by consolidating them into its own.

To an accountant: The *book value* (also known as *net worth* and *shareholders' equity*), which is the value of what the company owns (its assets) less all its debts. In theory book value should be the absolute or real (true) value of the company, but it's merely a bench mark, because the value of assets written into the books may bear no relationship (for historic-cost accounting reasons) to the price at which they could be sold to pay off the debts.

To a raiding corporation: The raider has two choices: to build plants itself or buy a company with plants. Its decision must relate to the *replacement cost of the target company's assets* — in other words, what it would cost more or less to duplicate them identically? Replacement cost isn't truly a *value* of the company; it's merely an indicator of whether the target is a good buy. Its use can also involve complex calculations because no two factories are ever

216

identical, more modern ones usually being more efficient than older ones, and replacement cost must be examined in the light of earning power.

A raiding corporation must also look at all the other measures of value because it will become an investor and a parent company, will employ accountants to write its newly bought acquisition into its own books and must justify the price paid for the target company's shares to its own shareholders.

Note 5:

About Domtar's accounting of its Price holdings.

Domtar carried the Price shares on its books at historic cost — even though that was meaningless in terms of inflated value paid — because, if they were carried at market price, losses and profits would have to be accounted for each year. The company would be expected to resist selling the shares at less than the meaningless historic cost, because to let them go at less would involve a big writeoff in the year they were sold.

Note 6:

About Domtar's sales and profits.

Total sales in 1974 rose by 37% to $898 million. Net profit doubled to $82.5 million from $40.5 million in 1973. Here are the contributions to sales by division:

	1974	1973
Pulp & paper*	$623 million (69%)	$442 million (67%)
Construction materials..	$144 million (16%)	$122 million (19%)
Chemicals	$131 million (14%)	$ 92 million (14%)

*Newsprint accounted for about 12% of total sales or less than one fifth of total pulp and paper sales.

DAY SIX

Note 7:

About Domtar's view of the Arthur D. Little study.

It's known that Domtar was less impressed by the optimism of the study than Abitibi, but it's not known why. It's possible that Little's credibility as a consultant of international stature had been damaged by its experience with the Manitoba government over the Churchill Forest Industries (Manitoba) Ltd. complex at The Pas.

The Manitoba government claimed that Arthur D. Little's performance as a consultant to the Manitoba Development Fund (which was disbursing public funds for construction of the complex) was a factor in a $35-million fraud allegedly perpetrated on the fund by the owners of Churchill Forest Industries. A negligence suit was launched against Arthur D. Little by the government of Manitoba. The suit was still on early in 1976.

An inquiry commission into The Pas complex also concluded that Arthur D. Little had used unrealistically low wood-cost figures in a study in the early 1960s designed to attract a paper-mill builder to The Pas.

Note 8:

About certain costs and benefits of the takeover to Abitibi.*

1. Servicing the debt (cash flow concept).
(a) At a bid price of $20 per Price share:
Price capitalization: 9.8 million common shares.
Cost of 4.8 million shares (49%) comes to $96 million.

---

* Normal practice would be to make a financial analysis over a period of perhaps five years. However, no earnings projections have been made available to the author, and 1975 earnings of Price and Abitibi were badly distorted by the effects of a strike. The analysis therefore has been limited (unsatisfactorily) to 1974 results. If a five-year period could be examined, it would be possible, for instance, to calculate a return on the Abitibi investment.

Interest charges on $96 million at 10% come to $9.6 million a year (pre-tax earnings).

Interest cost in after-tax earnings (tax rate, 42%) amounts to $5.6 million.

Price's dividend rate (established for 1974 on November 1) equals $1 per share.

Dividends payable to Abitibi (with 49% of the stock) amount to $4.8 million (tax-free).

(b) At a bid price of $18 per Price share:

Cost of 4.8 million shares (49%) comes to $86.4 million.

Interest charges on $86.4 million at 10% amount to $8.6 million a year (pre-tax).

Interest cost in after-tax earnings comes to $5 million.

Dividends accruing to Abitibi amount to $4.8 million (tax-free).

Therefore, assuming that Price's dividend rate could be held up once control had been achieved, the dividends paid to Abitibi would almost entirely cover interest payments.

2. Earnings purchased.

Price's 1974 earnings amount to $3.22 per share.

Attributable to Abitibi's 4.8 million shares: $15.45 million.

Cost of purchasing those earnings: $5 million to $5.6 million.

Net earnings gain equals $9.85 million to $10.45 million.

These earnings aren't payable to Abitibi. They represent dividends payable and retained earnings — which remain in the company and increase its net worth to the owners.

3. When would Abitibi start to lose by the investment?

Cost of purchasing Price control equals $5 to $5.6 million.

Number of shares purchased: 4.8 million.

Therefore, Price earnings must fall below $1.10 per share (one third of its 1974 earnings) before Abitibi would be taking a loss on

DAY SIX

the investment.* (And this completely ignores the synergism effect.) Earnings forecast (made in November 1974) for Price Co. for 1975 — came to $2.75 a share.

4. Forecast effect on Abitibi's earnings per share.

Earnings to Abitibi: $15.45 million (on the basis of 1974 results) plus $3.5 million for synergism.† Less the $5-million cost of acquisition.

Abitibi's earnings per share in 1974: $2.65 (as anticipated in November).

Abitibi's net earnings gain: $14 million (1974 basis) on 18 million shares.

Net earnings gain per share forecast: about 75¢ per share.

Therefore, after the acquisition, Abitibi's earnings per share would rise from $2.65 to $3.40 on a theoretical 1974 basis. Benefits should accrue to Abitibi shareholders in higher dividends and higher market prices for their stock.

* Any reduction of the Price dividend would reduce Abitibi's cash flow.
† Six-million-dollar total savings due to transportation savings resulting from one mill delivering to nearby customers of the other, rationalization of production among the mills and so forth. Part of these savings would go to Price; $3.5 million was the Abitibi share, forecast in November 1974.

DAY SEVEN

Note 1:
The work list of Ian McGibbon was a remarkable document. While it dealt with the specific business at hand, it also was a brief guide to the whole complex art of takeover — an art that was, of course, McGibbon's specialty. His work list follows. (In the "second-letter" code, B is Abitibi and R is Price.)

Legal matters

U.S. anti-trust questions:
— Is the transaction likely to be attacked [by the Justice Department] and if so, would the attack be successful? What remedies are available? And how quickly could they be enforced? Could either B or R be forced to divest itself of its U.S. mill?
— In what way can B structure the transaction to minimize the risks involved? [Would it make any difference if Abitibi bought, say, 40%, 49%, 51% or 80% of Price first, then the rest of the shares later, or all the shares at once? As a parent company moves along the 0%-100% ownership spectrum of its subsidiary, all sorts of legal effects are triggered as it passes various magic numbers.]
— Is there any way to obtain advance assurance on these questions from a U.S. government agency on a confidential basis? [Wishful thinking. No government agency would give assurances on a takeover in which the companies weren't identified.]

Canadian legal questions:
— Verify that the combined company would not dominate any part of the Canadian market to a degree that would present a problem under Canadian combines legislation. [Baillie had given assurances, but a written legal opinion was needed.]
— How does the Ontario Securities Commission interpret the exemption available for a stock-exchange transaction? [A delicate question from which success might hang by a gossamer thread.]
— Educate McGibbon on the conventional takeover ap-

221

DAY SEVEN

proaches that do not rely on the exemption. [Just in case . . .]

— Does the Quebec Companies Act permit a shareholder with 90% (or other high proportion) of a subsidiary's stock to force the remaining shareholders to sell in their shares? [The 1973 Ontario Select Committee on Company Law summarized the matter this way: "The legislation of certain jurisdictions in Canada affords an offeror corporation in connection with a takeover bid the opportunity to acquire 100% of the shares of the offeree corporation . . . where . . . the offeror corporation has acquired 90% of such shares. This right is given by the Canada Corporations Act, and by the . . . Companies Acts of the provinces of Alberta, British Columbia, Nova Scotia, Quebec and Saskatchewan. The right existed in Manitoba but was dropped . . . a few years ago. The right has never existed in Ontario nor . . . in the United States."]

— What procedures are available under Quebec Companies Act for electing a majority of R's board of directors after B acquires controlling ownership of R's shares? [Normally, directors resign when their company is no longer in control. In a contested takeover, they might refuse to go.]

— Assess any influence of the Foreign Investment Review Act on the takeover. Could Associated Newspapers, controlled as it is in Britain, compete with Abitibi under the act for control of Price? [Associated was already in effective control, so what did the act say about its increasing its holdings?]

— Ensure that in Stage Two [Abitibi's bringing its Price holdings up to 100% prior to merger] B does not become non-Canadian under the act. [That is, by giving Abitibi stock to foreigners such as Associated Newspapers in exchange for Price stock. The foreign-investment act presumes a public corporation is a "non-eligible person" (non-Canadian) if 25% of its stock is held by non-Canadians or if 5% is held by any one non-Canadian. Stage Two of Abitibi's plan existed as a theoretical concept necessary for the proper analysis of Stage One.]

222

DAY SEVEN

Financial questions

— Analyze the trust deeds and share conditions of both B and R to determine the restrictions on the first and second stages of the takeover, and B's ability to finance the takeover. [Abitibi mustn't generate borrowing needs greater than permitted in the trust deeds. Both companies had to be analyzed, because after the takeover Price's borrowing power would be added to Abitibi's]

— Develop a five-year projection of B's and R's external cash requirements. [How much more than the cost of Price's shares will Abitibi have to borrow for itself and Price between 1975 and 1980?]

— Would the borrowing needed exceed Abitibi's limit? [These questions were part of an attempt to think the takeover "right through," insisted on by Charles Gundy and James Tory, who were concerned that Abitibi might gain control of Price only to find it had bitten off more than it could chew. Equally, they wanted Abitibi to make sure the option of going forward to Stage Two was open even though the company might later say no.]

— Is B limited by borrowing capacity or any other factor from acquiring 51% of R's shares in the first stage of the takeover?

— Should the first stage be limited to acquiring only 49% of R's shares? Is there a designated surplus problem?

— Verify that the interest on the funds borrowed to finance the takeover is tax-deductible. [This would have a powerful effect on the value of Price to Abitibi. If interest weren't tax-deductible (it is), cost of the financing would be almost double.]

Political questions

— Would B headquartered in Ontario face any political problems in Quebec by acquiring control of R? [Would the Quebec government, anxious that control of Price not leave the province, prevent an Abitibi takeover or attempt to buy control of Price itself? Only events would show.]

DAY SEVEN

— Are there any Newfoundland problems an Ontario company would face in acquiring a Quebec company with a mine in Newfoundland? [Another question asked more out of prudence than real concern.]

— Might the takeover be attacked for Canadian federal government political reasons? [Improbable.]

Business questions

— What will be the problems and lost opportunities in B, R and B-R between the first stage of takeover [49%-51%] and the second-stage concept [100%]? [In other words, how fast should Abitibi go to 100% once that move was decided?]

—Is D* really planning a takeover of R, and what lead time might D have over B? If true, what can B do? [That is, how could Abitibi thwart a rival takeover?]

— Arrange for Wood Gundy's stock trader to enquire of his contact in D if its 7% block of R shares would be available if Wood Gundy had a customer. Bean indicates this is a question normally asked in the course of business and should arouse no suspicion. [If Domtar weren't planning a takeover, maybe it would sell.]

Structuring the takeover

— Pros and cons of purchasing either or both of the large blocks prior to, or coincident with, the first stage. Determine how D's 7% block could be locked up prior to our offer without arousing suspicion. [The only possibility seemed to be buying it through Wood Gundy.]

— Can anything other than cash be offered in the first stage — B's common stock, redeemable preferred or debentures, or some combination? [It depended on the route: only cash if the stock-ex-

---

* Domtar. Here McGibbon broke away from the "second-letter" code.

change route were taken, cash or securities if there were a formal offer.]

— Have we irrevocably rejected an approach to R leading to a friendly amalgamation of B and R? [The answer would be yes. Nobody at Abitibi was confident that such talks would be any more fruitful than in 1969.]

— Is it practical to consider a gradual acquisition of R's shares beginning with, say, acquisition of D's block? [No. Abitibi would have to declare its Price holdings above 10% each month and above 20% within three days of each 5% increase. The cat would then be out of the bag and among the pigeons.]

— If cash is used in the first stage [49%-51%], the sellers of R's shares will have to pay capital-gains tax. [The eight-year high of Price stock since a split in 1966 was $18⅞ in 1973. If $18-$20 were paid by Abitibi, many Price shareholders would show a capital gain.] Can the purchase of stock at any stage be designed so that it will not attract capital-gains tax for the seller and therefore make the sale of shares to Abitibi more attractive]?

— Can we trace the identity and residence of R's shareholders [in case a a circular was to be mailed] without arousing undue suspicion? [By law any person can buy one share of a company and exercise his shareholders' right to demand that the trust company acting as transfer agent show him the list of shareholders. But a transfer agent will usually report such requests back to the company, and that would arouse suspicion.]

Note 2:
About the Royal Bank of Canada.

The Royal was Canada's biggest bank (and it still is). At October 31, 1974, the bank operated 1,382 branches and sub-branches in Canada and 88 in other countries, while subsidiaries and affiliates operated 89 locations. It had close to 30,000 employees.

The bank was originally chartered as the Merchants Bank of

DAY SEVEN

Halifax under the laws of the province of Nova Scotia in 1869. Since 1871 the bank had been a chartered bank under the Bank Act (Canada). In 1901 the name was changed to the current one and the bank's head office was moved from Halifax to Montreal in 1907.*

Fiscal year	Total assets	Loans	Share-holders' equity	Total revenue	Net income
		(in thousands)			
	$	$	$	$	$
1974	21,669,880	12,713,031	516,786	1,917,154	62,102
1973	18,363,535	9,972,051	491,274	1,251,797	57,894
1972	14,767,516	8,111,053	442,309	943,128	51,399

Note 3:

About Charles Gundy's directorships.

The Gundy entry in the 1973-74 edition of Directory of Directors read as follows:

"GUNDY, Charles L., LL.D. (hon.); chm. Wood Gundy Ltd., P.O. Box 274, Royal Trust Tower, Toronto-Dominion Centre, Toronto, Ont. M5K 1J5; vice-pres. and dir. United Corporations Ltd.; dir. of: Massey-Ferguson Ltd., Domtar Ltd., Simpsons Ltd., Canadian Niagara Power Co. Ltd., Canron Ltd., The Dominion Life Assurance Co., Abitibi Paper Co. Ltd., Simpsons-Sears Ltd., Canada Cement Lafarge Ltd. Home: 43 Russell Hill Rd., Toronto, Ont. M4V 2S9."

*All data from Financial Post Corporation Service.

DAY EIGHT

Note 1:
About Abitibi's sensitivity to anti-trust matters.

The company's attitude could be attributed to the "race memory" of the newsprint industry, which sorely recalled being probed, investigated, analyzed, challenged, abused and bullied by American publishers, government committees and senators — all of whom had tried to prove for decades that the industry was monopolistic, addicted to price fixing, a cartel or a hated "trust." As recently as 1957 one senator had told the Senate that the newsprint industry "resembled a colossal spider web spanning the whole of Canada, extending across the United States border and down into our own Southern States. Lurking somewhere within that web is the spider himself . . . Like helpless flies, the smaller publishers have been squeezed to death. Larger publishers fight for their lives . . ."

Before the 1920s, when there'd been attempts at forming steel, cement and soap trusts, there may have been some truth to the accusations that the industry's ambition was to deliberately control prices, markets and production for its own benefit. Some manufacturers had even been fined for attempting to do so. In the 1930s, Canadian governments had encouraged newsprint companies to hold uniform prices; this had been done to help a shattered industry recover from the Depression. Yet for 40 years, successive United States government committees, set up almost every time the price of newsprint had risen, had found no evidence of pernicious business practices. Several of them, though, had felt free to claim they believed there were such practices, despite the lack of proof. In more recent years, the absurdity of these repetitive, futile committees had been recognized, and complaints against the industry seemed to have died away.

The newsprint industry had suffered more anti-trust investigations than any other because its customers, newspaper publishers, had practical politics as well as sacred ideology on their side. What publicity-hungry senator would dare tell a united newspaper industry it was being unfair or paranoid when it complained about

DAY EIGHT

"conspiracies" in the newsprint industry? Equally, the press could condemn increases in the price of newsprint with such emotion-charged language as "a tax on knowledge" or an "economic attack on the freedom of the press." If the newsprint industry sold its product to candy manufacturers, the story would have been different.

American newspapers had started to abandon high-quality rag papers for wood-pulp newsprint paper in the 1870s, and, from the beginning, the newly established newsprint manufacturers found they'd built too much capacity for the market.

What happened between 1878 and the turn of the century was only the first example of the dreary, inevitable cycle — of high prices, anti-trust investigations, business slump and low prices and of attempts to discipline production being disrupted by rough competition from mavericks — that would characterize the industry until now, and maybe always.

In 1878, the melancholy manufacturers in the United States had formed the American Paper Manufacturers Association, through which they attempted to co-operate to cut production and hold up prices, but the scheme failed because some mills refused to honor the agreement.

In 1879, an unexpected boom had created a shortage and the price of newsprint rose sharply. The publishers were reluctant to allow the laws of supply and demand have their unbridled effect on price, and at their instigation several bills were introduced into Congress proposing removal or lowering of tariffs on newsprint and pulp. The idea was that competition from Canada would help keep the American industry healthy.

After the brief boom of 1879, overproduction and declining prices had followed for a decade and a half, and various attempts were made by the manufacturers to ease their lot. In the mid-1890s a trust agreement appears to have been attempted, and initial steps taken towards an agency that would control the sales of the larger mills, but it wasn't set up. The third measure taken had been the creation of International Paper Co., with mills previously owned

228

by 19 other companies. In the words of a trade journal, "it was born out of the fear of bankruptcy and ruin, as competition among the manufacturers had gone beyond all reasonable bounds." International Paper controlled almost three quarters of the total American production of newsprint.

Another price boom had occurred in 1899, followed by successive swings to high prices, which brought the usual demand from publishers for anti-trust investigations and tariff removal. On one occasion, at the Mann Committee Hearings in 1909, it was proved that the publishers' spokesman had exaggerated their charges against the mills and used inaccurate statistics. The Mann Committee concluded: "Considerable evidence was presented which might excite suspicion that such a combination had been made and was in existence."

Despite the lack of any real evidence of collusion among the American manufacturers, the newsprint tariff was completely removed by 1913, by which time the American producers had already started to move mills to Canada. It was in the period of the tariff battle that Frank H. Anson had converted two students' vision of a mill on the Abitibi River into reality.

The Canadian industry grew rapidly. In 1909 the United States had produced all its own newsprint. By the mid-1920s Canadian newsprint production had surpassed the United States' even though most of it was sold below the border.

Prices remained stable through 1913-1916, but World War I and all the news it created caused a shortage in the latter part of the decade, which had an inevitable effect on prices. In 1915 there was still oversupply as a result of the rush to build new mills in Canada with American and Canadian capital (81 new companies were incorporated in 1911 alone). Most of the producers on both sides of the border united to set up the News Print Manufacturers Association, an attempt to reduce the crippling competition among its members by moving their product through a small number of sales agencies which could prevent the publishers playing one supplier off against another.

DAY EIGHT

In the first half of 1916, the average cost of producing a ton of paper was claimed by a United States government agency to be $33, but a boom in that year pushed prices up from $40 a ton to about $65 a ton in 1917.

The United States Justice Department set dates for the trial of the manufacturers belonging to the News Print Manufacturers Association. All the defendants pleaded "nolo contendere," thereby agreeing not to contest the government's case though at the same time not pleading guilty to violation of the Sherman (anti-trust) Act. By paying fines totaling $11,000, the defendants also made no claims of innocence, and the News Print Manufacturers Association was wound up. For all the investigatory energy expended between the 1870s and the 1970s, there'd be only one other "successful" United States government case against newsprint manufacturers, and that would be in the 1930s.

In early 1918, the American government fixed the price of newsprint initially at $60 per ton, later at $75, to prevent any further hanky-panky by the manufacturers and to ensure that the publishers enjoyed a reasonable price during the shortage in the latter part of the war. Wartime controls on the use of paper were removed in 1919.

By 1920, demand had far exceeded supply, and the price had soared up to $112.60 a ton. A period of powerful expansion, which would last well into the 1920s, was under way and the usual investigations were called for in Congress. The charges were made that "the manufacturers were conspiring to regulate production so that prices might continue to mount." The price was certainly high. It wouldn't reach this level again for many years. But in 1921, a recession started the price on its way downward and the accusations against the manufacturers petered out.

In response to the high prices at the turn of the decade, capacity expanded greatly.Total North American newsprint capacity rose from 2,564,000 tons in 1920 to 5,589,000 tons in 1930. The capacity utilized fell from 97% in 1919 to 73% in 1930, and prices steadily drifted down year after year from the $112.60 in

1920 to $62 in 1930 and they'd fall much farther. By 1928 the situation looked serious, though not critical, and in Canada the remedy attempted was, in two or three cases, to consolidate many companies into one — the same response to overcapacity that had led to the creation of the International Paper Co. Abitibi swelled by merger to an ungainly size, still acquiring other companies until 1930, and a couple of other pulp and paper giants were also formed in this period.

Another response to overproduction and falling prices was to form associations to prevent price cutting and minimize competition between members.

Price competition is particularly damaging to the newsprint industry because fixed costs (carrying costs of mills and machinery) are such a high proportion of the total cost of the product, and because the demand for newsprint isn't elastic in response to changes in price. If the price of newsprint declines, publishers aren't likely to publish bigger papers, because the size of the paper is a response to the amount of space purchased by advertisers, not the cost of the newsprint. A fall in price isn't ameliorated by greater sales, so it must come almost straight out of newsprint producers' profits. And the newsprint manufacturers' fixed costs are high and rigid. If the price of newsprint falls below them, the producers can't escape loss by laying off workers and shutting down mills. If ever a case could be made for benign production control to preserve and nurture an industry, newsprint would be the prime candidate. It has been attempted in bad times in earlier years, but with a few exceptions it hasn't worked.

Late in 1930 it was clear that selling associations weren't going to work. So corporate consolidation — which had the same effect, but legally — was pushed to its logical conclusion. One huge company was to be formed to unite Abitibi and the other four largest companies in the industry. It would have brought under one corporate umbrella a large part of Canada's newsprint capacity. But no agreement could be reached on the relative values of the individual companies' securities, and the merger was aborted.

DAY EIGHT

American anti-trust officers argue that any combination to reduce competition is harmful because, although profits may not be pushed to unreasonable levels, the incentive to cut costs is destroyed, and waste is built into the price. That may be true, but, if competition knocks out capacity in bad times, publishers would have to pay all over again through higher prices in good times the cost of rebuilding the lost capacity. Which is the more expensive alternative?

The price continued to fall until by 1932 it had reached $48, and several of the largest companies in Eastern Canada, including Abitibi and Price, had defaulted on interest payments and had taken 58% of Canada's capacity into receivership, bankruptcy or voluntary reorganization.

In 1936, the "one big company" idea came to the surface again and with it an attempt to merge four major Canadian companies including the bankrupt Price Co. and Abitibi in receivership, but it fell through.

The newsprint price reached rock bottom at $40 a ton in 1934 and 1935, and despite the financial wreckage most of the industry had become, the American publishers vigorously fought any attempts to bring it back to profitability through higher prices, despite their dependence on the industry. As early as 1930, the American Newspaper Publishers Association "viewed with deepest concern the continued effort being made to negative the operation of the law of supply and demand . . ." (It had howled just as loudly when the "law of supply and demand" had forced the price up in 1920.)

At the same time, the premiers of Quebec and Ontario were so alarmed by falling prices that they threatened International Paper Co. and others with dire consequences if they didn't raise prices. The price was raised temporarily by Abitibi and another paper company to please these governments, but the general industry decline continued.

Early in 1934, the United States government, through the National Industrial Recovery Act, tried to elevate the price of news-

232

print to $41 a ton, but the publishers attacked the National Recovery Administration as the "Godparent . . . of a monopoly in the manufacture and sale of newsprint paper for use in the United States . . . with absolute power over the price to be extracted from consumers of newsprint paper . . .The proposal is . . . repugnant not only to the anti-trust laws of this country but to the expressed prohibition against monopolies in the National Industrial Recovery Act. It is violative of sound business economics. And it is contrary to the public interest." The proposal was also attacked as' a danger to "freedom of the press." The publishers prevailed.

By 1933, however, demand started to increase slowly and the price rose naturally again. On March 19, 1937, International Paper Co. established itself as price leader with a 1938 price of $50. Most Canadian companies followed International's lead. Great Northern Paper Co., which had been the price leader, replied to International by announcing that its New York price would remain at $48. International's response ushered in a new approach to overcapacity. International held its price at $50, and it *cut back production*. The Great Northern move wasn't sufficient to break the Canadian price. From this point on, the industry would be more sophisticated in handling competition, and there'd be no further need for hospital-ward consolidation, price-fixing associations and provincial interference to prevent the industry from cutting its own throat in bad times.

As prices rose in the mid-1930s, they brought with them the inevitable cries of "cartel" and "price-fixing." John H. Perry, president of the American Press Association and publisher of many southern newspapers, stated that the Canadian price increases seemed to be "arranged as part of a conspiracy to gouge the American publishers." And the Federal Trade Commission began an investigation of "monopoly in the newsprint industry."

On July 12, 1939, indictments were brought down against seven newsprint companies on the American West Coast and in Canada for fixing the price of newsprint between 1935 and 1937, at a time when the price was still badly Depression-depressed. The price fix-

DAY EIGHT

ing was obviously part of a continuing attempt at survival. In 1941, several of the West Coast companies entered no-contest pleas against the indictment and paid fines, which terminated the government's action. (The western producers really comprise a distinct industry, their costs, markets and trees different from those in the East.)

In the years immediately after World War II there were tight prices, more investigations and familiar charges, such as that the producers were "charging all the market can bear" — in keeping with the law of supply and demand.

The United States Justice Department tried to subpoena records from Canadian newsprint producers, some of them subsidiaries of American companies, but the companies refused to produce them. The Ontario government passed a law making it a criminal offence for companies in the province to provide records in compliance with any judicial process outside the province.

In 1949, the American Newspaper Publishers Association again called on Congress to "conduct an investigation of newsprint prices and . . . profits, and . . . to reactivate anti-trust proceedings against the price-fixing corporations dominating the newsprint market." Vigorous investigation continued unabated into 1950, when prices were rising and capacity was running flat out. Onto the scene came the most famous antagonist of the Canadian newsprint industry, Emanuel Celler, chairman of the House Committee on the Judiciary, who stated publicly that the price of newsprint was being "jacked up" by a lot of "monkey business."

In mid-1950, R. M. Fowler, president of the Canadian Pulp and Paper Association, pointed out the absurdity of the publishers' constant bleating about prices, which had reached another crescendo at that time. Fowler spoke these words to the American newspaper proprietors: "I am sure you know that increased newsprint production, even by the method of speeding up machines . . . requires large capital investments and considerable time. In the last six or eight months Canadian producers have been bombarded by U.S. publishers with protests against the present price of newsprint which would have made any sensible manufacturer hesitate in embarking on new, heavy capital expenditures. These protests, taken at their face value, would make anyone think that American publishers would rather have lower prices than new capacity. You certainly can't have both."

On June 19, 1950, the Celler Committee, whose chairman had already been accused of "making accusations and pronouncing his verdict before hearing any evidence," opened its proceedings. The purpose of the investigation was "to determine whether present or threatened shortages result from any violation of existing anti-trust laws or any worldwide cartels."

Prof. John A. Guthrie of the State College of Washington, who made an extensive study of the newsprint and paper industries, told the committee: "The record of prices and profits in newsprint does not . . . bear out the charge that producers have, over the years, exercised an undue amount of monopoly power. Because of the very nature of the newsprint industry, fewness of firms is not undesirable, but rather it contributes to the achievement of greater efficiency and stability and lower costs and prices." He agreed that a system of pricing newsprint in the U.S. by zone then in use "in part restricts competition. But I do not feel there has been any unusual amount of that. I don't think in an industry of this type you can get away from attempts of that kind completely." In contrast with the inviolable doctrine of the U.S. anti-trust statutes, he also felt that "too much price competition" in the newsprint industry was "undesirable."

The Celler Committee found no conclusive evidence that there were or weren't monopolistic practices in the newsprint industry, though it did condemn certain practices such as the zone pricing system. Celler's personal bias was given full reign, and he forcefully expressed his own belief that the Canadian industry was organized and operating under cartel-like arrangements.

When a Canadian company had the temerity to increase prices in October 1950, Celler wrote to the United States Attorney-General urging anti-trust action against American mills if they fol-

DAY EIGHT

lowed suit, and asked to re-open his committee. On March 6, 1951, the Celler Committee was empowered to continue its investigations: it looked as though the shortage would get worse. After its hearings, the committee (naturally) condemned Ontario's Business Records Protection Act and recommended that the Department of Justice study the committee's report for evidence on "possible agreements fixing prices and allocating markets . . ." (even though none had been found). The committee also recommended that the Federal Trade Commission study statistical exchanges between United States, Canadian and Scandinavian producers' trade associations "for evidence of monopolistic tendencies."

In 1952 and 1953 there were more price increases and more investigations and the Celler Committee came lamely to the conclusion that "anti-trust implications are inherent in the structure of the industry."

Investigations continued at a quiet level in 1954. A shortage-induced price increase in 1955 led to the novel charge that the company leading the price increase was "asking the publishing industry to finance its expanding plant." The Department of Justice once again conducted its dreary investigations. Emanuel Celler stated publicly that a price investigation would be futile and that "a tight cartel operating with the connivance of the government of Canada holds the whip hand and there isn't a damn thing we can do." His beliefs didn't seem to have been modified by the failure of his committee to find any evidence of monopoly. Official investigations continued, then and in 1957, when there was another price increase. Sen. Charles E. Potter likened the industry to a colossal spider web, but admitted he couldn't find the spider.

In the spring of 1957 a number of producers, belatedly realizing it was time to put forward a few facts about the industry, established the Newsprint Information Committee, operating out of New York, which still sends a concise, fact-packed letter on newsprint to anybody with a productive interest.

In 1958 another United States government investigation tried hard, but was only able to come to the conclusion that "no firm conclusion is possible as to whether agreements presently exist in the industry to fix the price of newsprint in the United States." It also wrote its conclusion another way to make it sound a little more damning: "There can be no feeling of assurance that competition regulates this industry's course." In the 20 years since the combines action against the West Coast producers in 1939, this was the strongest conclusion any of the numerous committees that investigated the newsprint industry had been able to reach, notwithstanding the highly colored views of Emanuel Celler.

The price remained steady in the late 1950s, but in the early 1960s it again began its gradual upward trend*— not without cries of "monopoly" and "cartels" and some investigative interest south of the border. But the beavers of the Senate and the Justice Department seemed to have at last recognized the futility of the process.

Note 2:
About various facets of anti-trust and combines thinking.

The guidelines of the United States Department of Justice governing horizontal mergers state the following enforcement policy:

"With respect to mergers between direct competitors (i.e., horizontal mergers), the Department's enforcement activity under Section 7 of the Clayton Act has the following interrelated purposes: (i) preventing elimination as an independent business entity of any company likely to have been a substantial competitive influence in a market; (ii) preventing any company or small group of companies from obtaining a position of dominance in a market; (iii)

---

*The rise in newsprint prices wasn't enough to produce any bonanza for the producers. Aside from a few exceptional years, the Canadian newsprint producers worried along with earnings that represented a pretty unexciting return on investment. Refer to the notes to Day One.

DAY EIGHT

preventing significant increases in concentration in a market; and (iv) preserving significant possibilities for eventual deconcentration in a concentrated market . . .

"In a market in which the shares of the four largest firms amount to less than approximately 75%, the Department will ordinarily challenge mergers between firms accounting for, approximately, the following percentages of the market:

Acquiring firm	Acquired firm
5%	5% or more
10%	4% or more
15%	3% or more
20%	2% or more
25% or more	1% or more"

The approach of the Organization for Economic Co-operation & Development has been spelled out in its *Mergers and Competition Policy: Report of the Committee of Experts on Restrictive Business Practices*, published in Paris in 1974. It states:

". . . Only five Member countries — Canada, Germany, Japan, the United Kingdom and the United States — have specific systems of merger control within the context of their competition laws. To this must be added the rules of the Rome and Paris Treaties establishing the European Communities which also contain provisions permitting action to be taken against mergers . . .

"In Canada, no action has been taken pursuant to Section 33 of the Combines Investigation Act against a merger involving a foreign and a Canadian company. In fact only six proceedings have been instituted by the Department of Justice under this provision against mergers between Canadian companies only. Four were unsuccessful, one resulted in a plea of guilty and one is still in progress [in 1974]. The penal character of Section 33 would appear to be responsible for difficulty in bringing successful actions against national and international mergers . . .

"The United States is the only country which in recent years actively applied its legislation to international mergers, primarily un-

238

der Section 7 of the Clayton Act. Some of these cases have involved foreign companies which have acquired United States companies or their assets . . .

". . . The United States has also applied its legislation to mergers abroad which have or are likely to have a substantial adverse effect on American commerce. This has invariably involved acquisitions of foreign companies by United States companies, although in one case Section 7 of the Clayton Act was applied in the United States to contain aspects of a merger between two non-American companies each of which had an American subsidiary . . .

". . . In the Ciba Corporation et al. case, the Department of Justice attacked a merger between two Swiss companies, Ciba and Geigy, alleging that the merger would substantially lessen competition in the United States between their wholly owned subsidiaries in the manufacture and sale of dye-stuffs, certain drugs and herbicides. The merger was allowed pursuant to a settlement requiring the sale of certain assets of the American subsidiaries to restore competition lost by the merger . . .

"With respect to *the application of national laws to mergers and acquisitions involving foreign enterprises and any conflicts which may arise* from such an application, Member countries are invited to have recourse to the OECD Council Recommendation of 1967 concerning co-operation between Member countries in the field of restrictive business practices affecting international trade and to the OECD Council Recommendation of 1973 concerning a consultation and conciliation procedure on restrictive business practices affecting international trade."

Two judgments defining the interpretation of the Canadian Combines Investigation Act had been delivered in two cases in 1960.

In Regina v. Canadian Breweries Ltd., Chief Justice McRuer of the Supreme Court of Ontario said:

". . . If I am correct in applying, by analogy, the language of Cartwright J. in the Howard Smith case [1957] to the Combines

DAY EIGHT

Act, it must be interpreted as differing from the Clayton Act in this important respect: under the Combines Act it must be demonstrated beyond a reasonable doubt that the merging of competitive corporations is likely to put it within the power of the merger to so extinguish competition as to affect prices by monopolistic control. As long as the evidence shows there is strong virile competition in the market notwithstanding the merger, I do not think the merging of competing companies comes within the standard of proof required in a criminal case . . ."

In Regina v. British Columbia Sugar Refining Co. Ltd., and B.C Sugar Refinery Ltd., Chief Justice Williams of the Manitoba Court of Queen's Bench went even further:

"I should say here that in my opinion the Crown in this case must not only establish that as a result of the merger the accused acquired the 'power' to dictate trading practices referred to in the cases decided under . . . the Criminal Code: It must also establish excessive or exorbitant profits or prices . . ."

The merger of the two sugar companies had placed virtually all refineries west of Manitoba under the ownership of a single company.

". . . The Crown has not attempted to establish exorbitant profits; its attempt to establish exorbitant prices fails . . . The Crown must also establish a virtual stifling of competition . . ." Chief Justice Williams stated.

At the time of the Abitibi-Price takeover planning, new developments had been taking shape in Canadian competition policy. This was how a report of the Organization for Economic Co-operation & Development described them in 1974:

"The Government introduced the Competition Act, Bill C-256, in June, 1971. The Bill was comprehensive, and it was made clear at the time that the immediate intention of the Government was not to proceed with enactment but rather to await public reactions. Many representations were received, and it was concluded that revisions were required. The Bill had not been enacted when the

240

Session of Parliament ended in January, 1972, at which time it automatically lapsed. The Government concluded that a new competition policy should be enacted in stages. In that way, Parliament could be asked to make decisions more quickly on those matters which were urgently in need of attention and did not require reconciliation with broader policy issues still under review. The first stage was incorporated in Bill C-227, which the Honorable Herb Gray, Minister of Consumer and Corporate Affairs, introduced in the House of Commons on 6th November, 1973, towards the end of the Session. An identical measure, Bill C-7, was introduced in the House of Commons on 11th March, 1974. It passed second reading and was referred to a Committee of the House of Commons for detailed study. On 8th May, before the Committee had completed its work, the Government was defeated on a want-of-confidence motion. On 9th May, Parliament was dissolved and an election was called for 8th July, 1974."

Note 3:
An interesting comment on the relationship between Canadian newsprint producers and their American customers appeared in Pulp and Paper, an important American trade journal, in June 1972. It was written by Albert W. Wilson, senior editor.

"Not only is Canada subsidizing the American press by cutting down forests which take 60 to 100 years to mature, losing money doing it and imperiling their very survival," Wilson wrote. "Most U.S. newsprint mills are little better off. In effect, both nations are virtually giving away a precious patrimony — forests used for newsprint. In contrast, profits of a dozen of the largest U.S. newspapers and chains average five times that of 15 major Canadian newsprint manufacturers and 3½ times that of seven of the largest U.S. companies whose newsprint is a major portion of their output.

"To be specific, 13 major Canadian newsprint producers reported sales of $2,787 million in 1971 of which only 1.2% was net

DAY EIGHT

profit. Three of them reported appalling losses, 20.5%, 7.8% and 5.8%, partly due to a similarly depressed pulp market. Seven leading U.S. newsprint producers totaled $5,324 million in sales with average net profit of only 1.8% despite the fact their lumber divisions were very profitable. In contrast, a dozen leading U.S. newspaper publishers — eight of them chains of scores of newspapers — reported sales of $2,561 million for 1971 and a net profit of 5.9%. For five years these publishers' profits held reasonably steady as a group, dropping only one percentage point. On the other hand, Canadian mills' average profits skidded from 4.8% to 1.2% and American mills from 5.7% (5.8% in '69) to 1.8%.

"Canadian mills are taking losses of millions of dollars since the floating of the Canadian dollar at U.S. request, generally up to 10%. Canada has exported over six million tons of newsprint to the U.S. every year for seven years. This is an important two thirds of the U.S. supply. For 40 years newsprint prices have increased only $39 per ton. For eight years — 1958 to 1966 — the price never budged from $134 per ton. This year an increase of only $5 to $165 (Northern) and to $163 (Southern) was effected after much difficulty. An attempted boost of only $8 had to be rolled back, despite continuing skyrocketing labor and distribution costs, besides the devaluation crisis . . ."

DAY NINE

Note 1:

About the Thomson connection.

The long association between Abitibi and the newspaper peer Lord Thomson went back to the early 1930s when Thomson bought the weekly Timmins Press and converted it to a daily. Thomson recently recalled: "We had no money and no credit standing. We bought our newsprint COD from Abitibi which was a neighbor at Iroquois Falls."

There was an even earlier connection, however, dating to the late 1920s. Thomson had a chain of electrical hardware stores and a distributorship for a major electrical appliance firm. Dealers were appointed where Thomson had no stores of his own. At that time there was no local radio station, and in the late fall and early winter the northern lights created so much interference that residents of northern Ontario couldn't receive stations they could hear at other times of the year — those in Pittsburgh, Schenectady, New York City and other powerful American stations. But Christmas time was also the big radio selling season, when many sets were bought as presents. Thomson decided that a local radio station was essential to keep sales strong in the months of bad interference — and to keep happy those people to whom he had already so ably sold so many sets.

At that time Ottawa was revising its radio broadcasting policy, and had stopped issuing licenses. The only existing license in the area was held by Abitibi, which the company had obtained for communication in the woodlands. It was, however, an entertainment license and therefore inoperative for that purpose. Thomson sent one of his associates over to say to the Abitibi people: "Look, the government will cancel your license if you don't use it. I suggest you lend it to us and let us start a station. At the end of the year we'll give the license back, if you ask for it. But if you don't, we keep it."

That was the license for Thomson's first radio station — and his license to continue his hectic selling of radio sets. Thomson later bought the Timmins Press and, with it, Abitibi's newsprint.

DAY NINE

At the time of the Abitibi-Price takeover, the Thomson organization controlled more than 100 newspapers in North America — and 50% of their newsprint came from Abitibi mills.

Note 1:

How much could Abitibi raise in debt?

Abitibi's most restrictive covenants are set out in the trust indenture to the Series A debentures issued in 1965 to Metropolitan Life Insurance Co. as a private placement. The covenants provide that Abitibi or any of its designated subsidiaries* will not issue any senior debt** unless (a) the consolidated net tangible assets† of Abitibi and its designated subsidiaries would be not less than 225% of the principal of all senior debt, and unless (b) the average annual consolidated net earnings†† of Abitibi for the two preceding fiscal years shall have been at least equal to four times the aggregate annual interest requirements on all senior debt and junior debt° of the company. At the end of 1973 Abitibi's net tangible assets had been about $453 million, which gave the company a senior-debt ceiling of about $200 million — about $100 million more than the debt already out.

About consolidation.

Full consolidation of financial statements generally can be practised only where the parent has 50% or more of the subsidiary's stock. Earnings consolidation is generally acceptable at less than 50% if there is some degree of control.

About Abitibi's thinking on the long-term financing.

Premise: Long-term financing must be arranged for the greatest possible benefit to the existing Abitibi shareholders. Four basic

* A parent company can raise debt on the borrowing power of a designated subsidiary, but it also accepts the responsibility of providing the subsidiary with the financing needed.
** Senior debt: debentures or mortgages. (Abitibi's first mortgage bonds would be fully paid off in 1977 and future senior debt would be debentures.)
† Net tangible assets: total assets less entries representing expenditures for which no concrete value has been received.
†† Before interest, tax and depreciation.
° Junior debt: notes and other unsecured instruments coming after debentures in line of seniority.

ways of raising the money long-term for the Price acquisition were available to Abitibi.

Internal sources: At the end of 1973 Abitibi had cash and liquid investments of about $35 million. In 1974 there was an unusual cash drain. Two small acquisitions in early 1974 had called for cash. In addition, inflation-fueled capital expenditures were unusually high at $24.6 million (they'd been $8 million to $14 million annually in the 1970-1973 period). On top of that, a partially inflation-fueled sales expansion (from $403 million in 1973 to $551 million in 1974) had locked cash away in accounts receivable and inventory. In November, "cash" of $14 million or $15 million was still available for the purchase of Price shares. Because the entire return from investment of company cash accrues to existing shareholders, the use of funds from internal sources would be *desirable*.

Common stock issue: This was the least favored form of long-term financing. In 25 years Abitibi's number of common shares outstanding had risen by only 22%. Common stock is more flexible than debt, because there are no fixed interest obligations. But a new issue of common stock brings little or no benefits to the existing shareholders. Assuming all company funds are invested at the same rate of return (not true), the return on the new equity funds flows into the current dividend payments extended to the new shareholders and also start to pass into retained earnings. The retained earnings of the company are re-apportioned (in a book sense) among existing and new shareholders without distinction. Therefore the value within the company (net worth) assignable to each existing shareholder is reduced by the issuance of the new common stock. The reduction of the net worth per share can be reflected in the market price of the stock. Therefore, although a new common stock issue may not affect the company's ability to maintain the current dividend rate, it will likely reduce the market value of the existing shareholders' stock. Because of this dilution effect, Abitibi considered a stock issue *unacceptable*. Another temporary factor would be that Abitibi's common stock was undervalued in the market at $9 a share at a time when the net worth per common share was greater than $12 a share. As new common could only be successfully sold at market or less, Abitibi would probably be selling its assets at less than their value. (Depending on the number of new shares issued.)

Preferred stock issue: This route is less flexible than common stock, but more flexible than debt. Dividends can be omitted in bad times, but may accumulate for later obligatory payment. It's more acceptable to existing shareholders: there's no dilution effect (claim on retained earnings is limited to capital paid into the company for the shares), and preferred stock can be redeemed (bought back by the company to terminate the need for preferred dividend payments). However, preferred stock is much more costly than debt. Interest payments on debt come from pre-tax company earnings. Preferred dividends come from after-tax profits. A 10% preferred issue would require dividend payments equivalent to perhaps 18% in pre-tax earnings. For this reason Abitibi considered this route *undesirable.*

Debt (debentures): In good times this method is the most beneficial to the existing shareholders.

Assuming that money raised can be invested in the company's business at a 25% return (pre-tax), that return is distributed as follows:

If raised by a common stock issue: A 6% dividend rate would be equivalent to about 10% pre-tax (dividends come out of taxed profits). Any benefit to existing shareholders in the 15% (pre-tax) remaining on the new money after the new shareholders get their dividends could be wiped out by the dilution effect on the market price of the stock.

If raised by a preferred stock issue: A 10% dividend rate would be equivalent to about 18% pre-tax and the returns on the cash raised would almost all be paid out in dividends, leaving little for the existing shareholders.

If raised by a debentures issue: A 10% interest rate would be equivalent to 10% pre-tax dollars, leaving for the existing shareholders a 15% (pre-tax) return on the money raised.

DAY TEN

Obviously a debt issue would be most acceptable to the existing shareholders. Abitibi's covenants permitted a further $100 million of new senior debt — more than enough needed for the Price take-over. Wood Gundy advised that a new debt issue could be marketed, judging from the outlook for the 1975 securities market in late 1974.

Tentative conclusion at that time: Abitibi would try to raise all the long-term financing by means of senior debt, which would bring the greatest benefits to the existing shareholders of the company. Later this intention had to be altered.

DAY SEVENTEEN

Note 1:
About long-range defenses against a takeover.

Price was caught unawares by Abitibi, but some companies prepare themselves against takeover well in advance. Here are some of the techniques possible.

1. Establish control by management by one of several methods.

(a) Have management buy a large block of stock either collectively or as individuals.

(b) Lock up a large block of stock under management control by other means. Early in 1976, Donald F. Hunter sold part of his control block of stock in Maclean-Hunter Ltd. to a holding company, which was itself controlled by Maclean-Hunter's senior management and Maclean-Hunter subsidiaries through stock of the holding company held by those subsidiaries. Obviously Maclean-Hunter management controls both its own stock in the holding company and the M-H subsidiaries' stock by virtue of management's de facto control of Maclean-Hunter. It becomes more difficult for a raider to unseat M-H management.*

(c) A trust-company management can exercise control when the company's trust accounts hold a substantial number of the trust company's own shares. Management has the right to vote the stock of many trust accounts, and, in this case, can do so in its own favor. This seems to be in conflict of interest — the interest of the trust-account beneficiaries and the interest of trust-company management. Nevertheless, at least one Canadian company is believed to be controlled by management in this way.

2. Involve government in any takeover.

(a) Buy a radio station, then any takeover of your company

---

* Under both Ontario and federal law, a subsidiary may not buy stock of a company that controls it, or, if it holds such stock, may not vote it. The law attempts to prevent management perpetuating itself in office in this way. In the Maclean-Hunter case, the intervention of a holding company makes the arrangement legal.

must be approved by the Canadian Radio-Television Commission. A quick raid becomes impossible and everybody becomes alerted to the raider's intentions early.

(b) Buy an airline, then any takeover will be scrutinized by federal authorities. Before the Alberta government made an exchange raid on Pacific Western, a private corporation had submitted an application to Ottawa to take over the airline. It was probably that application to government that alerted Alberta.

(c) If the threat comes from the United States, buy a subsidiary in the same business down there and the raider then has to worry about the anti-trust implications of any takeover of the Canadian parent. Classic example: Schlitz's difficulties in trying to take over a Canadian brewery that had an American subsidiary.

(d) If the threat is from the United States, buy assets in certain states that don't allow changes of ownership without a hearing or adherence to certain state regulations.

3. Build defenses into the company's bylaws or trust indentures or what have you.

(a) Adopt a bylaw that permits only, say, one fifth of the board to come up for election each year (ostensibly for continuity of management). If the company is taken over, it would take the raider years to gain control of the board and to revoke the bylaw to enable him to vote in at one go his own nominees.

(b) Have a clause written into trust indentures making change of ownership of the company a default of the loans outstanding. Any raider eyeing the company will realize a takeover could lead to the company's falling apart.

4. Place a few tripwires in the capital structure of the company (or nearby).

(a) Grant an option on a large block of treasury stock to a third party. If a bid is made for 50% of the outstanding stock at an attractive price, the optionee will exercise his option and buy stock in order to tender to the bidder. The issuance of that stock would force the raider to buy more stock than he was prepared to in order to achieve the 50% he wants. It just might scare him off.

(b) Put out a big issue of convertible preferred stock or debentures. Any would-be raider will have to take into account the likelihood that if he takes over the company and makes it perform well the preferred stockholders or debenture holders will convert their securities to common and dilute his control. To get around this problem, the raider would have to initially bid for 50% of not only the outstanding common, but also the common that would be created by conversion. That increases the cost of the takeover and acts as a deterrent.

DAY EIGHTEEN

Note 1:

The history of Associated's Price shares.

The Price stock held by Associated Newspapers and the Harmsworth family dated back to the 1909 founding of Anglo-Newfoundland Development Co. by Lord Northcliffe and his brother, Harold (the first Viscount Rothermere and Vere Harmsworth's grandfather). The company operated a mill at Grand Falls, Newfoundland, that took three years to build and had been, at the time, dismissed as a "wild-cat proposition." In 1961, Price Co. obtained control of Anglo-Newfoundland from Associated by offering two Price shares for 11 Anglo-Newfoundland shares. The effect, however, was to catapult Associated into effective control of Price — a *reverse* takeover.

In 1962, Price made an offer for all the remaining Anglo shares at $9 and ended up with 99%. Anglo-Newfoundland then changed its name to Price (Newfoundland) Pulp & Paper Ltd. In Associated's 1974 annual report, its Price holding was carried at a cost of £1.7 million, which appeared to be close to the original investment in Anglo-Newfoundland.

Note 2:

About direct investment.

Harmsworth's difficulty in pre-determining the type of Associated's investment in Price can be appreciated by glancing at the maze of regulations governing "direct" investments. The following excerpt is taken from the Bank of England Notice to Authorized Banks and Authorized Depositories (December 10, 1974):

"For the purposes of Exchange Control, direct investments are:

"(a) those in which the investor establishes, expands or consolidates an economic enterprise with the intention of participating in its management and operation; and

"(b) trade investments, where the investor establishes or maintains commercial links with other companies to further his existing business.

"As direct investments outside the Scheduled Territories normally involve the acquisition of assets against payment in one form or another to non-residents, permissions under the Exchange Control Act 1947 are required. The permissions needed are usually for payments (including loans) to non-residents, whether effected by purchasing or borrowing foreign currency, the export of goods free of payment or on credit terms in excess of six months, or the issue or transfer of shares to non-residents . . .

"Permission is required for any act whereby a company, wherever incorporated, which is controlled directly or indirectly by residents of the United Kingdom ceases to be so controlled . . .

"H.M. Government attach importance to overseas investment and the resulting benefits in the form of invisible earnings and trading, technological and other advantages. At the same time, balance of payments considerations require that outward direct investments and their financing should be subject to control. Accordingly, applications are considered in the light of the probable impact of the investment on the United Kingdom balance of payments, and the expertise of the investor in the particular field involved. The Exchange Control rules are not designed to prevent or restrict genuine, profitable outward direct investment projects, but relate primarily to the method of financing. This should be emphasized when proposals are discussed with customers or clients and no intending investor wishing to seek permission should be discouraged from applying to the Bank of England.

"The balance of payments benefits referred to in this Notice will usually comprise foreign currency and external sterling received in the United Kingdom as a direct result of the investment in respect of one or more of the following:

"(a) exports to countries outside the Scheduled Territories;

"(b) interest, dividends and profits;

"(c) royalties, licence fees, management fees and other payments for technical 'know-how'.

DAY EIGHTEEN

"In addition, the maintenance of existing benefits which would otherwise be lost or the avoidance of outflows from the official foreign exchange reserves which would otherwise be incurred in maintaining existing trade may also be taken into account in computing the total benefits which will flow from the investment.

"Note. Benefits are measured on the basis of foreign currency and external sterling received in the United Kingdom as opposed to the value of unpaid exports or sums which have become due to the United Kingdom but remain outstanding. Allowance should therefore be made, when estimating or assessing benefits, for any element of credit involved . . .

"Direct investments outside the Scheduled Territories are divided into two categories:

"(a) those in which the Bank of England are satisfied that the super-criterion is met, i.e., investments which directly promote exports of United Kingdom goods or services and promise additional benefits to the United Kingdom balance of payments, being benefits which would not occur without the investment and which will at least equal the total cost of the investment within eighteen months and continue thereafter. The use of official exchange, i.e., foreign currency purchased at *the current market* rate in the official foreign exchange market, is permitted within limits for such projects;

"(b) those investments which do not meet the super-criterion but which nevertheless promise additional benefits to the United Kingdom balance of payments. The basic principle applied in such cases is that the investments should be financed in such a way that their cost does not fall directly upon the official foreign exchange reserves.

"Super-criterion projects

"Super-criterion projects may, subject to the permission of the Bank of England being obtained, be financed with official exchange up to £250,000 or 50% of the total cost of the investment, whichever is the greater. Any balance should be financed in one or more of the ways described in paragraph 14.

DAY EIGHTEEN

"Other investments

"In cases where investments do not qualify to be financed with official exchange under the terms of paragraph 13 (or investors do not wish to use any entitlement to official exchange), such investments may, subject to the permission of the Bank of England being obtained, be financed in any or a combination of any of the following ways:

"(a) by the use of foreign currency purchased in the investment currency market (see paragraph 30 concerning sales and liquidations);

"(b) by the export, free of payment, of capital equipment and stock-in-trade of United Kingdom manufacture forming an integral part of the investment;

"(c) by the use of borrowed foreign currency (see paragraphs 15-16);

(d) by the issue or transfer of shares to non-residents on appropriate terms (see paragraphs 17-18);

(e) by the capitalisation of an overseas subsidiary's current account indebtedness to the United Kingdom parent company . . .

"Exchange Control permission is, in general, required for United Kingdom companies to dispose of interests, whether controlling or not, in direct investments outside the Scheduled Territories. Permission for sale is normally given provided that the Bank of England is satisfied that, in all the circumstances, the terms of the transaction are fair.

"The foreign currency proceeds of sales and liquidations by United Kingdom residents of direct investments outside the Scheduled Territories, whenever made, should be offered for sale to an Authorised Bank at the current market rate in the official foreign exchange market unless the specific permission of the Bank of England has been obtained for them to be disposed of in some other manner.

"Where a United Kingdom company, as part of a group reorganisation, sells or liquidates direct investments outside the Scheduled Territories and wishes to reinvest the disinvestment

255

DAY EIGHTEEN

proceeds in further direct investment outside the Scheduled Territories, the Bank of England will normally, on application, consider giving permission provided that:

"(a) the sale/liquidation is associated at the time with the intention to reinvest; and

"(b) any shortfall on the two-thirds profit remittance requirement in respect of the subsidiary sold/liquidated has been rectified and any outstanding debts of a current nature to the United Kingdom parent company have been repaid; and

"(c) the reinvestment takes place within six months.

"In all cases of sales to other residents for sterling, any permission for the transaction may be conditional upon the official reserves being compensated to the extent of any 'shortfall' in profit remittances by purchasing an equivalent amount of foreign currency in the investment currency market and offering it for sale to an Authorised Bank at the current market rate in the official foreign exchange market . . ."

Note 3:
About the many facets of Abitibi's $18 bid.

To Associated Newspapers and Vere Harmsworth, the Abitibi bid of $18 a share had many different values depending on what course of action Harmsworth took.

The value would be $18 — if Harmsworth agreed to a direct share exchange with Abitibi for its stock. As Abitibi was bidding $18 for the stock, that's the valuation it would be expected to put on Associated's Price stock in calculating the basis for the exchange.

The value would be about $21.50 — if the investment were classified as portfolio, and if Harmsworth repatriated it. The value would include the premium on the premium currency, less capital-gains tax.

The value would be $15 — if the investment were classified as direct, if capital-gains tax were paid and the proceeds were repatriated (at no premium).

The value would be $12 — if a direct investment (no premium) were repatriated, and the double-taxation relief were thereafter lost on dividends from Associated's remaining Price holdings.

About the value of Abitibi's $18-a-share bid, if the Bank of England classified Associated's holdings as a *portfolio* investment.

Associated's proceeds from the stock sold = $18 plus a 62% premium. (This figure must be adjusted as a result of the Bank of England's rule that only 75% of the proceeds of a portfolio investment may be sold back into the investment currency market at a premium, in order to enable British reserves to benefit from investors' fortunes abroad. The remaining 25% of the investment currency is repatriated as normal currency. The premium on the 25% effectively passes into reserves.)

Associated's net proceeds from stock sold = $26.36 a share (before capital-gains tax and the other tax effects).

Capital-gains tax: The valuation base was about $11; rate, 30%.

At this stage, the portfolio investment = $26.36 less 30% of $15.36 = about $21.50.

Devaluation effects: Between November 1974 and November 1975, the pound sterling fell in value from $2.30 to about $2, a drop of about 13%.

So, the final portfolio investment = proceeds worth about $19 one year later. The proceeds from the portfolio investment would still be worth more than the $18 Abitibi bid price, after tax and devaluation effects.

A portfolio classification would also offer the alternative of reinvesting most of the $18 proceeds from the sale to Abitibi in other North American securities to protect the proceeds from the devaluation of the pound.

Then there was the matter of lost dividends. In 1974, Price established an annual dividend rate of $1 per share. Associated would receive this dividend tax-free because, holding more than 10% of Price, it was eligible for double-taxation relief in Britain.

(a) If the portfolio investment were repatriated to Britain, the $21.50 net proceeds could probably be invested at that time at 10% for a return of about $2. Assuming a tax rate of 50%, the net proceeds would be $1. (This would have to be adjusted for devaluation or inflation in Britain.) Therefore the net proceeds would be no less than the lost dividends.

(b) If the portfolio investment were rolled over in Canada, almost all of the $18-per-share proceeds, gains-taxed down to $16, could easily at the time have been reinvested in other stocks for a $1 yield (6%), as in Price. But double-taxation relief might have been lost if Associated bought less than 10% in another company, and in that case the net proceeds to Associated would be 50¢. (However, the capital would be shielded from devaluation of the pound.)

The conclusion had to be that classification of Associated's investment as portfolio would be more profitable for the company and allow more flexibility of reinvestment than if it were classified as direct.

About the punishing tax effects faced by Harmsworth, if the Bank of England classified Associated's holdings as a *direct* investment.

Assumption one. If Harmsworth tendered *all* of Associated's stock, if 49% were taken up by Abitibi, if Associated were left with 8% or 9% of Price:

Bid price per share of Price stock = $18 (A).

Capital gains tax = 30% on gains above $11 = $2.10 (B).

Dividends on remaining Price stock (1974 rate) = $1 a share.

Tax triggered by the holding's falling below 10% (at a 50% rate) = $0.50 a share.

The dividend loss capitalized at the prevailing 10% market interest rate. (Dividends were paid every year. What sum of money would bear 10% interest for 50¢ a year? Answer: $5) = $5 (C).

Value of the $18-per-share proceeds to Associated = A minus B minus C = $10.90. (Assuming number of shares sold = number kept, then the $5 lost on each held share can be deducted from the proceeds of each sold share.)

That value less the 10% decline in the value of the pound sterling within six months of bid = $9.81.

The conclusion had to be that, if Associated tendered all its stock, Abitibi's bid was worth less than the market price ($12).*

Assumption two: If Harmsworth tendered *one million shares* to Abitibi, and only 49% of these were taken up:

Value of the sale to Associated = $18 per share, less capital gains tax ($2.10), less a 10% loss due to conversion into weaker sterling currency = $14.40. (Note: The proceeds would have to be converted into sterling if the investment were classified direct.)

---

* The difficulty in accurately assessing the value of the $18 to Harmsworth is that loss of double-taxation relief would wound the remaining investment in Price without actually affecting the value of that stock. (It could, of course, always be sold at market.) How to relate this wounding to the decision to sell half the Price stock, a decision that would cause the wounding? The author has capitalized the loss of dividends at 10% (an arbitrary percentage) and applied that to the $18. Advisers disagreed on the appropriate percentage to use, though some said that 10% was too high. The other difficulty was that there was no knowing how long Associated would keep its wounded investment in Price. The above calculation assumes the investment would continue to be held forever. But if, for example, Associated sold the rump-end of its Price stock after one year, it would lose only a 50¢ dividend per share (through loss of double-taxation relief) — not $5 per share.

DAY NINETEEN

Note 1:
The Canada Permanent letter

"November 18, 1974
"Arthur S. Pattillo, Esq., Q.C.
Chairman,
Ontario Securities Commission,
555 Yonge Street,
Toronto, Ontario.

"Dear Mr. Pattillo:
"This is further to the conversation which my associate, Mr. C. N. Halford, had with Mr. Bray this morning regarding the Abitibi offer for 49% of the Price Company.

"We hold 128,000 shares of Price on behalf of 157 trust clients serviced by 22 of our branches. While part of this represents accounts such as pension funds which are managed in Toronto on a discretionary basis, the majority of stock is held for individual trust accounts where client consent is required before any investment action may be taken. We are now trying to contact each client owning Price to explain the offer and obtain a decision, but in view of tomorrow morning's deadline, we may not be able to reach everyone in time to act on their behalf. We therefore urge you to take whatever action would be appropriate to extend the offer for several more days, and we suggest Monday, November 25, 1974, as a reasonable date.

"We have been greatly concerned over the lack of adequate protection for the small investor in takeover bids of various kinds. In this case we feel that the period of time between the original announcement and the date for tendering shares is so short as to be contrary to the interests of many individual shareholders of Price.

"Yours truly,
"John P. S. Mackenzie
Vice-president, Investments"

Note 2:

Why Domtar was willing to sell at $18.

As Domtar held only 7% of Price and didn't have effective control, it couldn't consolidate Price's earnings into Domtar's accounts. At the 1974 dividend rate ($1 per share), the return on the book value of the Price stock ($18 per share) was only 5½%. Domtar's best policy was to take the one-time opportunity of selling the stock at book value ($18 or more) and reinvesting the proceeds in Domtar's business for a return of, say, 15%, or in some other profitable area. By selling the stock at or above book value, Domtar avoided having to show a loss in its financial statement that year. A sale at above $18 a share would create a book profit.

Domtar was probably relieved to get out of Price at $18 a share or more. Not only would it be unusual for the market price to reach that level (it happened only once, in 1973: high, $18⅞; low, $13), but Price's earnings per share hadn't grown significantly for at least 25 years. In 1950, earnings per common share had been $4.12 (before a 1966 three-for-one stock split). In 1973, earnings per common had been 78¢ ($2.24 before split). Earnings per share of $3.22 in 1974 ($9.66 before split) would mark the first time earnings had exceeded the 1950 level.

Note 3:

About double-taxation relief in Britain.

British taxation laws permitted an investor to receive dividends free of British tax, provided that the dividends came from the taxed profits of the dividend-paying corporation and that the investor held more than 10% of that company's stock. This concession (which was available in similar terms under Canadian tax law) gave major investors relief from double taxation: at dividend source and then later in the investor's pocket. Double-taxation relief wasn't available if the investor held less than 10% of the dividend-paying company.

261

DAY NINETEEN

Note 4:

The Foreign Investment Review Act.

These excerpts from the act cover the areas that most concerned some of the participants in the takeover dealing.

"This Act is enacted by the Parliament of Canada in recognition by Parliament that the extent to which control of Canadian industry, trade and commerce has become acquired by persons other than Canadians and the effect thereof on the ability of Canadians to maintain effective control over their economic environment is a matter of national concern, and that it is therefore expedient to establish a means by which measures may be taken under the authority of Parliament to ensure that, in so far as is practicable after the enactment of this Act, control of Canadian business enterprises may be acquired by persons other than Canadians, and new businesses may be established in Canada by persons, other than Canadians, who are not already carrying on business in Canada or whose new businesses in Canada would be unrelated to the businesses already being carried on by them in Canada, only if it has been assessed that the acquisition of control of those enterprises or the establishment of those new businesses, as the case may be, by those persons is or is likely to be of significant benefit to Canada, having regard to all of the factors to be taken into account under this Act for that purpose . . .

" 'Non-eligible person' means

"(a) an individual who is neither a Canadian citizen nor a landed immigrant within the meaning of the *Immigration Act* and includes

"(i) a Canadian citizen who is not ordinarily resident in Canada and who is a member of a class of persons prescribed by regulation for the purposes of this definition, and

"(ii) a landed immigrant who has been ordinarily resident in Canada for more than one year after the time at which he first became eligible to apply for Canadian citizenship,

262

"(b) the government of a country other than Canada or of a political subdivision of a country other than Canada, or an agency of such a government, or

"(c) a corporation incorporated in Canada or elsewhere that is controlled in any manner that results in control in fact, whether directly through the ownership of shares or indirectly through a trust, a contract, the ownership of shares of any other corporation or otherwise, by a person described in paragraph (a) or (b) or by a group of persons any member of which is a person described in paragraph (a) or (b) . . .

"Presumption as to non-eligible persons. Where, in the case of a corporation incoporated in Canada or elsewhere,

(a) shares of the corporation to which are attached

"(i)   25% or more of the voting rights ordinarily exercisable at meetings of shareholders of the corporation, in the case of a corporation the shares of which are publicly traded, or

(ii)   40% or more of the voting rights ordinarily exercisable at meetings of shareholders of the corporation, in the case of a corporation the shares of which are not publicly traded,

are owned by one or more individuals described in paragraph (a) of the definition 'non-eligible person' in subsection (1), by one or more governments or agencies described in paragraph (b) of that definition or by one or more corporations incorporated elsewhere than in Canada, or any combination of such persons, or

"(b) shares of the corporation to which are attached 5% or more of the voting rights ordinarily exercisable at meetings of shareholders of the corporation are owned by any one individual described in paragraph (a) of the definition 'non-eligible person' in subsection (1), by any one government or agency described in paragraph (b) of that definition or by any one corporation incorporated elsewhere than in Canada,

the corporation is, unless the contrary is established, a non-eligible person . . .

DAY NINETEEN

" The acquisition by any person or group of persons of shares of a corporation to which are attached

"(i) 5% or more of the voting rights ordinarily exercisable at meetings of shareholders of the corporation, in the case of a corporation the shares of which are publicly traded, or

"(ii) 20% or more of the voting rights ordinarily exercisable at meetings of shareholders of the corporation, in the case of a corporation the shares of which are not publicly traded,

shall, unless the contrary is established, be deemed to constitute the acquisition of control of any business carried on by the corporation . . .

"Notice of proposed acquisition of control. Every non-eligible person, and every group of persons any member of which is a non-eligible person, that proposes to acquire control of a Canadian business enterprise shall give notice in writing to the Agency of such proposal in such form and manner and containing such information as is prescribed by the regulations . . .

"Review and assessment by Minister. Following receipt by the Agency of a notice under subsection 8(1), (2) or (3), the notice shall be referred by the Agency to the Minister who shall thereupon review

"(a) the information contained in the notice,

"(b) any other information submitted to him by any party to the proposed or actual investment to which the notice relates,

"(c) any written undertakings to Her Majesty in right of Canada relating to the proposed or actual investment given by any party thereto conditional upon the allowance of the investment in accordance with this Act, and

"(d) any representations submitted to him by a province that is likely to be significantly affected by the proposed or actual investment to which the notice relates,

for the purpose of assessing whether or not, in his opinion, having regard to the factors enumerated in subsection 2(2), the investment is or is likely to be of significant benefit to Canada.

"Recommendation by Minister to Governor in Council. Where the Minister, on completion of the assessment referred to in section 9, is of the opinion that the investment to which the assessment relates is or is likely to be of significant benefit to Canada and less than sixty days have elapsed since the date of receipt by the Agency of the notice under subsection 8(1), (2) or (3) relating thereto, the Minister shall.

"(a) recommend to the Governor in Council that the investment be allowed; and

"(b) submit to the Governor in Council in support of such recommendation a summary of the information and written undertakings to Her Majesty in right of Canada, if any, on the basis of which the recommendation is made . . ."

Note 5:
What is a contract?

Bell's criticism that Harmsworth reneged on a "deal" was unfair to Harmsworth. Harmsworth's "promise" and "handshake" was merely a statement of information, a statement of his intention at that time, and it could only be regarded as a deal in the context of his knowledge at that time. As for it being a legal contract, there wasn't any question of that. Only mutuality of promises, intended by the parties to be legally enforceable, *are* legally enforceable. And the parties didn't get into that kind of action.

Moreover, Harmsworth's legal responsibility was to the shareholders of Associated, not to a promise given to Bell on the basis of mistaken information. And Bell, by mounting a fast raid on Price, had forced on Harmsworth a very complex decision that had to be made in a very short time. Fairness to Harmsworth demands sympathy with his predicament.

DAY NINETEEN

Note 6:

About Harmsworth's alternatives. Which was the best?

1. He could sell *all* of Associated's Price stock to Abitibi. *Advantages:* Entire holdings sold at a price ($18) 50% above the market. No residue of double-taxation-relief problems. *Objections:* Abitibi wouldn't agree.

2. He could sell *no* stock to Abitibi. *Advantages:* No double-taxation-relief problems. Newsprint contract would probably continue. Might get a good price if Abitibi merged with Price and *had* to get Associated out of the way. *Objections:* Loss of a good price for at least some of the stock (the market wouldn't likely reach $18 again for a long time). Danger that Abitibi might not want to merge with Price or might not want to for a long time, and Associated would have lost control with no compensating gain.

3. (a) He could tender *one million* shares to Abitibi (hoping only 49% would be taken up, to leave Associated with about 12% of Price). (b) Alternatively, Harmsworth could tender *all* of Associated's stock, have 49% taken up, and be left with 8%-9% of Price, losing double-taxation-relief, for all the disadvantages of 3 (a) with none of the advantages. (c) He could tender some stock, and then use the proceeds to buy even more Price on the market after the takeover. *Advantages:* Each of (a) and (c) would get some advantage of Abitibi's $18 offer without losing double-taxation relief on the remaining Price holdings. He'd remain in a strong position to get a good price for the remaining Price stock if Abitibi wanted to merge with Price. *Objections:* In (a), there'd be a danger that only a few Price shareholders would tender and Abitibi would take up much more than 49%, leaving Associated with less than 10%, with the resultant loss of double-taxation relief. Either way, Associated

would end up with a big position in a company in which it had lost control. In (c) Harmsworth would achieve a big position, but control would be lost.

4. He could try to switch from more than 10% of Price to more than 10% of Abitibi by tendering any amount of shares (all, or a million) and buying Abitibi stock on the market with the proceeds from the stock taken up by Abitibi. *Mechanism:* 49% of Associated's 17% of Price's 10 million shares sold at $18 would buy about 7%-10% of Abitibi's 18 million shares at $9 a share. Harmsworth could buy more Abitibi when Abitibi merged with Price and bought the remaining Price stock. If Associated tendered only one million shares, it would retain 10% in Price until a Price-Abitibi merger, when it would move into 10%-plus of Abitibi, always being in a 10%-plus position of one or the other company. *Advantages:* He'd move from effective control of Price to high influence or even, conceivably, effective control of Abitibi.* *Objections:* First, it would depend on Associated's investment being classified as portfolio so that it could be rolled over without repatriation. Second, it might require the Canadian government's okay for a

* How the British group would have moved into Abitibi:
Forty-nine percent of the English holdings = about 800,000 shares.
Proceeds of sale (at $18 a share) = $14.4 million.
Proceeds net of British capital-gains tax = about $12.8 million.
Market price of Abitibi stock = $10 a share.
If proceeds invested in Abitibi stock = 1.3 million Abitibi shares.
Abitibi's capitalization = 18 million common shares.
Percentage bought by the English = about 7%.
Needed to bring holdings over 10% = 3% or 540,000 Abitibi shares.
Remaining holding of Price = about 800,000 shares.
In the market, Abitibi's stock had historically traded at lower prices than Price's stock. Even if an exchange of one Abitibi share for each share of Price would be negotiated when the two companies were to be merged, the English group could easily bring their holdings in Abitibi above the 10% necessary to overcome the British tax penalties again — and also to threaten Abitibi's "Canadian" status under the Foreign Investment Review Act, which classifies non-resident companies as those owned more than 5% by a non-resident.

DAY NINETEEN

non-resident to buy more than 5% of a Canadian public company.

Alternative 4 would be the only course of action whose outcome could be affected by the Bank of England's ruling on the status of Associated's investment. If the investment were ruled to be direct (as it was), the proceeds of the sale of shares to Abitibi would have to be repatriated to Britain and permission obtained from the Bank of England before they could be reinvested in Canadian stocks such as Abitibi. The danger would be that once the proceeds from the sale of, say, one third of Associated's holdings were repatriated, the Bank of England might rule that any new investment with this relatively small amount of money was a "portfolio" investment and had to be made with "investment currency" bought at a 60% (or whatever) premium in London.

The value of the sale proceeds to Associated would thereby be reduced by about 38% before they could be reinvested in Abitibi stock. The $18 Abitibi price would fall to about $15 after capital-gains tax, and might fall again to about $9 by passing through the London investment currency market. This would frustrate Associate's plans, because Abitibi stock was selling at about $9 a share and Associated would be able to exchange only one Price share sold to Abitibi for $18 for one Abitibi share bought on the market for $9. As Abitibi's capitalization was about 18 million shares, half of Associated's 17% holding in Price would be exchanged for about 5% of Abitibi and double-taxation relief might be lost permanently in both Price and Abitibi.

What was Harmsworth's most favorable course of action?

Before the Bank of England's ruling was known, he should try to achieve Alternative 1, until it became clear that Bell wouldn't agree. Then he should try to make do with Alternative 3 as a second best. When the Foreign Investment Review Act's influence and the Bank of England's ruling became known, it might be possible to go from Alternative 3 to Alternative 4, but in any case Alternative 3 was a better course of action than Alternative 2.

DAY NINETEEN

On the afternoon of Day Nineteen when it appeared that the bid would close early the following morning, *it didn't matter what the Bank of England would rule.* Harmsworth's best course of action was Alternative 3 — regardless.

Note 7:
About the cease-trade period.

These paragraphs of the Ontario Securities Act govern the duration of a suspense of trading ordered by the Ontario Securities Commission:

"(1) The Commission may, where in its opinion such action is in the public interest, order, subject to such terms and conditions as it may impose, that trading shall cease in respect of such securities for such period as is specified in the order.

"(2) No order shall be made under subsection 1 without a hearing unless in the opinion of the Commission the length of time required for a hearing could be prejudicial to the public interest, in which event the Commission may make a temporary order, which shall expire fifteen days from the date of the making thereof, but such order may be extended for such period as the Commission considers necessary where satisfactory information is not provided to the Commission within the fifteen-day period."

Note 8:
Harmsworth's behavior on Day Nineteen raised several questions:

1. Why hadn't Harmsworth sought a Bank of England ruling on Associated's investment in Price long before, in preparation for such an eventuality? Harmsworth must have realized Price was vulnerable to a takeover bid when it was cash-rich and the biggest shareholder held only 17% of the stock. Perhaps the Bank of England would only give a ruling when a specific situation had arisen.

269

DAY NINETEEN

2. Why didn't Harmsworth leave instructions at Baring Bros. or at Associated that he was to be informed immediately about the Bank of England's ruling? England was five hours ahead of central Canada, and, even if the bank's decision had been reached at 8 p.m. British time, it could have reached Harmsworth in Canada while he was talking to Bell at Abitibi at about 3 p.m. Perhaps Harmsworth had arranged for the bank's ruling to be rushed to him immediately wherever he was — and somebody goofed.

3. Would Harmsworth have acted differently if he *had known* the Bank of England's decision before meeting Bell? The only alternative to tendering to Abitibi (or so it appeared that afternoon) would have been to sit tight in Price. And the only justification for that would have been that, if Abitibi merged the two companies later, Associated would be able to demand a good price for its stock. But what if Abitibi didn't seek merger, or didn't seek it for many years? Associated would have lost control of Price, lost the chance to sell some stock at a nominal $18 a share, and perhaps remained with a minority position in a company (Price) whose parent (Abitibi) was hostile and resentful of Associated. At this stage, all Harmsworth's courses of action seemed to be damaging for Associated.

4. During Harmsworth's luncheon decision, did it matter what the Bank of England's ruling was? If Associated tendered one million shares and only 49% of that stock were taken up, Associated would retain more than 10% of Price and wouldn't lose double-taxation relief. The value of the $18 Abitibi payment for the shares sold would be about $16 a share after capital-gains tax had been paid, even if the Bank of England classified it as direct. That was better than the market price of $12 a share, and, by tendering almost two thirds of its stock, Associated would gain Abitibi's friendship. This would seem to have been the best possible course of action, out of a bad lot, for Harmsworth to take, regardless of the Bank of England's ruling, which would merely determine whether Associated received $26 a share (portfolio) or $18 a share (direct) — something out of Harmsworth's control.

DAY NINETEEN

The extension of the bid gave Harmsworth an opportunity to find another way out — one that might be more attractive than selling less than one third of the stock at $16 a share.

DAY TWENTY

Note 1:
About the special deal Abitibi offered to Harmsworth.

The basis of the valuation was that Abitibi shares would be assigned a value of $10 a share (close to market) and Price shares, $18 a share (the value of Abitibi's bid). Associated held close to 20% of Price.

To get 10% of Abitibi, Associated would need two million shares (10% of 18 million plus the two million new treasury shares issued). At $10 per share, those two million shares were worth $20 million. At $18 a share that $20 million equaled about 1.2 million Price shares, or about 65% of the total Harmsworth and Associated holdings.

With 1.2 million Price shares removed from circulation by this special deal, there'd be only about 8.6 million Price shares (less the half-million still held by Associated) that could be tendered under Abitibi's public bid. Abitibi had bid for 4.9 million shares and that would involve taking up about 60% to 65% of the eight million of the remaining shareholders' holdings (assuming they all tendered). Under this arrangement, Abitibi would be treating everybody more or less equitably. Both Associated and the remaining shareholders would have 60% to 65% of their stock taken up.*

The only extra cost to Abitibi would be the issuance of two million treasury shares to Associated.

Note 2:
At the Quebec National Assembly there was some concern about out-of-province ownership:

"Débats de l'Assemblée Nationale . . . Mardi 19 Novembre 1974 . . .":

President: Order, messieurs, order. Order, please! I have received a note from the honorable deputy from Chicoutimi which

---

* The deal assumed that Harmsworth couldn't tender twice.

DAY TWENTY

reads as follows: "Would you please be advised that before the announcement of the business of the day at the next sitting I intend to propose an emergency debate to discuss an important matter that lies within the powers of the Assembly, and whose examination is urgent, to wit — the offer to buy the Price paper company by Abitibi Paper Co. of Toronto." I received this note in time and I would invite the deputy, briefly, to provide me with an explanation.

Marc-Andre Bédard (Member for Chicoutimi):
Monsieur le Président, I presented this motion under Article 68 and I respectfully submit to you that the urgency of this question is evident, in my humble opinion, because without rapid intervention by the government, it is probable that tomorrow morning, between nine o'clock and 10 o'clock, a majority of the shareholders of Price Co. will accept the offer to sell their shares to Abitibi Paper Co. of Toronto.

I would point out to you that the Caisse de Dépôt [a provincial investment institution] is also a shareholder of Price. As for the importance of the transaction, as you know, Mr. President, it concerns one of the most important companies in the pulp and paper sector.

Price produces about 20% of Quebec's newsprint. It also has its head office in Quebec City and has always been Québecois by the location of its operations. Even if Price does have some plants in the Maritimes, the great majority of its investments are in Quebec.

Monsieur le President, what's most important is that this company, in the course of recent years, has generated accumulated important profits in its Quebec activities. At this time the company's working capital is estimated at $130 million and grows by $40 million a year. What's important, Mr. President, is that the working capital has been built up . . .

President: I think you're going into the facts of the matter.
Bédard: No! No!
President: You presume I will accept your emergency debate. What would you have left to say if I did agree?
Bédard: There are three elements, Monsieur le President, in

273

DAY TWENTY

favor of the motion: to show urgency, importance and, equally, the consequences. The importance is proved by the consequences that may result if one decides not to agree to an emergency debate. It is in this sense that I wish to intervene.

What is important, Monsieur le President, is that the working capital of which I have spoken, which has been built up in Quebec, risks being moved outside of Quebec.

President: Order! Excuse me, you go too much into details, into the facts of the matter. Just tell me why it's necessary to have an emergency debate. True, it's very difficult, but you must touch only on the question, without expanding on it.

Bédard: Monsieur le President, the urgency is that it's *tomorrow* that a decision could be made which can affect . . .

President: That is your best argument.

Bédard: It's not long, but I really ought, I think, to give a few more details, concerning the importance and the consequences. Because, Monsieur le President, as I have said, the working capital could be moved beyond Quebec. I stand on that point.

Concerning the consequences, I submit that the urgency with which this subject should be discussed resides precisely in the consequences, which are the following. First, one can ask what will become of the head office and employees if this company is displaced by Abitibi which, itself, has its head office in Toronto. First point.

Second point, this purchase could represent an important flight of capital from Quebec, since the important assets and investments of the company could easily be applied to projects outside of Quebec, perhaps in Ontario or British Columbia.

Moreover, among the consequences, Monsieur le President, this purchase could mean the cancelation of important investment projects in Quebec, among them one of $20 million in a pulp mill and $16 million in a sawmill in Lac St. Jean.

There are then, Monsieur le President, several existing jobs at head office and many hundreds, even many thousands of future jobs in plants that risk disappearing. This is without counting the indirect losses caused by the fact that Abitibi Paper will take to its

274

DAY TWENTY

own account the policy of buying and hiring favorable to Quebec which was naturally practised by the Price company.

I conclude, Monsieur le President, by saying debate should be allowed on this urgent question and that the government ought to intervene rapidly for the first reason I explained just now, because on the basis of $18 a share, it's for only about $90 million one could buy majority control.

President: Order! I believe I have been sufficiently enlightened. You said to me three or four minutes. Listen, after all . . .

Bédard: Monsieur le President, for all these reasons, taking into account the various interests, taking into account, in particular, working capital of $130 million of which I have spoken and all the jobs that could be affected now and in the future, following this transaction, I submit respectfully that the emergency debate ought to take place in order that the government can intervene to safeguard Quebec interests concerned in this matter.

President: I received this notice, I believe, at three minutes to two.

You have caught me, as President of the Assembly, a little unawares, I must say. I am not versed in the matter. It is very difficult for a President to know what goes on in every corner of Quebec. Following this reasoning, you tell me it ought to be tomorrow morning or in the days . . .

Bédard: At nine tomorrow morning, Monsieur le President.

President: I would wish on the other hand . . . Listen, I have many points to question. Is it, first of all, a matter for the Assembly? In this event there are two private companies. Bon! One moment. I let you speak; let me speak for a while. There are criteria to respect for an emergency debate. Should one permit emergency debates on any subject, on every offer one company can make to another? For these reasons I shall not go into it and I shall not render my final decision today. I regret that even if it should be made tomorrow morning I cannot make a decision for the Chamber. I do not have all the components today to be able to permit, at the present moment, an emergency debate. Moreover, I have permitted

DAY TWENTY

you, I do believe, to elaborate practically as long as if you had been granted your emergency debate. You would have had the right to speak . . .

Bédard: Oh no!

President: . . . pretty near, I believe, 10 or 20 minutes. In any case, I reserve my decision to tomorrow, if possible.

Note 3:
About the final deal between Harmsworth and Consolidated-Bathurst.

English holdings: 1,860,770 Price common shares. Market price: $12 a share (at suspension).

Consolidated-Bathurst payment: 930,385 treasury shares. Market price: about $25 a share.

Why the voting trust wouldn't work for the English. If a trust were created under which others jointly voted the English group's Price shares, the group's ownership of these shares would become clouded, as would the group's right to double-taxation relief in Britain on dividends from the shares. (See Note 3, Day Nineteen.)

Why the stock swap would work for the English. First off, there was the matter of double-taxation relief. The English still qualified for that in Britain because they now held 13% of Consolidated-Bathurst. Then there was the British classification of the investment. The English now became part of the Consolidated-Bathurst control group (with Power Corp.). The English got two directorships and the trappings of a friendly arrangement with Power Corp. Associated also would be able to shift its newsprint contract from Price to Consolidated when it came up for renewal. Because of these business and "control" ties with Consolidated, Associated's overseas investment probably remained "direct" rather than "portfolio" — that is, the deal merely involved the rollover of a direct investment in one company to a direct investment in another.

The Bank of England, which had informally told Harmsworth

276

to do "what is best under the circumstances" within certain limits, would probably be least likely to object to such a rollover. Without the flavor of "control," the investment might perhaps be deemed a rollover from a trade investment to a portfolio investment (because Power Corp., not Associated, had control). The Bank of England might be unlikely to favor such a fundamental change in the type of investment involved, and, even if it did, the complications created by making allowances for currency premium might prove insurmountable.

DAY TWENTY-ONE

Note 1:

Should Consolidated-Bathurst have been allowed to buy Associated's shares of Price privately while Abitibi's bid was on the exchange?

A submission to the Quebec Securities Commission by the Montreal Stock Exchange (dated May 5, 1975) recommended negatively:

"The . . . rules . . . [propose] a halt in trading [in the bid for stock] following the acceptance by the Exchange of the notice [of the bid] . . . This rule would be of doubtful significance if the Securities Commission did not come into play by disallowing all private transactions during this period . . . trading is suspended . . ."

Note 2:

About the factors behind Harmsworth's final decision.

A comparison may be useful. The following table shows the value of Price, Abitibi and Consolidated-Bathurst stock in the proportions in which Associated *would have* received Abitibi stock and *did* receive Consolidated stock under the two offers.

	Price (1 share)	Abitibi* (1.6 shares)	Consolidated (½ a share)
1974 earnings/share	$ 3.22	$ 3.60	$ 3.15
1974 indicated dividend rate	$ 1.00 (50¢)†	$ 1.04	$ 1.00‡
Net worth	$11.00	$21.00	$10.00
Directors	4	2	3
Market value, mid-November 1974	$12.00	$16.00	$13.00
High-low, 1975	$12¾-$18½	$13¼-$18⅝	$11-$14⅛

* In the Abitibi column, earnings/share has been calculated on the basis of 20 million shares (18 million plus two million issued to Associated). The dividend rate and market prices are actual.

† If Associated had accepted Abitibi's special offer, its holdings in Price would have fallen below 10% — with loss of double-taxation relief in Britain and decline of the $1 dividend to a 50¢ taxed dividend.

‡ Plus 25¢ extra in January 1975.

DAY TWENTY-ONE

On first glance, it seemed reasonable to conclude that Abitibi's offer to exchange two million Abitibi shares for 1.2 million Price shares (a ratio of 1:1.6) was in some ways more advantageous to Harmsworth than the Consolidated offer to exchange one Consolidated-Bathurst share for two Price shares (a ratio of 1:½). But, in terms of dividend flow, it was less advantageous. It was also less attractive in that Associated would have ended up in two companies, Price and Abitibi, whereas with the Consolidated deal Harmsworth converted his entire Price holding.

In a letter to Associated shareholders Harmsworth explained: "Your Board was concerned to retain an interest in the manufacture and supply of newsprint in Canada and, after considering the exchange control and taxation implications, *the constraints imposed by Canadian legislation designed to control foreign investment* in Canada, and other relevant Canadian laws and regulations, Associated Newspapers agreed to exchange its holding in Price for shares in Consolidated-Bathurst on the basis of one common share in Consolidated-Bathurst for every two shares in Price." [Italic emphasis is the author's.]

Harmsworth seemed to have been concerned that any purchase of 10% of Abitibi by Associated might be disallowed under the Foreign Investment Review Act. Power Corp.'s control of Consolidated-Bathurst didn't, of course, come into dispute as a result of Associated's purchase of Consolidated shares.

Note 3:
How to calculate the value of a bid.

If one bidder offers $20 for 50% of the shareholder's stock and another bidder offers $23 for 35% of the shareholder's stock, which is the more valuable bid to the shareholder if the market price of the stock is $10 a share?

Bid one: The total value of 100 shares of the target stock to a shareholder is $20 times 50 shares = $1,000 plus $10 times 50 shares (= $500) = $1,500.

Bid two: The value of 100 shares is $23 times 35 shares = $805, plus $10 times 65 shares (= $650) = $650 + $805 = $1,455.

Although the second bid appears better because the price per share is higher, the first bid is of greater value to the target-company shareholder.

DAY TWENTY-TWO

Note 1:
About the benefits to Abitibi at $25 a share. (The reader might compare these calculations with those in the notes for Day Six — the benefits at $18 to $20 a share.)

1. Servicing the debt (cash flow).
Cost of five million shares (51%) = $125 million.
Interest charges on $125 million at 10% = $12.5 million (pre-tax earnings).
Interest cost in after-tax earnings (tax rate 42%) = $7.25 million.
Price's dividend rate = $1 per share.
Dividends payable to Abitibi with 51% of the stock = $5 million.
(These calculations would be altered by the issuance of preferred stock instead of debt. See below.)

2. Earnings purchased.
Price's 1974 earnings attributable to Abitibi's five million shares = $16.1 million.*
Cost of purchasing these earnings = $7.25 million.
Net gain in earnings on consolidation = $8.85 million.

3. When would Abitibi start to lose by the investment?
Cost of purchasing control of Price = $7.25 million (post-tax earnings).
Number of shares bought = 5.0 million.
Therefore Price earnings had to fall below $1.45 per share before Abitibi was losing on the investment.

---

* Assuming the overall synergism effect of $6 million, with $3.5 million of the increased earnings attributable directly to Abitibi, Abitibi's share of the synergistic earnings would be $3.5 million plus 51% of Price's synergistic earnings, or $3.5 million plus $1.2 million.

DAY TWENTY-TWO

At January 1976, a forecast of Price's earnings for 1975 was $1 to $1.25 per share, down from $3.22 in 1974. Industry strikes and a cyclical softening of demand had contributed to the decline. Earnings were expected to resume their upward trend in 1976.

4. Effect on Abitibi's earnings per share.

Abitibi's estimated 1974 earnings per share assuming no Price acquisition = $2.46.*

Abitibi's estimated consolidated earnings per share, assuming the investment in Price had been made on January 1, 1974 = $2.97.†

Note: If Abitibi issued $40 million of the long-term financing as 10% preferred and the rest as debentures, the annual servicing cost in after-tax earnings would rise from $7.25 million to about $9.3 million, because, unlike debenture interest, preferred dividends come out of taxed earnings. If preferred were issued, the gap between Abitibi's share of Price dividends and the servicing cost would rise to about $4 million or $5 million, and the net earnings gain would fall to $6.85 million. The point where Abitibi would start to lose by the investment would rise to $1.86 of earnings per Price share.

---

* Abitibi's actual 1974 earnings per share came to $2.50, which included a Price contribution for December.

† Abitibi's 1974 annual report: "Assuming that the investment in Price had been made as of January 1, 1974, that financing costs of the bank loan had been incurred for the full year and without ascribing potential economies to be derived from the acquisition, it is estimated that Abitibi's consolidated results for the year ended December 31, 1974, would have been as follows: net sales — $834.9 million, net earnings — $54.4 million, net earnings per common share — $2.97." From these figures it can be assumed that Price contributed about 4¢ a month to Abitibi's earnings. In future years the net increase in earnings due to the Price acquisition would be adjusted to take into account the positive synergism effect and the negative effect of any preferred stock issued.

DAY TWENTY-TWO

Note 2:

Which system of counterbidding should have been used?

Only three principal auctioning systems are in general use.

1. *Dutch auction:* Auctioning begins at a high price which is gradually lowered in silence until one bidder shouts a "buy." He stops the auction, and wins. This wouldn't have worked on the stock exchange, because counterbidding only occurs after an initial bid and progresses upwards from that level.

2. *Sealed bids:* The bidders submit their bids in envelopes, which are opened by an exchange official. The stock goes to the highest bidder. A major objection to this system was that it destroys the principal of disclosure, on which the market system is based. It also might permit the kind of hanky-panky that sometimes occurs in construction-contract bidding by sealed tender. Furthermore, it doesn't really result in the highest value being placed on a target company's stock. Since the bidders work in the dark, both bids could be at a low level.

3. *Leapfrogging:* One bid is announced, the competitor announces a higher bid and so on until one drops out. This had some drawbacks, too. The process might go on for a long time, up 25¢ or so at a time, causing an unduly long suspension of trading. What's more, it could be confusing to shareholders, depending on number of shares taken up and so forth.

On balance, leapfrogging was considered the best method during the Price takeover.

Note 3:

About the Consolidated-Bathurst stock deal.*

Whether Consolidated-Bathurst made a profit, broke even or lost during its Price adventure depends on the value placed on the

---

* Pertinent calculations based on Consolidated's 1974 annual report.

DAY TWENTY-TWO

treasury stock issued by Consolidated-Bathurst for the English group's Price stock. This valuation obviously becomes extremely important in assessing any tax effects of Consolidated's transactions.

Here's an account of the treasury-stock exchange taken from a prospectus issued by Consolidated:

"Pursuant to an Agreement made November 20, 1974 [Day Twenty-One] with Associated Newspapers Group Ltd. of London, England, and others, the company has issued as fully paid 930,385 common shares . . . without nominal or par value of its capital stock at a stated value of $50 per share totaling $46,519,250 in consideration for the transfer to the company of 1,860,770 common shares of The Price Company Limited."

The author could think of at least five ways of valuing the Consolidated-Bathurst treasury stock, all of which presented problems.

1. As Consolidated stock was trading at about $25 a share and the last trade of Price before suspension was about $12, and as Consolidated stock was exchanged one for two with the Price stock, then the value of the Consolidated treasury stock was $24-$25 a share (close to market). Problem: This valuation fails to take into account a bid of $18 a share, on the exchange at the time, for 50% of the Price stock. In view of the value created by that bid, was $12 a share a reasonable value to place on the Price stock?

2. As there was an $18 bid for 50% of the Price stock, and the market price (suspended) was $12, then the value of any shareholders' parcel of Price stock was an average of $15 a share, and so the value of the Consolidated treasury stock was $30 a share. Problem: A federal income tax official told the author stock should probably be assigned open-market value rather than the value of a one-shot exchange bid.

3. There had been a report that the Consolidated board didn't ratify the Consolidated-Associated share exchange until the afternoon of November 21 (Day Twenty-Two) when Abitibi's bid was up to $25 a share. That then could become the effective Price figure, and a valuation of the Price stock would be an average of $25

DAY TWENTY-TWO

and $12 or $18.50 a share. The value of the Consolidated treasury stock then would become $37 a share. Problem: Two facts indicate the agreement was firm in the early hours of November 20 (Day Twenty-One): (a) Robert Morrow was able to make his "It's all over and you're out" phone call to Rosier; (b) Consolidated was prepared to make a $20 bid for more stock later that morning. In that case, one might expect the valuation time to be early Day Twenty-One.

4. Because of the $25 bid extant when the agreement was approved, and since Consolidated-Bathurst could have been the only Price shareholder tendering to Abitibi (theoretically anway), all its Price stock might have been taken up at $25. Therefore, the value of every Price share held would be $25 and the value of the Consolidated treasury stock would be $50. Problem: First of all, the same problem as with the third valuation. And then it was also well known on the street that most Price shareholders would tender and that only about half of each parcel would be taken up.

5. Ultimately, Consolidated received for each of its treasury shares $25 in cash plus an entry in its books of one Price share at a cost of $25. This was the argument made by one Consolidated official to the author to explain the valuation of the Consolidated stock at $50 a share. Problem: (a) A question arises. Why not the notion that Consolidated entered *two* transactions — one for the Price stock, and then the sale of the Price stock at a profit? (b) It's a circular argument, depending on what Consolidated decides is the book cost of its remaining Price stock.

What's the effect of valuing Consolidated treasury stock at $50 a share?

First, the company broke even on the sale of half its Price stock to Abitibi at $25 a share. In such a case, no capital-gains tax would be applicable.

Second, Consolidated exchanged Price stock valued at market for its own preferred stock valued at market with a Quebec financial institution shortly after the Abitibi deal. As the stock was sold for less than its cost ("$25"), Consolidated may have had a tax loss.

DAY TWENTY-TWO

There are also some random consequences of the $50 valuation.

— If the Consolidated treasury stock was worth $50 when issued, Consolidated was paying the British $25 a share for their Price stock when there was a bid on the exchange at $18. (The financial accounts of Associated Newspaper later suggested that the British sold their Price stock for $12-$13, in their view.)

— After supposedly paying the British $25 a share for their Price stock, Consolidated was prepared to offer only $20 for more stock in a counterbid against Abitibi on the exchange. When the bidding rose to $25 a share, Consolidated backed out. Also, shortly after Consolidated's $20 per share bid was announced, Bill Turner was reported to have said that it was "more attractive" than the deal given to Associated. This suggested that Turner also believed at the time that the British got $12 a share not $25, which would place the value of the Consolidated treasury stock at $24.

— The stated value per share of $50 for the treasury stock compares with a book value per share at the time of the transaction of about $25 a share. As a result of the treasury-stock issuance, common share capital rose from 6.3 million shares in 1973 valued at $42 million to 7.2 million shares in 1974 valued at $88.6 million. On the asset side of the balance sheet, Consolidated received cash of about $42.5 million and has entered its remaining Price stock at a cost of $25 in long-term investments. At December 31, 1974, the market value of the investment in Price Co. was $7.2 million below cost. Book value would also be overstated by that amount if the market value of the Price stock was a more valid valuation than the value on Consolidated's books.

Note 4:
About Wood Gundy's fee.

Reliable sources in the investment district say Wood Gundy's fee during the takeover came to close to $750,000, which would be the biggest ever in Canada. This could be a reliable estimate. The firm's compensation would come from two sources:

1. As Abitibi's (the buyer's) agent: A letter dated November 14, 1974 (Day Fifteen) addressed by Abitibi Paper and Abitibi Finance authorized Wood Gundy to make the bid on the Montreal and Toronto stock exchanges and agreed to pay Wood Gundy a fee of 10¢ per Price share acquired. (That would come to about $500,000.)

2. As seller's agent: A Price shareholder would accept Abitibi's bid by instructing his own broker to tender his stock to Wood Gundy acting as Abitibi's agent. If that broker happened to be Wood Gundy, then the firm would receive the sell commission as well as the buy commission.

The sell commissions might well have totaled another $250,000. In takeovers of this kind, investors like to tender their target stock directly to the buyer's broker. It reduces the possibility of confusion.

The author,

while a writer and senior editor on the staff of
The Financial Post, over many years made a
reputation as one of Canada's best investigative journalists. Born and educated in Britain, Philip Mathias currently works for the
Canadian Broadcasting Corporation as an associate producer in public affairs television
programming.

The Risk Takers, by Alexander Ross, a lively study of real-life Canadian entrepreneurs and how they made their dreams come true.

Galt, U.S.A., by Robert L. Perry, an award-winning study of the "American presence" and foreign ownership in a small Canadian city, seen through the eyes of its people.

Women in Business, by James E. Bennett and Pierre M. Loewe, the first popular study of the dangers and implications of the shocking treatment of women in Canadian organizations.

Also from Financial Post Books:

Your Money: How to Make the Most of It
Your Guide to Investing for Bigger Profits
Life Insurance & The Businessman
Real Estate for Profit
Running Your Own Business

Financial Post Books
481 University Avenue
Toronto, Ontario
M5W 1A7